The Atl   Conne

Focusing on the interconnections of the Atlantic world from 1450–1900, *The Atlantic Connection* examines the major themes of Atlantic history. During this period, ships, goods, diseases, human beings, and ideas flowed across the ocean, tying together the Atlantic basin in a complex web of relationships. Divided into five main thematic sections while maintaining a broadly chronological structure, this book considers key cultural themes such as gender, social developments, the economy, and ideologies, as well as:

- the role of the Atlantic in ensuring European dominance
- the creation of a set of societies with new cultural norms and philosophical ideals that continued to evolve and transform not only the Atlantic but the rest of the world
- the contestation over rights and justice that emerged from the Atlantic world which continues to exist as a significant issue today.

The Atlantic Connection is shaped by its exploration of a key question: how did Europe come to dominate the Atlantic if not through its technological prowess? Adeptly weaving a multitude of events into a larger analytical narrative, this book provides a fascinating insight into this complex region and will be essential reading for students of Atlantic history.

Anna Suranyi is associate professor in the Department of Humanities at Endicott College. Her publications include *The Genius of the English Nation: Travel Writing and National Identity in Early Modern England* (2008).

The Atlantic Connection

A History of the Atlantic World, 1450–1900

Anna Suranyi

Routledge
Taylor & Francis Group

LONDON AND NEW YORK

First published 2015
by Routledge
2 Park Square, Milton Park, Abingdon, Oxon OX14 4RN

and by Routledge
711 Third Avenue, New York, NY 10017

Routledge is an imprint of the Taylor & Francis Group, an informa business

British Library Cataloguing-in-Publication Data

Library of Congress Cataloging-in-Publication Data
Suranyi, Anna, 1967-
  The Atlantic connection : a history of the Atlantic world, 1450-1990 / Anna Suranyi.
    pages cm
  Includes bibliographical references and index.
  1. Atlantic Ocean Region—History. 2. Slavery—Atlantic Ocean Region—History. 3. Europe—Relations—Atlantic Ocean Region. 4. World politics. I. Title.
D210.S87 2015
909'.09821—dc23
2014046586

ISBN: 978-0-415-63985-9 (hbk)
ISBN: 978-0-415-63986-6 (pbk)
ISBN: 978-1-315-71432-5 (ebk)

Typeset in Sabon
by Apex CoVantage, LLC

MIX
Paper from
responsible sources
FSC
www.fsc.org   FSC® C013604

Printed and bound by CPI Group (UK) Ltd, Croydon, CR0 4YY

Contents

Figures

Acknowledgments

Many people provided support while I was writing this book. The editorial staff at Taylor & Francis have been exemplary with their encouragement, patience, and gentle nudging. Also, I owe much to Endicott College and especially Provost Laura Rossi-Le, who provided me with institutional support in order to pursue my writing and research. I would like to express gratitude to a number of current and former colleagues who have helped and encouraged me, offered suggestions and new lines of inquiry, and generally helped me to prevail over adversity. They include Sam Alexander, Sara Allen, Arianne Chernock, Amy Damico, Bill Fowler, Chris Gilmartin (who sadly did not live to see the completion of this book), Harvey Green, Mark Herlihy, Clay McShane, Sharon Paradiso, Steve Slocomb, and Hilda Smith. I would also like to credit Geoffrey Plank for his careful reading of the manuscript and mention my appreciation of reference librarian Betty Roland of the Halle Library at Endicott College for her inexhaustible ability to find whatever I needed. I would also like to thank Catherine Wood of the Norman B. Leventhal Map Collection at the Boston Public Library for facilitating access to a number of maps. I dedicate this book to my family: Tim, Thalia, and Jesse. I am grateful to all of those listed here, as the book has profited from their support in multiple ways.

Preface

The Atlantic world is usually seen as the region comprising the rims of the four continents that border the Atlantic Ocean, including North and South America, Europe, and Africa, as well as the islands located within the Atlantic Ocean basin. Following Columbus' historic voyage of 1492, this area developed a regional system of political, economic, and cultural connections that gradually became the most important economic and political hub on the globe. It continued to exist as a tightly connected system until the end of the nineteenth century, when it was superseded by a broader and more globalized orientation in the realm of politics and world economies. Although the individual components of this system, such as particular regions, processes, or events, continue to be the subject of intensive historical study, this region is also worth studying as a whole because of the many dynamic exchanges and processes which were transnational but were also centered in and around the region of the Atlantic.

Studying the Atlantic as a whole instead of focusing on disparate national histories or, alternatively, on individual incidents allows historians and students to see the underlying patterns, connections, and causes of historical events on a larger scale. These include the voyages of discovery, the Atlantic slave trade, abolitionism, the Atlantic trade nexus, the growth of new ideologies from the Enlightenment, the movement of revolutionary ideals, the changing patterns of social identities, the adjustment of Native American culture and society, the colonization of Africa, the global struggle for political representation, and many other topics. Not only did these developments first arise in the Atlantic, but they also continued to cross-influence each other within the region, setting the stage for further transformations. While Atlantic societies continued to interact with other regions of the world as well as with those within the Atlantic basin, it was the Atlantic itself that served as a center and an origin for many aspects of modern world society. Indeed, the Atlantic encounter between Europeans, Africans, and Native Americans was crucial in establishing many aspects of modern reality, shaping politics, economics, and social and intellectual life.

This book takes its place among a considerable body of literature about Atlantic history. The importance of this field has been increasingly recognized in the past two decades, and the number of works on Atlantic history has proliferated. Most works concentrate on specific aspects or historical events, but there are some which take the general span of Atlantic history as their theme, as this one does. This book differs from such works in providing a narrative discussing Atlantic history that is accessible to those who do not come to the study of this field of history already possessing the background to focus on a more specialized analysis. For those who wish to read more broadly in Atlantic history, in the final section of this book entitled "Sources for further reading" I have listed some of these other generalist works mainly directed toward more advanced students; collections of essays on specific topics within Atlantic history; and a number of books that focus on historiography, scholarly debate, or theoretical approaches to the study of Atlantic history rather than primarily emphasizing the presentation of history.

This book shares much with the aforementioned kinds of works – some of which have influenced it – but also differs in its focus. My emphasis is primarily on interpretations of pervasive trends in Atlantic history, such as long-term trajectories and crucial events that shaped human societies, particularly emphasizing the relationships and transformations that occurred in or affected the Atlantic rim regions. Consequently, it is thematic rather than chronological in form, though it does adhere generally to a chronological structure. It also does not detail every event that took place in the four continents that surround the Atlantic. As such, I hope it will also prove useful to both beginning and more advanced students who are searching for a more thorough understanding of the connections present throughout Atlantic history. In order to make this book accessible to students and general readers, it does not contain footnoted references other than to direct quotes within the main text. However, inquisitive readers can find these sources listed in the section at the end of this book, which will hopefully serve as a guideline to those who are interested in learning about the numerous facets of Atlantic history in greater detail.

Introduction

The period described in this book is one in which the political, social, cultural, and economic relationships of human beings in the world were fundamentally reorganized. In 1492, human civilizations that had been separate for millennia were reunited, bringing Europeans, Native Americans, and Africans into interactions that included cooperation, conflict, and exploitation. In the course of this, Western Europe was transformed from a remote backwater into a region that dominated the rest of the world. During this time, the Atlantic can be identified by connections – between populations; between geographical regions; between biological organisms, including diseases, plants, animals, and humans; and between technologies and ideas – all of which circulated around and across the Atlantic basin. Transnational and intercontinental networks wove together events in Africa, the Americas, and Europe. The motor driving this vast mechanism was human movement, including both voluntary immigration from Europe to the Americas and the slave trade. Yet instead of the actions of individuals, it was the activity of human populations that was central to the pattern of changes in Atlantic history. Indeed, these changes occurred not because of qualities intrinsic to the societies that clustered along the Atlantic rim; rather, it was a mixture of environmental constraints and historical contingencies that shaped events. The place of individual human actions was not so much to instigate massive changes as it was to leave particular imprints shaping important events. This human movement continued through the nineteenth century as the main form of global connections, but the nineteenth century was also an era during which opposite but parallel eastward movement also increased, such as the advance of European colonizers into Asia. The nineteenth and especially the twentieth centuries were also characterized by a more globalized series of connections, broader than the Atlantic, as the economic, social, political, and biological connections that characterized the period from 1492 to 1888 drew to a close to be replaced by a broader and less geographically centered web of economic, military, and cultural exchanges.

A central theme of this book is to explain the historical context of how Europeans succeeded in their domination of the Atlantic world and to explain how this process was possible. I also concentrate on the interconnectedness of the societies of the Atlantic world and on long-term trends in Atlantic history, particularly focusing on social developments, ethnicity and gender, the economy, and changing ideologies. In addition, I aim to show how the wealth and the cultural challenges emanating from the Atlantic helped spur major European intellectual, economic, and political developments in the eighteenth century, fostering the growth of new forms of society, as well as the contestation of justice and human rights that emerged from the Atlantic encounter which continues to exist as an important current in today's world.

This book is divided into five parts. The first, "Explorations and first contacts," depicts the societies of the Atlantic rim prior to 1492 and explains the interconnections that already existed in Eurasia and Africa before Columbus' voyage. It also discusses the Portuguese voyages of discovery and the forces that led Europeans to cross the Atlantic. The second part of the book, "Colonization and conquest," situates Christopher Columbus within the European context and examines the motivations for his initial trans-Atlantic voyage. It discusses the "Columbian Exchange" or the first interaction between the human and biological features of the Western and Eastern Hemispheres, especially the effects of European and African diseases on Native Americans. This section also details the development of the early settlements peopled by migrants from Spain, Portugal, and northwestern Europe and examines settlement patterns from national and economic perspectives. Part III, "Connections, journeys, and war" covers the rise of political and social imperialism, illustrating the rise of European empires, especially the British Empire, in the Atlantic and the growth of Atlantic trade. It focuses particularly on the growth of slavery and the slave trade and the organized struggle of Native American groups to retain political and social autonomy. The fourth section, "The age of ideas," considers the European Enlightenment and its consequences, as well as the Atlantic's age of revolutions that spread revolutionary ideologies across the Atlantic basin. The growth of ideologies of human rights is also shown to inspire the rebellions of disenfranchised peoples as well as to accord with the political aspirations of middle-class reformers, resulting in movements which sought to abolish slavery and expand the electorate. The final section, "The paradox of modernity," examines the culmination of many of the developments reviewed in the book, including the growth of industrialization, wide-scale European migration in the nineteenth century, the growth of European colonialism, and the shape of nineteenth-century societies in the Atlantic.

The span of this book covers what historians call the "early modern period" from the end of the Middle Ages in the mid-fifteenth century through the radical political and intellectual changes of the late eighteenth century and continues until the end of the nineteenth century, at which time the idea of an Atlantic world begins to lose its coherence. Indeed, while the entire period covered by the book is one of increasing globalization, by the end of the nineteenth century, the rise of new technologies and new forms of mechanization resulted in a far more globalized world than could have been imagined previously. There were a number of far-reaching transformations that resulted in a considerably greater internationalization of economies and political affairs than in previous centuries. These included the establishment of rapid long-distance forms of communication such as the telegraph and telephone, transcontinental rail travel and transoceanic travel by steamboat and, soon after, the advent of air travel, with the result that the world suddenly became a much smaller place. The cultural and physical coherence which had connected the Atlantic world had thus faded by the end of the nineteenth century.

Although most books about Atlantic history end at the beginning of the nineteenth century, this book argues that the nineteenth century was a transitional period in which the early modern and late modern coexisted rather than an abrupt break with the past. It was during this period that many – perhaps most – people first encountered the intellectual and political promise of the eighteenth-century Enlightenment, including the growth of public education and literacy and the increasing attempts to enable larger segments of the population to vote. The nineteenth century saw the beginning of deep-rooted and sustained political movements to fight for equality for various groups, such as women, slaves, ethnic minorities, the poor, and others. The period also saw the culmination of many political, social, and cultural trajectories that had been initiated in the 1490s. Atlantic slavery, inaugurated in the fifteenth century, ended in 1888. Spain's Atlantic empire finally collapsed. A series of revolutions on both sides of the Atlantic in Europe and Latin America aiming for political freedom were the culmination of ideologies developed during the Enlightenment, which had seen their earliest expression in the American and French Revolutions. Also during the late nineteenth century in Africa and Asia, a new form of direct colonialism by European imperialists replaced earlier, more equitable and flexible relationships during the late nineteenth century. Economically, the growth of industrialization resulted in an increase in cheap commercial goods and the development of an urban working class who operated industrial machines. Most of these changes were not fully realized until the end of the nineteenth century, and most were likewise a culmination of trends that had begun much earlier – in some cases, centuries previously. At the same time, new global connections and networks were emerging which would challenge the westward orientation of older routes. By the end of the nineteenth century in 1900, the close Atlantic connections that had emerged over previous centuries were merely some among a number of international crosscurrents tying together an increasingly globalized world.

The dominance of the West

A number of scholars studying global history have addressed the issue of the growth of the political, military, and economic geopolitical dominance of the West which emerged during the eighteenth century. This is a question particularly important to our understanding of the significance of Atlantic history. While older works tended to credit the West's rise to its moral, philosophical, or intellectual superiority, more modern scholars have come to doubt these ascriptions and have located Western dominance in geography, climate, and historical contingency. Jared Diamond, in *Guns, Germs, and Steel* (1997), argued that climate zones, shaped by geography and latitude, helped determine the lifeways of peoples of the earth. Those who came from the temperate zones found more animals that could be domesticated and soil more suitable for agricultural production. These factors bolstered the development of human societies in these regions and continued to do so. In addition, constant close contact with domesticated animals provided contact with infectious microorganisms spread by animals which constituted the majority of human diseases and eventually provided partial immunity to endemic diseases. Thus, certain societies and regions were fortunate from the outset in being able to devote less time and resources to the difficulties of survival, providing the opportunity to turn to developments in other directions. Simultaneously, some societies and regions were stymied in their expansion because of acute obstacles to growth. Alfred Crosby, in *The Columbian Exchange* (1972), examined the effects of the first encounter between Europe and the Americas, especially the biological consequences, elucidating the devastating effects of disease on Native American populations and demonstrating the major and far-reaching demographic consequences of the Columbian encounter, especially in preventing Native Americans from being able to effectively counter the European conquest. In *The Great Divergence* (2000), Kenneth Pomeranz explores the reasons for the ascendency of the West rather than China by the eighteenth century, despite the latter's previous technological superiority. Ultimately, he ascribes the rise of the West to the Atlantic encounter. The tremendous productive powers of the resources of the two continents of North and South America, as well as the Caribbean, once conquered and harnessed by Europeans, provided the resources and capital necessary for investment in rapid and sustained growth. In addition, the prevalence of navigable rivers and local coal supplies within Europe provided further preconditions for industrialization. Together, these factors stimulated the eventual Western domination of the world. Likewise, Immanuel Wallerstein's contribution to world systems theory in *The Modern World System: Capitalist Agriculture and the Origins of the European World Economy in the Sixteenth Century* (1974) demonstrates the close relationships between historical events around the world and locates the rise of modern capitalism in fifteenth-century European historical events, allowing Europeans to become the dominant power on the globe. Janet Lippman Abu-Lughod, on the other hand, in *Before European Hegemony: The World System A.D. 1250–1350* (1989) argues that the preconditions for European political dominance included the increasing structural weakness of the previous nexus of international trade in the Indian Ocean. Together, these scholars seek to explain how Europe, a relative backwater in the fourteenth century, was able to dominate the world by the eighteenth century. Their theories, focused on geography, biology, economic trends, and historical contingency, replace earlier explanations that asserted that the cause of European hegemony was the intrinsic superiority of European values.

Part I
Explorations and first contacts

1 The Atlantic world before 1492

Prior to 1492, the human world was divided into several realms. Although there are many ways to define the environmental and cultural divides among human societies of the time, in the most basic form these comprised three main geographic regions: the connected continents of Europe, Asia, and Africa – the "Old World" – which were somewhat separated by geographical obstacles but were also in constant and increasing contact with each other by the fifteenth century; the South Pacific, which had sporadic interaction with Asia; and the Americas, which, despite a few minor and infrequent contacts, had been essentially separate from other human-inhabited regions since they were cut off from the rest of the world some 13,000 years ago. Each of these regions contained many thousands of individual human societies. It should be immediately apparent, however, that the Americas were far more isolated than other parts of the world. In some ways, this made little difference – there were a number of parallel developments that made human cultures translatable to foreigners, even as each society also retained unique and sometimes mutually incomprehensible characteristics. This pattern of similarities and differences prevailed in all parts of the world. It meant that, often, human societies encountered foreigners as enemies or invaders, but also as allies and trading partners. However, the isolation of the Americas resulted in some very significant biological differences, especially in human disease ecology and in diversity of animal and plant life that would have very important consequences for the peoples of these continents when they were reunited with Europeans and Africans in 1492.

As a whole, human societies in the Americas, Africa, and Europe followed similar trajectories. They exhibited a great variation in lifeways that ranged from settled civilizations with entrenched social hierarchies; complex systems of exchange, transportation, and religion; and large-scale architectural infrastructures to village-based societies that engaged in agriculture or animal herding and, more rarely, to less sedentary societies that subsisted by hunting, fishing, and gathering wild foods. As urban centers developed, an increasing trend all over the world during the fifteenth century, they often dominated the surrounding countryside, a trend exacerbated by the increasing consolidation of large national states or empires in many areas.

The shape of interactions among regions in the Old World was based on a combination of geography, availability of resources, and historical events. During the Middle Ages, the centers of economic activity lay in two great commercial nexuses: the Indian Ocean, which connected East Africa, the Middle East, and South Asia, and the Mediterranean Sea, which connected southern Europe, the Middle East, North Africa and, to some degree, West Africa. The regions that were far away from these two epicenters of commercial activity were relative backwaters, including southern Africa, eastern and northern Europe, northern Asia, and the South Pacific. However, this would change when Western Europeans developed ships that were capable of crossing the Atlantic Ocean. The Atlantic would prove to be a basis for wealth and power that surpassed the capacity of previously established commercial hubs.

Although it was not obvious during the early Middle Ages, Western Europeans turned out to have been geographically lucky. They occupied a temperate zone that is suitable for agriculture and possesses adequate water. Much of the Old World in general was suitable for animal husbandry, a factor that greatly increased the transmission of epidemic diseases but that also, over time, decreased the biological susceptibility of the peoples of the Old World to many bacterial and viral infections. In addition, Western Europe was geographically oriented toward the Atlantic. During the Middle Ages and earlier, this factor was not a significant benefit, as the Atlantic was turbulent and unnavigable, but by the fifteenth century, it was stimulating Europeans to develop more efficient shipping and navigation. European sailing ability became more important after 1453, when the Ottoman Empire conquered Constantinople and cut Europeans off from the Indian Ocean and some Mediterranean ports. It was the gradual advances in shipbuilding and navigational technology that made Columbus' voyage possible and thus enabled Western Europe's subsequent accumulation of great wealth. West-facing European regions such as Spain, Portugal, Britain, France, and the Netherlands were fortuitously located on the western fringes of the known world, giving them greater access to the Atlantic and an incentive to develop sophisticated nautical and navigational technologies. On the other hand, West Africans, although also located on the Atlantic rim, did not benefit from the same opportunities, as the coasts of their region were hampered by south-going Atlantic currents that made ocean navigation difficult. They also remained connected to overland commerce with both the Mediterranean and the Indian Ocean, creating less of an incentive to establish advanced navigational technologies. Centuries later, Western Europe's aggregation of capital from the Atlantic, coupled with its possession of navigable rivers and its large and conveniently located deposits of coal, would enable its rapid industrialization.

2 Europe

A new age of trade and travel

Europe was at a time of transition in the fifteenth century during which Europeans were experimenting with new ideas and leaving behind some aspects of medieval life while at the same time clinging to traditional values. Europe was primarily agricultural in the Middle Ages, and social interactions were based on deeply entrenched hierarchies. In Western Europe, the Catholic Church controlled many aspects of cultural mores, with the Orthodox Church taking that role in eastern Europe. Yet at the same time, changes were developing in technology, educational possibilities, political ideology, and international connections. At the end of the medieval era and the beginning of the early modern period, the Atlantic encounter of 1492 would permanently reorient European society.

Traditional values persisted in Europe and would continue to do so for centuries. Most people were peasants, and society was based on a system of privileges based on birth, determining social roles based on whether one was born a noble or a commoner and, if the latter, a peasant or perhaps someone born into a family of artisans or merchants. However, new opportunities were also appearing. In the growing urban areas, there were increasing numbers of professionals such as doctors, lawyers, university professors, clerks, and public officials, as well as expanding roles for artisans and merchants. In addition, there was a greater presence of the working poor, including porters, dock workers, sailors, hired laborers, peddlers, domestic servants, washerwomen, seamstresses, prostitutes, and the like.

There were approximately 80 million people in Europe in the year 1500, with about three quarters of the population concentrated in Western Europe. The nuclear family predominated, with people marrying relatively late in life, usually in their mid-twenties or later, once both partners had established the wherewithal to set up an independent household. Noble families followed a different pattern in which youths were married off early to cement family alliances. Men were seen as the heads of households, and fathers were owed deference and obedience by wives, children, and servants. There were few restrictions on the power of fathers and husbands, who were expected to discipline their subordinates, even by violence, though at the same time consideration and companionate marriage were also urged by religious institutions and, to some degree, expected by peers. Women's autonomy was actually decreasing during the fifteenth through seventeenth centuries, because as the state became more centralized and adopted Roman law instead of customary traditions, women's roles were increasingly circumscribed by legal strictures that had not been clearly defined during the Middle Ages. Women had few rights and often did not possess independent adult status, in many areas lacking the rights of owning property, retaining custody of children, representing themselves in court, restraining abusive husbands, or running a business. However, the reality was more complex, with many women evading such restrictions through skillfulness, family connections, or wealth.

Despite traditional expectations, society was not entirely static, especially in Western Europe. The most dynamism was occurring in coastal regions, either in the Mediterranean, such as in the case of Italy, or in Atlantic territories such as Portugal. Incentives for change included increasing contact with other Mediterranean cultures, especially in the Middle East, and renewed knowledge of pre-Christian classical literature. New economic developments included growing urbanization; the growth of large-scale industry; an increasingly money-based economy, with financial innovations in banking and lending; the rise of long-distance trade; and economic competition. Cultural changes also included a growth in literacy, a new acceptance of individualism, and an increase in skepticism. One of the most important innovations was the development of the printing press by Johannes Gutenberg in the 1450s, which allowed the rapid accessibility and dissemination of ideas. These factors occurred in tandem with increasing centralization of the state, advances in weaponry, and the intensification of national tensions.

A further important change developed shortly after 1492 as new vistas opened to Europeans after Columbus "discovered" the Americas (a region often called the "New World" to distinguish it from the better-known "Old World" of Africa, Asia, and Europe). Beginning in 1519, Europe experienced the Protestant Reformation in which long-standing religious grievances; the disruption of the Papal Schism of a few decades before; the growth of money-based markets that created economic disruption; and the growth of humanistic ideals promoting literacy, free speech, and intellectual inquiry led to an increasing desire for theological innovation. Earlier heretical movements led by John Wycliffe in England and Jan Hus in Bohemia had been suppressed, but in the early sixteenth century the printing press allowed rapid distribution of Protestant ideas, while the threat of the Ottoman Empire initially prevented German rulers from containing the new theology. Frederick, the ruler of Saxony, protected Protestant innovator Martin Luther from retribution by the Catholic Church, both for spiritual reasons and because he saw Luther's ideas as a way to bolster his regional interests. The Reformation amplified increasing distrust and eventually warfare between emerging European nations in the sixteenth century.

Prior to 1492, Europeans were beginning to develop a number of new technologies that enabled Columbus' historic voyage, especially a series of innovations in shipbuilding and navigation. If the Americas had not been reached accidentally, putting all of their valuable resources in the hands of Europeans, these technological developments would likely have created subtle alterations in the balance of power within early modern Europe and between European states and the Ottoman Empire. It is doubtful, however, that these new capabilities alone would have been sufficient to propel Europe to the level of global political domination that it began to achieve by the mid-nineteenth century.

The voyages of discovery

A number of factors came together to start Western Europeans on the path to the Atlantic voyages of discovery. During the late Middle Ages, economics were a powerful stimulant, particularly the drive to gain access to the Asian spice trade. Spices, especially salt, pepper, cinnamon, nutmeg, ginger, and cloves, were extremely important to the European economy. They were used as a preservative for meats from the annual fall slaughter of livestock, as flavorings for otherwise bland foods and, most importantly, as medicines. Salt mainly came from Portugal, but the other spices came from Africa, India, China, and the islands of the East Indies. They were prohibitively expensive because of the logistics of transporting them, traveling with Muslim merchants across the Indian Ocean and overland through the Ottoman Empire and thence to Venice and were also difficult to purchase because Europeans produced few trade products of any value for the more sophisticated Asian empires. However, commerce continued because the potential profits were enormous – up to six times the value of the original investment.

At the same time, increasing contact with other regions meant that Europeans were beginning to gain knowledge of the rest of the world and develop a sense of their own distinctiveness. In particular, there was a sense of antagonism toward the Islamic regions abutting Europe to the east and south, which dated from the crusading movement of the twelfth century, and extended to economic competition with the Ottoman Empire. There was also a need to guard against Ottoman encroachment in eastern Europe, while Spanish Christians sought to drive the Muslims out of Spain. Once the *Reconquista* (or reconquest) of Spain was completed in January of 1492, the Spanish monarchs undertook supporting Columbus' initial voyage. In the meantime, while Spain had been preoccupied with its war with the Muslims, Portugal had established control over the sea routes along the coast of Africa, which pushed Spain and other countries to look westward in their attempts to gain access to the lucrative spice trade.

There had already been some attempts to explore the Atlantic Ocean during the Middle Ages, particularly from coastal areas. The earliest Europeans to reach the west side of the Atlantic were eleventh-century Vikings sailing with Leif Erikson from the Norse settlement of Greenland to the briefly settled site of L'Anse aux Meadows on the Newfoundland coast. The Greenland settlement itself only survived into the fifteenth century but during its existence may have continued to send some expeditions to North American shores in search of timber. The Vikings were followed two centuries later by the Vivaldi brothers, who were lost at sea after they sailed from Genoa in 1291 intending to sail to Asia, though it is unknown whether they aimed to sail south along the African coast or west across the Atlantic. There were also many medieval stories about voyagers such as the Irish monk Saint Brendan, who reportedly found a mysterious island in the Atlantic. The reality of such tales is discounted by scholars, but they were widely believed in the late Middle Ages and inspired the curiosity and interest of other explorers. During the fourteenth century, the first sustained movement into the ocean occurred with Spanish and Portuguese expeditions to the Atlantic islands off the coast of Africa. In addition, beginning in the 1480s, expeditions sailed from the English port of Bristol in search of mythical islands like Atlantis, the Fortunate Isles, and Hy-Brasil, likely bolstered by the many reports of actual islands encountered during the previous century. During the same period, a more practical cohort of fishermen from Bristol were returning to England with large stores of codfish from unknown northern regions. These sailors were likely traveling to fishing grounds off the coast of Iceland, Greenland, or even Newfoundland. There were also tales, which Columbus may have heard, of Basque fisherman frequenting mysterious cod fisheries in the North Atlantic. All of these stories contributed to a European desire to explore or even cross the Atlantic Ocean, but this was always tempered by the knowledge of the vast reaches of open water that a ship would have to traverse.

Portugal and Africa

Although it was ultimately the Spanish who sponsored Columbus' historic voyages, it was Portugal that led in the voyages of discovery. Bracketed on one side by the Atlantic Ocean and on the other by its competitor, Spain, Portugal was by necessity oriented toward the ocean. The fish and salt trades were major supports of the Portuguese economy, and the Portuguese were becoming advanced seafarers, interested in expanding into other profitable ventures made possible by their close proximity to Africa such as commerce in spices, gold, ivory, and slaves. Development in this realm was supported by a member of the royal family, Prince Henry (1394–1460), known as the Navigator for his encouragement and financing of voyages of discovery and his promotion of the study of navigation, astronomy, cartography, and shipbuilding and the development of navigational instruments, all of which were necessary for sailors and explorers to venture into the ocean out of sight of land. Prince Henry was interested in promoting Portuguese interests by increasing trade and exploring the African coastline for possible sources of wealth, as well as gaining access to the sources of the fabled trans-Sahara trade routes. He was also impelled by crusading ideals, hoping to circle around Muslim territories, convert non-Christians, and ally with the mythical Christian ruler Prester John, who was rumored to live in the heart of northwest Africa.

Portuguese expeditions along the coast of Africa began with the 1415 attack of Ceuta, a Muslim town along the Strait of Gibraltar possessing a Mediterranean harbor. Ceuta's capture meant that the Portuguese had advanced out of Europe, establishing a foothold in Africa. Thereafter, the Portuguese gradually crept along the African shoreline, sometimes engaging in trade with African kingdoms on the coast. Initially, they were hampered by a number of difficulties, especially the inability of ships to move far from the coast and imaginary fears of the unknown, which included the belief that the southern seas would be boiling hot or filled with sea monsters. In particular, European sailors were daunted by Cape Bojador, a projection of land off the northwest coast of Africa just south of the Canary Islands, which featured dangerous winds and currents and was perceived as the boundary of the known world. In 1434, Prince Henry finally persuaded Captain Gil Eanes to sail around the cape, demonstrating that the ocean was unchanged on the opposite side, after which sailors were soon exploring much farther down the coast. In 1441, a ship returned to Portugal bearing gold and slaves, demonstrating the lucrative possibilities of continued voyages. In less than a decade, many hundreds of slaves were being brought back to Portugal, resulting in the establishment of a Portuguese trading post in 1448 for purchasing slaves from African suppliers on Arguin Island south of Cape Bojador. Initially, most of these slaves were employed as household servants for wealthy nobles or sometimes returned to Africa as interpreters for African sailing ventures.

In the early fifteenth century, both the Portuguese and the Spaniards sent voyages into the Atlantic in search of new territories. The incentives for this came from two sources: factual reports from sailors about islands they had glimpsed far out to sea and the prevalent legends about mysterious Atlantic islands. These expeditions reaped tangible rewards for Europeans, resulting in the acquisition of a number of Atlantic islands off the coast of Africa. The Canary Islands had been known to Europeans since ancient times, and their conquest by the Spanish began in 1402. However, thereafter, the Spanish monarchy became distracted by its ongoing battles with Muslim kingdoms in Spain and took little part in Atlantic expeditions until the end of the century, allowing the Portuguese to surge to the fore in the colonization of Atlantic islands. The Portuguese settled the previously uninhabited Madeira and Azores islands, the latter almost halfway across the ocean, which had been charted on maps since the mid-fourteenth century, by 1419 and 1431, respectively, and also discovered and then settled the Cape Verde Islands beginning in 1456.

Islands in the Atlantic were central to the early conceptualization of colonialism that shaped European endeavors in the Atlantic. The Canary Islands were inhabited prior to European colonization, and it was to take almost a century before they were fully under Spanish control, primarily because of the vigorous resistance of the Guanches, the indigenous inhabitants. The Spanish, however, saw control over the islands as their prerogative, and the Catholic Church encouraged the conquest, though for the purposes of conversion rather than enslavement. The Canaries were to prove to be a valuable acquisition to the Spanish as a stopping-off and reprovisioning depot for later Atlantic voyages, a role also filled by the Portuguese Azores and Cape Verde Islands. The Atlantic islands were also the location where Europeans first pioneered plantation slavery, the harshest form of slave labor. By the 1450s, Prince Henry was already sponsoring sugar plantations in Madeira, which became the center of the European sugar trade.

In addition to backing African voyages, Prince Henry strove to ensure political legitimacy for his ventures, obtaining a number of rights from the Pope, including plenary indulgences for his sailors who died en route, as were typically granted to crusaders, and the responsibility of converting Africans. The Portuguese king gave Prince Henry the prerogative of trading ventures along the African coast and the right to significant shares of the profits. Henry then reinvested the proceeds into continued exploration and development, establishing Portugal as the dominant state engaged in ventures along the African coast by the time he died in 1460.

After a brief hiatus, Prince Henry's aims were supported by John II (1655–95), who occupied the Portuguese throne from 1481 to 1495. Increasing voyages along the African coastline under John II firmly established the Portuguese as the main European slave traders in the fifteenth century. However, John II's vision was more expansive than Prince Henry's had been. In addition to controlling the African trade, John II hoped that the Portuguese could circumnavigate Africa to reach India and the spice islands in Asia. He also moved to consolidate his power over the African coast. In 1479, two years before officially ascending the throne but in fact already ruling, John II signed the Treaty of Alcáçovas with Spain. Both parties benefited from the agreement. The Portuguese crown agreed to give up its contested claim to the Spanish throne, but in return Portugal gained the monopoly over colonization and trade in territories south of the Canary Islands, as well as the verification of its claim to the island groups of Madeira and the Azores and the Cape Verde Islands. This treaty, which was ratified by the papacy, was initially intended to cover the African coastline and the known Atlantic islands but was to assume further importance with the discovery of new Atlantic territories thirteen years later. John II further consolidated Portugal's claim to coastal Africa by declaring that the Guinea coast – or eastward curve of the African continent south of the Sahara Desert – was under the exclusive control of the Portuguese and that any other European ships found there were subject to being sunk and their crews subject to execution. In 1482, John II established a large trading fortress at Elmina on the coast of present-day Ghana, then called the Gold Coast. Among the earliest crews who sailed to Elmina on trading ventures was a younger Christopher Columbus. Elmina was to become a major hub of the African slave trade for many centuries afterward, even after the bulk of the trade passed into Dutch and then British hands. Portuguese control over the southern route to Asia also had the further effect of impelling other countries interested in spices or Asian goods to face westward when they turned to exploration, especially after the Ottoman Turks conquered the city of Constantinople in 1453, blocking overland routes (see Figure 2.1).

Portuguese sailors and explorers sponsored by John II reached ever farther along the African coast, though they were surprised to find that the continent of Africa was much larger than they had expected. In 1487, John II funded the expedition of Bartolomeu Dias along the southern coast of Africa, which sailed past the southern tip of Africa in 1488. Undeterred by the region's storminess, John II named it the Cape of Good Hope. That same year, he sent an Arabic speaker, Pedro da Covilhã, to the Middle East to search for the sources of the spice trade. Covilhã traveled through the Mediterranean and East Africa, disguised as a merchant, and was able to send a report to the king that described the east African and west Indian coastlines, making it clear that circumnavigating Africa was achievable. Logistically difficult to plan and finance, the expedition did not sail until the 1497 voyage of Vasco da Gama. However, by then Columbus had already reached the Americas.

John II continued to promote Portugal's geographical interests after Columbus' voyage of 1492. Columbus himself insisted until the end of his life that he had reached Asia. However, on Columbus' return to Europe from his first voyage, bad weather forced him to dock at Lisbon, and it was immediately apparent to John II that Columbus had reached uncharted lands. The king instantly sent emissaries to Spain arguing that the new lands belonged to Portugal under the terms of the Treaty of Alcáçovas. Pope Alexander VI, a native Spaniard, favored Spain. Eventually the conflicting claims were settled by the 1494 Treaty of Tordesillas, which divided the globe into Portuguese and Spanish spheres of influence on a line of longitude set between the Cape Verde Islands and the new lands discovered by Columbus, with Portugal gaining any new lands to the east of the line, while Spanish territories stretched to the west. The treaty recognized Spanish sovereignty over the territories that Columbus had discovered in the Caribbean – at the time believed to be a group of islands – but gave Portugal rights to any undiscovered islands in between, to the African routes they already controlled and, eventually, to Brazil, which was not then known to exist. This treaty created immediate problems because of the lack of precision in accurate measurement and because the new lands were soon revealed to include entire continents. It became the basis for the initial Spanish claims to most of the Americas and the Portuguese claim to Brazil, which fell on the east side of the line. Coincidentally, it was a Portuguese sailor, Pedro Álvares Cabral, who was the first European to land on the Brazilian coast in 1500.

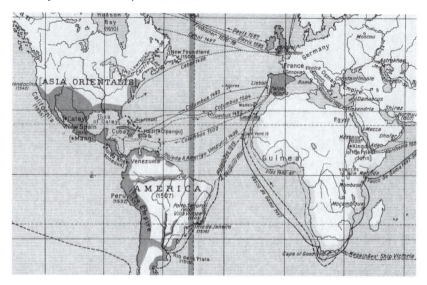

Figure 2.1 Section from "Europe in search of new routes to India and China, 1486–1616" by Albert Hermann (1935). Map reproduction courtesy of the Norman B. Leventhal Map Center at the Boston Public Library.

New European navigational technologies

The voyages of explorers like Columbus and da Gama would not have been possible without the growth of navigational and nautical science and a number of technological innovations developed or adopted by Europeans, especially the Portuguese, during the fifteenth century. These included developments in mapmaking and geography, astronomy, navigational instruments, gunnery, and shipbuilding. Many of these built upon technological advances originating in the Middle East, but the ocean-facing orientation of Western Europe allowed them to be utilized to the utmost extent.

In Columbus' time, a number of misconceptions about the globe were still current. Both Europeans and Middle Easterners relied upon the geographical works of the second-century Greco-Roman scientist Ptolemy. While recognizing that the world was round, Ptolemy had posited a symmetrical world with an extremely hot southern hemisphere that was about one sixth smaller than the actual globe. Arab geographers had contributed a belief that the southern Atlantic was an unnavigable "green sea of darkness." All of this was encapsulated in a 1410 work entitled *Imago Mundi* (or *Image of the World*) by French theologian Pierre d'Ailly, which initially dissuaded most sailors from sailing southward but later encouraged Columbus because it presented a globe with a small circumference. Once Prince Henry was able to persuade sailors to sail south of Cape Bojador and it became apparent that southern seas were no different from those in the north, there was a new surge of interest in exploration.

Meanwhile, mapmaking was becoming more sophisticated, developing in a piecemeal fashion during the fifteenth century as sailors gained increasing knowledge about ocean coastlines and currents. European maps were primarily based on Arab maps, which from the twelfth century described most of the Mediterranean coastline, and were gradually added to by European sailors moving along the Atlantic coast. Charts were drawn by hand, crafted for functionality by sailors, and gradually improved upon with more accurate drawings and plotted courses for sailing.

Mapmaking combined with geographical and nautical knowledge as voyages increased along the Atlantic coast. Among the most important vistas of new knowledge for Atlantic sailors was the *volta do mar* (or turn of the sea) technique, which took advantage of the continually rotating systems of winds and currents in the Atlantic, the clockwise North Atlantic Gyre and counterclockwise South Atlantic Gyre. These could be utilized to rapidly sweep ships a great distance across the water. Portuguese navigators became familiar with these during the course of the fifteenth century while piloting courses to the Atlantic islands, and this knowledge was essential for the success of the voyages of Columbus, Vasco da Gama, Pedro Álvares Cabral, and others. Nonetheless, navigation was not really accurate by modern standards. Navigators employed "dead reckoning," using approximations of speed, location, and time to project their course on a chart. Although this method was subject to considerable error, some mariners, such as Columbus, were exceptionally adept at predicting their routes. This technique demanded not only skill at estimating but also accurate maps.

Astronomy, like cartography, drew upon the works of Islamic scholars, who had combined the writings of Ptolemy with close observation of the movements of heavenly objects. Like Europeans, Muslim astronomers were interested in astrology as much as in science, but their data was used for practical purposes by navigators in the Indian Ocean and Mediterranean Sea, who used the stars to calculate direction. By the 1460s, Portuguese navigators were using the altitude of the Pole Star, which was approximately lined up with the earth's axis, to calculate latitude. Below the equator, where the Pole Star is not visible, the Portuguese used the angle of the sun from the 1480s onward.

In order for such calculations to be possible, there were two necessary requirements that developed at the same time: tables showing the locations of important celestial bodies at different days and times and an instrument to measure their height. An astronomical treatise including precise charts of the positions of the sun, moon, and planets was published in 1478 by Abraham Zacuto, a Jewish astronomy professor from Spain. Zacuto, one of the foremost scholars of his day, fled Spain in 1492 when Spain expelled its Jews and continued his research as royal astronomer at John II's court in Lisbon. After the king's death, his successor, Manuel I, initiated severe persecution of Jews beginning in 1497, and Zacuto escaped to the Middle East, eventually ending up in Jerusalem.

In addition to gains in astronomical and geographical knowledge, advances in technology were just as important in improving the ability of Europeans to navigate the Atlantic Ocean. The most important instruments were the compass, the quadrant, and the astrolabe, all of which were used to determine location at sea. The wet compass, which comprised a magnetic pointer floating in liquid, had been invented in China in the third century, reached Western Europe by the twelfth century, and by the fourteenth century was modified into a needle swiveling on a pivot over a card marked with the cardinal directions. In order to calculate latitude, sailors also required the astrolabe or the quadrant, instruments that measured the height of astronomical bodies. The astrolabe was an older but more complex instrument known since antiquity but modified by Muslim astronomers during the Middle Ages. It consisted of a disk with graduated angles and a swiveling pointer with sights through apertures at the end. It was very difficult to use on a moving ship until a heavier and simpler model was devised for sailors during the fifteenth century. The quadrant, invented in the Muslim world during the Middle Ages, was a similar instrument, covering a quarter circle only and including a hanging weight for accurate determination of vertical angles. Although less accurate than an astrolabe, it was also less difficult to use and therefore was preferred by many mariners, including Columbus.

Thus, by the end of the fifteenth century, navigators had been freed from the need to hug the coast and were able to contemplate long voyages out of sight of land with the expectation that they would be able to determine their location with reasonable accuracy. Nonetheless, sailors could easily go astray at sea, and determining longitude at sea was based on guesswork until the invention of the marine chronometer, an accurate portable clock, by Englishman John Harrison in the eighteenth century.

Among the most important navigational innovations of the fifteenth century were developments in shipbuilding. During the fifteenth and sixteenth centuries, European ships went from being slow, lumbering, single-masted or oar-driven ships to vessels that were superior in speed, seaworthiness, and ability to sail far from land. This was necessitated in part by the rougher waters of the Atlantic Ocean in comparison to the relatively calm Indian Ocean and Mediterranean Sea. Under the sponsorship of Prince Henry, the Portuguese developed two ship prototypes that would make the voyages of discovery possible. These were adopted by the Spanish by the end of the fifteenth century and by other European countries thereafter. They included the caravel, a small, fast, and maneuverable ship with one to three masts, such as Columbus' *Pinta* and *Niña*, and the carrack, a larger, heavier, and more stable ship like Columbus' flagship, the *Santa María*. Caravels often carried triangular lateen sails that could be turned into the wind, but both vessels could be rigged with a combination of lateen and square sails in order to take the best advantage of prevailing wind conditions. Both types of ships were crowded and uncomfortable, with one cabin for the officers, while the crew slept on deck or below. On-board life was difficult at best. Discipline was harsh, with severe floggings for small infractions. Constant leaking necessitated continual hand pumping of water, and the food for a long voyage consisted mainly of salted meat, legumes, hard ship's biscuits, wine, and water, which were subject to deterioration and pests. Cooking was done on an open fire on deck. Any fresh provisions were soon used up, leaving ships' crews vulnerable to scurvy, an often fatal illness caused by vitamin C deficiency, which sometimes carried off more than half of a crew during a long voyage. Nonetheless, even under these conditions, the new vessels represented a significant advance in the ability of Europeans to sail long distances out of sight of land.

In addition, another major innovation was ships' gunnery, which would be central to the ability of European captains like da Gama to subdue adversaries and would be crucial in competition between ships from various European countries. Cannons, a Chinese invention, were being used effectively by both the Ottomans and Europeans by the late Middle Ages and conferred a great advantage against weaker opponents. Caravels often had apertures in the gunwales or reinforced edges to allow broadside firing. Later ships became even more formidable, with built-up "castles" on the fore and aft decks to provide height, as well as heavier cannons.

Although these innovations were first developed by the Portuguese and then rapidly adopted by the Spaniards, other regions along the Atlantic – especially Britain, France, and the Netherlands – soon caught up and eventually surpassed their predecessors as the balance of power in Europe shifted during the sixteenth century. Altogether, a number of developments, including the crusading urge, economic competition, increasing interest and investment in trade, the rumors and realities of Atlantic islands, and new nautical knowledge and technologies, combined at the end of the fifteenth century to make Columbus' 1492 voyage possible.

3   Medieval Africa

Africa, Europe, and Asia had been in contact with each other since the dawn of humankind. Indeed, modern human beings had first developed in Africa and radiated outward to the other connected continents, and contact between them had never been lost. However, this connection underwent significant changes beginning in the early fifteenth century, commencing with the increasing presence of the Portuguese along the African coast. Although there were substantial changes to African society and culture as a result of the increased contact with Europeans – particularly due to the slave trade – there was also a considerable amount of continuity with the past. The sharpest transition in the structure of African societies occurred after the beginning of European colonialism in the 1880s, many centuries after the historic intersection of societies in 1492.

Medieval Africa was very diverse ethnically, with hundreds of languages and thousands of cultures, and contained approximately 80 million people. Because of the continent's vast size and varied geographical and climate zones, there was a greater diversity of political organizations than in a small region such as Europe, and Africa contained great empires as well as regions without a strong central government that were unified by kinship connections. The continent also had some semi-sedentary and non-sedentary groups, which prevailed in the Americas as well. In addition, there were a number of large deserts, wide plains, and thick forests in the interior, creating geographical and biological barriers within the continent. The largest barriers were the great deserts – the Sahara Desert and, to a lesser extent, the Kalahari and Namib Deserts in the south – and many smaller deserts throughout the continent. The Sahara in particular is the world's largest dry desert and has served to almost completely isolate northern, western, and sub-Saharan Africa from each other. This meant significant differences in lifeways, religions, and forms of livelihood. In parts of the south, the climate and insects, especially parasite-carrying tsetse flies, also contributed to a hostile environment for some domestic animals, particularly large livestock and transport animals such as cattle, horses, donkeys, and camels.

Rather than absolute monarchies as in much of Europe, many African states had a corporate identity in which elites within the government bureaucracy elected rulers from a royal dynasty and shared in the governance and profits of the state. In some cases, governance was by coalitions of traditional leaders or semi-democratic representative bodies, including elected officials, councils of elders, or coalitions of nobles. Larger African kingdoms typically incorporated smaller political entities with local rulers, who were semi-autonomous within their regions. During the fifteenth century, northern Africa was dominated by a Tunisian sultanate in the east, while the Mamluk sultanate controlled Egypt, its power extending into the Middle East. While Spain remained Muslim, there were close economic and cultural ties spanning the Mediterranean between Iberia and North Africa. In western Africa, there were a number of powerful and mainly Muslim city-states and empires. The state of Mali was the most prominent kingdom in West Africa, and along the southern curve of West Africa there was a string of expansionist states such as the Benin Empire, paralleling a number of powerful kingdoms along the east African coast. These states were partitioned by the inhospitable Sahara Desert covering much of the central part of North Africa.

Rather than private ownership of land as was found in Europe, African states typically controlled access to land, with peasant farmers possessing rights, regulated through fees and taxes, to cultivate the soil and to keep and sell the harvests. As elsewhere throughout the world, most people were peasants, though as in Europe, trade was becoming a more important source of revenue during the fifteenth century, especially in coastal regions. Like Europeans but unlike Native Americans, Africans used iron and steel weapons and possessed many kinds of domesticated animals. There were many cities, especially along trade routes in East and West Africa and along the Mediterranean and Indian Ocean coasts, that were comparable to European cities in size, complexity, and wealth.

African trade

Throughout the early modern period, Africans were active participants in the international Mediterranean and Indian Ocean trade systems and then in the Atlantic world trade system into the nineteenth century. African states had engaged in commerce among themselves and with Europeans and Middle Easterners for centuries, and large empires and kingdoms with trade-based economies existed throughout northern and sub-Saharan Africa. Prior to the development of an extensive Atlantic slave trade, these states traded ivory – both carved and raw – pepper, salt, gold, and human slaves – the latter mainly to the Middle East – in exchange for horses; raw iron and copper; guns; and luxury products such as steel goods, cloth, and beads. Gold and salt in particular produced great wealth for Africans. The horses, raw metals, and guns (at least initially) supplied local deficiencies, but the remainder of these products was also produced in Africa to equivalent levels of quality. However, foreign-made goods were seen as rare luxuries and were therefore desirable. Originally, many of these trade goods came through the Sahara Desert on camel caravans into western and southern Africa. On the east coast of Africa, a number of African city-states and kingdoms, including the cities of Mombasa and Malindi and the kingdom of Zimbabwe, served as hubs of the Indian Ocean trade network, which connected the cities of East Africa, the Middle East, India, and China.

During the Middle Ages, African trade was oriented northward and eastward, and African sailing ships were built to sail in the relatively calm Mediterranean Sea and the Indian Ocean rather than in the rougher Atlantic. Once the Portuguese began sailing along the west coast of Africa in the fifteenth century, a considerable system of exchange arose between the Portuguese and African states along the west African coast – for example, with the Benin Empire or the kingdom of Kongo. The rulers of these states utilized the economic and diplomatic ties that they formed with the Portuguese monarchy to bolster the strength of their regimes and their realms. They formed diplomatic ties with Portugal, received Portuguese ambassadors, and sent diplomats to Europe. They engaged in commerce with Portuguese traders to bypass the traditional routes of exchange through the African interior; purchased Portuguese firearms which they used to extend their territories; and, in the Kongo, the royal dynasty converted to Christianity.

Africans initially entered the Atlantic trade system from a position of strength. African wealth was considerable, and the continent supplied most of the gold in circulation around the globe. In fact, African gold was crucial to the commercial growth of medieval Mediterranean societies in Europe. The kingdom of Mali in the northwest dominated the world gold trade during the late Middle Ages. When Mansa Musa, Mali's fourteenth-century Muslim king, made a pilgrimage to Mecca, his lavish spending created a worldwide depression in gold prices for the next century. Mansa Musa was so famous that although he was a Muslim, some scholars have identified him as the source of the European myth of Prester John, the powerful Christian king believed by Europeans to rule a realm in northwest Africa.

African society

Northern Africa also provided a significant repository of knowledge that was highly important in the early modern world. During much of the Middle Ages, Europe abandoned and then lost the learning of the classical world, but classical knowledge and literature was preserved in the Muslim Middle East and in North Africa. Scholars in these regions continued to build upon ancient literary, philosophical, medical, and scientific knowledge, while Europe stagnated during the early Middle Ages. When Europeans came into contact with classical and Muslim learning after the Crusades, it came into the eastern Mediterranean, especially Italy, from the Middle East and into Western Europe through Muslim Spain via North Africa. For example, the city of Timbuktu in Mali contained a repository of hundreds of thousands of manuscripts containing much of the recorded knowledge of Africa, Asia, and Europe. Most of sub-Saharan Africa, on the other hand, was preliterate at the beginning of the early modern period, with traditions and knowledge passed on orally.

African religions also varied considerably. The two biggest religious traditions were Christianity in East Africa and Islam in West and northern Africa, and the regions that followed these faiths regularly engaged in warfare to extend their influence. However, the majority of Africans followed local traditional belief systems during the early modern period, sometimes combining them with Islam or Christianity. These religious systems included West African Vodun and the widespread Bantu tradition in the southern portion of Africa, as well as more localized traditions. Although there was considerable variation, there were also usually some shared similarities. These belief systems typically included belief in a creator god or goddess and lesser gods and goddesses who were often linked to natural forces and who inhabited a spiritual realm along with human ancestors. Gods, spirits, and ancestors communicated with human worshippers through dreams, visions, or spirit possession. Humans could ask spiritual beings to intercede in the affairs of humans, and divination and traditional healing were important practices. There was considerable spiritual equality in terms of gender, and both spiritual beings and religious practitioners could be male and female. Once the Atlantic slave trade was under way, African religious forms spread throughout the African diaspora.

African social organization showed both similarities and differences from that of Europe. Much as in Europe, there were traditional roles for individuals with particular occupations, including traders, peasants, and artisans who produced various kinds of goods. While kinship was important in Europe, it was a central organizing factor in African societies, with kin usually living in close proximity to their extended family. Society was governed by elders, especially in non-urban areas. In addition, southern and eastern African societies were also often divided along the line of age-sets in which cohorts of people of similar ages gained particular rights and obligations upon attaining chronological milestones and shared ties that in some circumstances might be more binding than extended kinship. Elders were particularly respected. Cultural variations existed between various ethnic groups, with different peoples emphasizing individualism or traditional values, for example. Social expectations tended to be stricter in Muslim areas, but because of the proximity to the Mediterranean and the Indian Ocean, there were also more opportunities for trade, scholarly endeavors, and cross-cultural contact in general within these regions.

Within the household, extended families prevailed. Monogamy was the norm, although polygamy existed and was typically a privilege of wealthy and influential men. In Muslim North Africa, gender norms were similar to those of Europe and the Middle East; women's lives were restricted, and they were expected to cover their bodies and heads and to adhere to a strict code of sexual morality. However, social expectations for women tended to be less rigid in Muslim West Africa or in non-Islamic regions. As elsewhere, men were officially in control, but in some non-Muslim areas women possessed a relatively high status, particularly because they controlled family interests in land or because family lineages conferring inheritance or political power were matrilineal.

Africa and Europe had always been in contact with each other, and during the period discussed in this book, contact continued to increase. The earliest intensive contact between Africans and Europeans was around the Mediterranean rim, as North African, Middle Eastern, and southern European regions interacted through trade and sometimes warfare, including the warfare between Rome and Carthage and the conquest of Spain by the North African Umayyad dynasty in the early eighth century. Spain remained Muslim and Moorish (North African Muslim) until the southward push of Spanish Christian kingdoms during the Reconquista, which culminated in the successful final conquest of Spain by the Catholic monarchs – Ferdinand II of Aragon and Isabella I of Castile – in 1492. In addition, African and eastern European slaves had sporadically appeared in both regions, mainly trafficked by Middle Eastern Muslim merchants. From the mid-fifteenth century, the increasing Portuguese proficiency at seafaring meant that the west coast of Africa came into increasing contact with Portuguese sailors, merchants, and diplomats. The influx of Europeans provided a challenge to African states but was seen by them as beneficial; the newcomers were unable to coerce the Africans for the most part. The two exceptions were territories that the Portuguese managed to occupy in Angola and in the Cape of Good Hope in South Africa (which soon became Dutch territory). Using a mixture of diplomacy and cannon fire, the Portuguese were able to establish small fortresses as footholds along the coast, but in general they remained subject to the power of local rulers and negotiated with African merchants on an equal basis. Larger west coast African states such as the Kingdom of Benin, the Kongo, and Luanda formed the strongest association with the Portuguese as the trade of western Africa began to reorient from the Middle East to the Atlantic.

The career of the early sixteenth-century king of Kongo, Affonso I, illustrates the mutual ties that bound the two regions; he was a Christian convert who supported many Portuguese political and economic interests in West Africa, sent his children to study in Europe, and promoted Catholicism and Western education. Throughout his reign, he judiciously selected those aspects of Portuguese culture that he judged were to the advantage of both his people and himself: he took advantage of Portuguese military support to establish himself on the throne and expand his realm but simultaneously retained autonomy, refusing cultural intrusions that he deemed negative. Thus, he opposed the Portuguese slave trade and refused to sell Kongolese land to the Portuguese.

In summation, Africans and Europeans were far more similar to each other than they would be to most Native American groups. They had been in communication for millennia and had had much physical, cultural, and intellectual contact, which included existing within the same zone of infectious diseases, sharing some religious beliefs, and engaging in trade. The two also had technological similarities, with widespread domestication of animals and the ability to fashion iron and steel tools and weapons. However, African technology on the west coast of the continent lagged behind European technology in two crucial areas: nautical technology and weaponry. While African societies that abutted the Mediterranean and the Indian Ocean possessed technologies similar to those in Europe, the use of small rowed vessels and the lack of guns on the west African coast weakened those societies in their encounters with the Portuguese. However, ultimately, even these technological benefits were not sufficient to give the Portuguese the upper hand, and most transactions were conducted on a relatively equal basis. As the Portuguese improved their ability to sail along the African coast, European and African societies came into extended contact along the west coast of Africa in the fifteenth century, significantly affecting the development of West Africa.

4   The Americas

The peoples of the Old World, composed of Asia, Africa, and Europe, had been in contact with their geographical neighbors for millennia – since the beginning of humankind. However, the peoples of the New World, the Americas, had been much more isolated. Indeed, the ancestors of most Native Americans had arrived during three waves of migration from 30,000 to 13,000 years ago and had mainly lost contact with the Old World at the end of the last period of major glacial advancement, although the Inuit continued to travel throughout the Arctic. Although in many ways human development was parallel in the two regions, in many other respects the Americas took different paths in both biological development and human social development. Unlike the peoples of Africa, Asia, and Europe, Native American peoples had few domesticated animals and, with the exception of dogs (and llamas and alpacas in western South America), did not employ draft animals for labor or warfare. They also lacked the knowledge of working iron and steel and thus lacked weapons made from these materials. Finally, they existed in a less virulent disease environment, in part because they had less daily contact with animals. As in other parts of the world, the two main types of civilizations in the Americas consisted of densely settled urban populations and a number of less sedentary populations, some of which migrated seasonally or every few years to new territories. In 1492, there was a total population of approximately 60 million Native Americans on the two American continents. As in other parts of the world, urban people made up most of the Amerindian population. Approximately 21 million in Mexico and another 6 million in Central America made up 45% of the entire Amerindian population, while 12 million people in the Andes added up to another 20%, leaving another 21 million people – or 35% of the total population – less densely settled in the vast reaches of North and South America.

After the first contact in the Caribbean, Europeans who arrived in the New World initially gravitated toward the urban populations which were similar to European societies and possessed assets desirable to Europeans such as precious metals, complex manufactured goods, and agricultural land. At the time of the Spanish arrival, these peoples included the Nahua in central Mexico, the Maya and Mixtec in Central America, and the Quechua of the Andes. Central Mexico and the Andes are frequently referred to as the Aztec and Inca Empires, but these terms are not fully accurate. The people often called the Aztecs usually identified themselves as the Mexica and were part of a larger cultural group called the Nahua which included hundreds of Amerindian cities and confederations that were often at war with each other. The term *Aztec* refers to those who came from Aztlán, a mythological place of origin for the Mexica. Likewise, the group often designated as the Inca were Quechua, although the ethnicity itself extended beyond the borders of the empire. The term *Inca* referred only to the ruling dynasty.

These large urban populations were organized as city-states and shared a number of similarities, with hierarchical societies that comprised rulers, nobles, and commoners; urban infrastructure including massive stone buildings; a state religion; well-established systems of trade; tribute and taxation; government control of assets such as farmland, militaries, and natural resources; private ownership of land and goods; a tradition of warfare and conquest; and, with the exception of the Quechua, writing. The rulers of these societies came from royal dynasties that engaged their regions in warfare against smaller weaker regions and sometimes united with other city-states in larger confederations, gaining control over larger empires. At the time of first contact with the Spaniards, both the Mexica and the Quechua were in a state of some political instability due to the resistance of surrounding communities to their continued imperial expansion which, in the case of the Inca Empire, had helped inspire an internal rebellion.

The lives of ordinary people in these societies were similar to those of Europeans within general parameters. Most ordinary people subsisted upon agriculture, employing a number of techniques to bolster agricultural fertility, including irrigation, terracing, and draining wetlands. Families controlled their own land and passed it on to their children, with men taking on the planting and harvesting and women processing agricultural produce. Unlike the Old World of Europe, Asia, and Africa, there were only a few domesticated animals: turkeys and Muscovy ducks in Mesoamerica; llamas, alpacas, and guinea pigs in the Andes; and dogs throughout the Americas. In more densely settled areas, urban professionals included merchants and artisans who lived and worked in special districts producing and selling cloth, including luxury fabrics, and ceramics, precious metals, and other products. Ordinary people were liable for taxes, labor, and military duty to the government, while the noble classes supplied military leaders and the priesthood. Less is known about women's roles than men's positions in society, but women were usually in charge of maintaining the household and were important in the manufacturing and selling of cloth, one of the most important trade goods, and other products. They had the right to own property, including land. Individual households centered predominantly around nuclear families, but men with wealth and status often had sexual access to a number of women.

Mesoamerica

The region best known to scholars today is Mexico because of the large number of surviving documents from both the natives and the invaders. In addition, because of the early contact with the Mexica, the Spaniards encountered a society that still existed in a preconquest condition, whereas Andean civilization had already been devastated by disease when the Spaniards first arrived.

Most of Mesoamerica was inhabited by the Nahua people, who spoke the Nahuatl language. The region contained hundreds of individual city-states called *altepetl*, a term meaning water and mountains that referred to the land controlled by a particular region. Individual altepetl often formed confederations with others for the purpose of conquest or defense, while smaller or weaker altepetl often paid tribute to larger city-states. Altepetl were separated into semi-autonomous individual districts called *calpulli*, which were defined based on administrative needs, kinship, or occupational relationships. Calpulli were governed by leaders who owed allegiance, taxes, and the periodic labor duty of their subjects to the altepetl's ruler or *tlatoani*. Although commoners did not ordinarily own land, they were allocated agricultural land by their calpulli, which also regulated education, although most people were probably not literate. Mesoamericans, including the Nahua, Maya, Zapotec, and Olmec, did have a writing tradition of over 2,000 years' duration in 1492; they used a variety of scripts with pictographic and phonetic characters on paper and stone. The Maya of Central America possessed the most developed script.

Mesoamerican religion was polytheistic, with a number of gods who commanded various forms of sacred power but who also demonstrated human-like traits such as anger, jealousy, or arrogance, much like the gods of the ancient Greeks. Most deities demonstrated both benevolence and aggression toward humans and had to be appeased by the actions of worshippers, usually through worship, tribute, and sacrifice during a cycle of annual religious festivals. Religious activities were directed by a priesthood drawn from the ranks of the nobility and closely tied to the state, and large stone pyramidal temples were a central fixture in population centers. A principle of gender complementarity in Nahua society ensured that there were dual institutions for males and females, including schools and public offices, and even deities imbued with particular qualities usually occurred in gendered pairs. Among the Nahua, in addition to being a separate political unit, each altepetl had its own version of the mythology, with special deities who were usually believed to be divine ancestors of the local ruler. The rulers of the altepetl and calpulli were central in leading worship and in supplying sacrificial needs, which consisted at various times of blood sacrifices given from the ruler's body, animal sacrifice, and human sacrifice. For Mesoamericans, these sacrifices not only propitiated the gods but ensured that the cosmic cycle of birth and death, which linked human life to the daily rise of the sun and the change in seasons, could continue. Among the Nahua, some of the more important deities included Huitzilopochtli, the warlike patron of the Mexica; his mother Coatlicue, a monstrous earth goddess; Quetzalcoatl, the feathered serpent, who was associated with knowledge, resurrection, and the creation of humans through sacrificing his own blood; Chalchiuhtlicue, goddess of water; and Tlaloc, the rain god. Mesoamericans also engaged in a ritualized ball game in which two teams aimed to propel a rubber ball through a stone hoop. Although the game was played recreationally, it was also part of formal religious festivals that may sometimes have involved the sacrifice of team members.

The Mexica (Aztecs)

The Mexica were relative newcomers to Mexico, probably arriving in the mid-thirteenth century and coming to dominate the region by the mid-fifteenth century. By the sixteenth century, they were at the head of a confederation of three altepetl, often termed the Triple Alliance, containing Mexico-Tenochtitlán, Tetzcoco, and Tlacopan. Through several generations of war, the Triple Alliance had conquered a large empire that controlled much of what is now central Mexico. Conquered altepetl retained internal self-sufficiency and kept their local rulers but owed a tribute of goods, labor, and sacrificial captives to the capital city of Tenochtitlán. The empire reached its greatest extent under the leadership of the ninth tlatoani, Moctezuma II, who encountered the forces of the Spaniards in 1519.

Tenochtitlán, the most important city, had a population of approximately 200,000 people, the largest city in the Americas in 1500, and bigger than most European cities. Indeed, it was much larger and wealthier than any Spanish city and had a sophisticated infrastructure containing sizeable public squares, an advanced system of aqueducts, great markets, massive temples, a zoo, gardens, and other civic buildings. The city was built on reclaimed land drained from Lake Texcoco and was spanned by numerous canals that were used for transportation. There were three main causeways connecting the city to the mainland, making it almost unassailable.

This defensibility was necessary, because as the Mexica Empire expanded, it had created mortal enemies along its borders among Nahua altepetl that had resisted its encroachment. The most powerful of these was the altepetl of Tlaxcala, which was later to provide crucial support to the invading Spanish. Opposition to the Mexica was based not only on resistance to invasion. The Triple Alliance had adopted a number of religious innovations that terrorized their neighbors. They had elevated the bloodthirsty god Huitzilopochtli to the head of their pantheon and had enormously amplified the role of human sacrifice in religious ceremonies, on some occasions sacrificing hundreds of victims who were violently slaughtered. In order to ensure the flow of captives, they engaged in what they termed "flower wars" which were fought to terrorize the surrounding areas and supply sacrificial prisoners rather than to expand the empire. This strategy amplified the fear and hatred of surrounding communities and eventually contributed to the downfall of the Aztecs.

The central Andes

The Andes region governed by the Inca dynasty is less well understood than Mesoamerica, in part because the society was in such disarray when European observers arrived, and also because of the lack of sources that describe preconquest Quechua society. The Quechua did not possess writing, though they employed a technique known as *quipu*, which consisted of intricately arranged knotted strings for recordkeeping and accounting.

Geographically, the empire ruled by the Incas was vast, controlling widely spread populations and rivaling the largest empires of world history. It stretched along the Andes Mountains in northwest South America, encompassing much of modern Ecuador, Peru, Chile, Bolivia, and Argentina. As a result, the government of the Incas, ruled from the capital of Cuzco in southern Peru, built an extensive system of roads, some of which still exist today, with storage depots at periodic intervals. In addition, the government developed an extensive infrastructure including temples, palaces, and fortresses that encompassed both local and more far-flung locations in what is now Chile as well as the famed mountain site of Machu Picchu in Peru, likely a retreat for the Inca emperor. The regime also controlled agricultural land; stores of goods and food; herds of animals; and the manufacture of goods such as cloth, bronze weapons, and precious metals.

The Inca Empire possessed a hierarchical society in which rulers, nobles, and priests possessed great power over the lives of common people. Large cohorts of ordinary people were periodically moved by the central government for the purposes of construction, agriculture, manufacture of goods, mining, or military service. However, a principle of reciprocity underlay the structuring of society and ensured that the state also assumed responsibility for guaranteeing that commoners were provided with food and supplies for living.

The nuclear family predominated for commoners, while the nobility were polygamous. In ordinary households, women maintained the home, while both spouses worked in agriculture. Men were often called away by the state for military or labor duties, called *mita*, while women might be drafted for cloth production enterprises. The state provided schools for upper-class men and women. The Quechua also practiced cranial deformation, in which the skulls of infants were shaped by binding.

The Inca Empire was assembled by both conquest and alliances beginning in the mid-fifteenth century, so it had only been in existence for about a century at the time of the Spanish conquest. Much like the empire ruled by the Mexica, the Inca Empire consisted of a number of smaller, semi-autonomous kingdoms with their own rulers and customs which paid tribute to the Inca dynasty in Cuzco. These kingdoms were subdivided into *ayllu*, similar to the Nahua calpulli.

The Quechua, like the Nahua, were polytheistic, but the Inca promoted the sun god Inti to the top of the pantheon and claimed him as the ancestor of the Inca dynasty. Other gods who mostly represented cosmic forces included Mama Pacha, goddess of the earth and fertility; Mama Quilla, goddess of the moon; Pacha Camac, creator of humans; Viracocha, who had created the world; and Illapa, a weather god, as well as many others. Quechua divinities were more predictable than Nahua deities, and some were benevolent. Nonetheless, they too were propitiated with sacrifices of animals, goods or, in some cases, humans. Upon the death of an Inca ruler, hundreds of court retainers and concubines were sacrificed to accompany him into the afterlife. At times of crisis such as famines, human sacrifices – often children – were offered to the gods, but unlike Mexica practices, these individuals, sometimes from the upper classes, were usually well treated, sedated prior to being put to death, and worshipped after sacrifice as deities.

Semi-sedentary and non-sedentary populations

Outside the two urban regions of Mesoamerica and the Andes, there were about 21 million people in the Americas in 1492, comprising many thousands of cultural groups, each with its own traditions, lifeways, and language. Most of this Amerindian population was semi-sedentary, living in villages and migrating seasonally in response to cyclical changes of weather or moving every few years to new areas with undepleted soil and sources of food. In addition, in some areas such as the eastern coast of North America and the Caribbean and possibly the Amazon, populations had settled relatively permanently in villages of several thousand people, but these areas were far less densely populated than in the more urban territories. Whether sedentary or not, these peoples tended to be organized around kinship rather than social hierarchies as in the larger empires. Tribes or bands were led by chiefs, called *sachems* in some northeast communities and *caciques* in the Caribbean, and by councils of elders. Leaders were sometimes hereditary and sometimes chosen through election by elders or tribe members and were usually, but not always, male. Semi-sedentary and village-based peoples lived by farming, hunting, fishing, and gathering wild foods. They constructed some urban infrastructure such as shared dwellings, farmlands, and irrigation canals or palisades around towns or villages, but they did not develop monumental architecture and also did not possess many other aspects of urban societies such as taxation systems, rigid laws, priesthoods, or marked social hierarchies. Social norms were decided by community consensus or the decisions of elders and were enforced through shaming and exclusion. Tribes were structured cooperatively, with food and resources being meted out equally. In most cases, chiefs and their families lived like other members of the group.

In addition, some inland groups followed partially or fully non-sedentary lifestyles, usually when living in regions with few resources such as deserts, arctic regions, or grasslands, areas in which obtaining necessary provisions required covering long distances. They lived in easily moveable homes such as the *tipis* of the Great Plains and were among the last Amerindians to come into contact with Europeans.

Gender norms for non-urban Amerindian groups tended to be less regimented than among the urban Indian societies or among Europeans. While labor was usually organized along gendered lines, with men hunting and women caring for the household and engaging in agriculture, and with both sexes involved in daily activities like the production of weapons and tools, there was some flexibility in many groups. Women governed the village while men were away hunting, and some women hunted or engaged in warfare from necessity or personal choice. Most tribes were matrilineal, with kinship defined through the female line, and women tended to possess higher standing than women from urban Amerindian societies or among Europeans. Many Amerindian village-based or mobile groups incorporated semi-egalitarian gender norms establishing the leadership of male and female assemblies of elders; equal inheritance of goods; and equivalent access to justice, marriage, and divorce.

Each tribal group followed its own religious traditions, with significant differences, but there were similar patterns across many groups. Most believed that the world was infused with spiritual power, with no separation between the secular and sacred realms. Some groups, like the Cherokee of southeastern North America, believed in a Great Spirit who had created the world and who continued to permeate the world with its essence. Many groups also held that spirit beings invested objects, animals, and powerful natural forces, such as thunder or fire, with sacred power. They accepted that visions and dreams held guidelines for human action and that spiritual practitioners such as healers and shamans possessed a special connection to the spiritual world. In addition to daily ritual practices, traditional worship at tribal gatherings incorporated dance, music, and storytelling.

Religious belief in the interconnectedness of the world helped shape social structures. Reverence for the sacred forces of nature meant respect for the land, not outstripping its resources. If angered, the spiritual forces of the land would retaliate against humans, but if respected and worshipped, the land and sacred spirits would be generous. There was no concept of private ownership of land, which was seen as a part of the whole of nature, which also included humans. This was to cause mutual incomprehension when these groups first encountered Europeans, who adhered to acquisitive, individualistic ideals and defined land as private property to be fenced in by its owners.

The Caribbean

The earliest groups of Amerindians to encounter Europeans were the Taíno people of the Caribbean, who were part of the larger South American Arawak language group which also populated the north coast of South America. There were approximately 1 million Taíno on the island of Hispaniola in 1492. Taíno society showed more social differentiation than many other native societies, with hereditary caciques whose households lived more loftily than other Taíno and a class of nobles. Rulers wore gold ornaments, which convinced Spanish conquerors that gold would be available in abundance. Taíno lived mainly in multifamily houses, and Taíno towns included plazas for ceremonial and recreational activities. They worshipped a number of spirits (or *zemis*), the most important of which were Yúcahu, creator and god of cassava, the staple food, and Atabey, goddess of fertility and bodies of water.

The other main group inhabiting the Caribbean were the Caribs, after whom the region was named. The people called Caribs mainly inhabited the remote Lesser Antilles – the southeast portion of the Caribbean islands – making them difficult to defeat. Like the Taíno, they subsisted mainly on fishing and agriculture, but they were also noted for their practice of raiding Taíno villages, taking goods and kidnapping women who were then incorporated into Carib society. There has been some debate among scholars as to whether the Caribs were a distinctly different group than the Taíno and whether they spoke another dialect of Arawak or a dissimilar language or if the conquistadors had created the distinction when they distinguished those groups that resisted conquest from the more peaceful Taíno. Further, while the Spaniards claimed that the Caribs were cannibals (indeed, the word Carib is the source of the European term "cannibal"), many scholars argue that this ascription was part of an attempt to vilify those groups that opposed the conquerors rather than an accurate description.

Caribbean societies rapidly disappeared after contact with Europeans, to some degree caused by ill treatment by Spaniards and other Europeans, but primarily as a consequence of contact with European diseases. By about 1700, the Caribbean population of Amerindians had almost disappeared. There is much debate today about whether any of the Taíno or Caribs still survive. For centuries, it was assumed that the native population of the Caribbean had entirely disappeared by the seventeenth century. However, there are several groups and individuals living in the Caribbean today that claim indigenous origins, and DNA studies have shown that many people in the Caribbean have some Amerindian ancestry. Further, many communities still uphold, at least in part, Amerindian cultural practices, including agricultural and fishing methods, celebratory festivals, and other traditions. There are still some Arawak groups on the South American mainland.

Eastern coasts of North America

In the eastern woodlands, there were many dozens of individual cultures who spoke a variety of languages and sometimes allied or fought with each other. People lived in villages of several thousand in portable individual homes such as *wigwams* or *wetus* or in communal longhouses used in colder weather (see Figure 4.1). The use of canoes enabled widespread transportation and contact with other groups.

Many Amerindian tribes joined confederations which allowed them to maintain trade or guard against adversaries. The eastern woodlands from New York to Pennsylvania were dominated by an expansionist group termed the Iroquois Confederacy formed in the late fifteenth century, primarily to unite against the rival Algonquian peoples. It consisted of five tribes – the Cayuga, Mohawk, Oneida, Onondaga, and Seneca – adding the Tuscarora in the early eighteenth century. Although the tribes did not always act in concert, the coalition allowed the Iroquois to dominate the region, reduced internal strife, enabled them to coordinate military policy and trade, and prepared them to more effectively resist the Europeans when they arrived.

Society was structured communally, with many important decisions made democratically by vote, with all members of the community, even children, taking part. Women held a high level of political influence. Iroquois society was organized around extended matrilineal kinship groups called *ohwachira*. Each ohwachira was headed by a woman elder, and women chose the chiefs of their clan. While these chiefs were ultimately the leaders, they could be dismissed if they failed to support the aims of their women constituents. These values were very different from those of Europeans, whose society was extremely hierarchical, with marked distinctions between people of different social status, men and women, and adults and children. This social pattern of confederated tribes with communal values predominated along the North American coast down to Mesoamerica, encompassing the Muscogee or Creek Confederacy in the south and the Algonquian peoples in the north, as well as many other groups.

In addition to maintaining communal values, individuals within the tribe were expected to take an equal share in the daily work of providing necessities. They were expected to behave with dignity, even under extreme conditions. Warfare occurred regularly, usually based on feuds and desire for vengeance between tribes or confederations, and military skills were highly prized. Brave and successful warriors were particularly admired, while defeated captives might be tortured, executed or, according to some reports, cannibalized, though they might also be adopted into a tribe, particularly when population levels dropped.

When the northern tribes first came into contact with Europeans, their traditional lifeways were so dissimilar that, at first, both sides had difficulty in understanding the other. Because of the later European contact with the northern regions, northern Amerindian societies gained some advantage

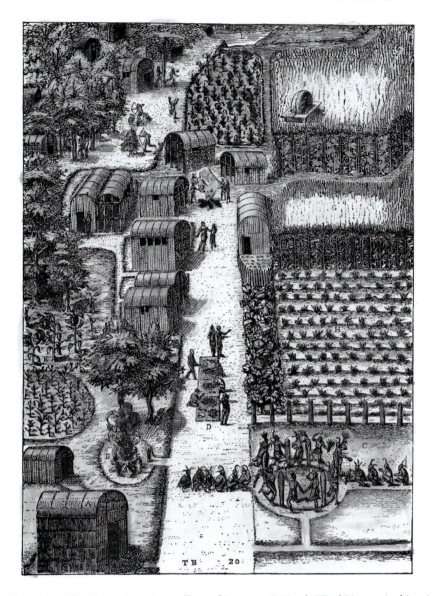

Figure 4.1 The Native American village of Secotan. © North Wind Picture Archives/ Alamy

through learning about Europeans more gradually, initially encountering only individuals or small groups. However, as a result of these early contacts, the transmission of epidemic disease from the Old World often preceded large-scale efforts at European settlement and placed northern Native Americans in a disadvantageous position which was exacerbated by the disparity of military technologies. For example, approximately half of the initial Iroquois population of 20,000 had died of smallpox by the mid-seventeenth century. Nonetheless, the mobility, cooperative values, and warlike traditions of semi- and non-sedentary populations meant that it would take a long time before Europeans were fully in control of the North and South American continents.

In 1492, the lives and societies of Europeans and Africans were already interwoven, while Americans had been mainly isolated for many millennia. Yet the new encounters caused by Columbus' first voyage would be a turning point for all societies involved. The populations of the four continents rimming the Atlantic – Africa, Europe, North America, and South America – came into abrupt and unexpected contact in 1492 when Columbus landed in the Caribbean on October 12, 1492. This encounter was to transform both the Old and New Worlds, which would develop new societies based on the interaction of people from these continents. The encounter would reorient the focus of global political and economic systems from Asia to the Atlantic.

Europe was uniquely poised to take advantage of this change. Although it took a long time, the Asian empires that had previously been dominant globally through military strength and control over trade gradually lost their control over these spheres during the succeeding centuries. The Ottoman Empire was essentially landlocked, without direct access to either the Indian Ocean or the Atlantic, while China was geographically blocked by the vast Pacific Ocean and remained largely content to invest in Indian Ocean trade. Africans were also oriented eastward and northward toward the Mediterranean and Indian Ocean trade systems, and once Portuguese voyagers began to sail along the west African coast, they had little need to develop their own shipping to advance commerce. Thus, 1492 was a pivotal year in the reshaping of power relations and political and economic systems around the globe.

Part II
Colonization and conquest

5   The voyages of Columbus

In 1451, Cristoforo Colombo (Christopher Columbus) was born in the port city of Genoa in northern Italy into a struggling family with many children. From the beginning, the young Columbus found himself in an environment which would shape his aspirations and expectations and mold him into the explorer he became in his later life. The Republic of Genoa had been an independent state for several centuries during that time and was known for its seafarers and explorers, many of whom had sailed under the flags of other Italian cities or for Portugal. Genoa had also involved itself in a number of colonizing ventures, controlling colonies in northern Italy, the Middle East, North Africa, and eastern Europe. The Vivaldi brothers who had sailed into the Atlantic in the thirteenth century were also Genoese. Columbus had much experience in sailing and navigation. He started his career at sea early, probably before he reached his teens. During this time, he acquired the navigational expertise that was to stand him in good stead during his famous expedition. He spent most of his youth and early life traveling around the Mediterranean and North Africa, including the Portuguese islands, and possibly even reaching Iceland, while engaging in commercial ventures, often through contacts with merchants from his home city or through family connections. He showed little allegiance to any state, and indeed his life exemplified the tradition of commercial travel that had been flourishing around the Mediterranean since ancient times and which had been expanding since the twelfth century.

Columbus' personal experiences also helped shape his behavior and expectations when he departed on his famous voyage. His private journals show that he was a deeply religious man, convinced that he had a divine mission to propagate Catholicism. Columbus was also an avid reader of travel and geographical works like the writings of the thirteenth-century Italian traveler Marco Polo, who had journeyed on a commercial expedition across Asia to China and later wrote a narrative about his travels. Columbus' own travels also helped form the framework for his later behavior. During his time in Africa, he spent time sailing along the African coast, where he was exposed to commerce in gold and human slaves. He also spent considerable time working in the Mediterranean islands; in Lisbon; and on the Portuguese island of

Porto Santo off the African coast, part of the Madeira group, where he was employed as an agent for a Genoese firm involved in the sugar trade. There he observed African slave labor on the sugar plantations and also married the daughter of a local nobleman. Columbus' family connections were also deeply important to his later career. Columbus' father-in-law, Bartolomeu Perestrello, had also been an explorer, one of the first Europeans to land on Porto Santo. Likewise, Columbus continued to maintain family connections later in life, and his brother and then his sons joined him on some of his journeys across the Atlantic. These experiences formed the context for Columbus' behavior and opinions during his voyages.

Columbus' mistake

Although no one was known to have successfully sailed across the Atlantic Ocean previously, there was great incentive to do so. Columbus' main intent was to gain access to the riches of the Asian spice trade, and he was also interested in the possibility of converting Asians to Catholicism. However, he had a difficult time finding sponsors for his enterprise. Columbus, together with his brother Bartholomew, a mapmaker, initially attempted to obtain funds and a charter from England and Portugal, regions that were extensively involved in Atlantic ventures; he also sought backing from some of the Italian city-states and France. He was repeatedly turned down, even though interest in the spice trade remained high. After these initial rejections, he eventually found a sympathetic reception with the Spanish monarchs. Columbus initially utilized his personal contacts among Genoese merchants and financiers to gain access to the Spanish court.

There were a number of reasons why most European rulers were hesitant to support or finance Columbus' voyage. The most important one was that it was too risky. Scientific advisors to these leaders correctly pointed out that Columbus' estimate of the length of a potential trans-Atlantic voyage was far too small. Since they were unaware of the existence of the American continents, according to the knowledge of the day, they believed that the Atlantic Ocean was actually three times the size that Columbus had claimed. No one had ever journeyed so far before. The ships of the period simply could not carry sufficient provisions or water for such a trip.

Although it is commonly believed that Columbus was the first to argue that the world was round since ancient times, this is a misconception. Instead, Columbus misunderstood the true size of the globe. Most educated men had known since the time of the ancient Greeks that the earth was round. This is amply illustrated by the use of the orb, a cross-topped sphere, by kings during the Middle Ages to signify royal and Christian authority over the globe. Sailors and navigators like Columbus routinely used the position of the sun and stars in the sky as a means of navigation under the assumption that they were revolving around a round globe. This would be disproved in the

"Copernican Revolution," in which sixteenth- and seventeenth-century scientists like Nicolaus Copernicus and Galileo Galilei showed that the earth actually revolved around the sun. However, in the Middle Ages, not only was the world known to be round, but the size of the globe had already been calculated with great accuracy in the third-century BCE by the mathematician and geographer Eratosthenes using calculations of the angle of the sun's rays at different locations. Nonetheless, some later geographers had made estimates that were less accurate, including the second-century astronomer Ptolemy, who miscalculated the size of the globe by about one sixth. As chance would have it, it was Ptolemy's works that were more popular and that fell into the hands of Columbus. Thus, while many scientists of the day accepted a fairly accurate assessment of the earth's size, Columbus, who was an entrepreneur and a sailor rather than a scholar, accepted Ptolemy's estimates. Even within the scientific community, there was some dispute about the exact circumference of the earth, because it was not entirely clear what measurements the ancient scholars had used. Columbus accepted the smallest possible calculation of global size in all of his estimates. He recognized a smaller measure of longitude than Ptolemy had used, thus accepting a figure for the circumference of the globe that was about 25% too small.

Columbus made further geographical mistakes because he was influenced by geographical errors that he found in the writings of Marco Polo. The latter believed that Asia was much larger than it actually is so that it took up more surface space on the globe. This misperception was also verified by Ptolemy's works. Further, Marco Polo had believed that Japan (which he had never visited) was over 1,500 miles from Asia, whereas it is actually about 120 miles from the Korean peninsula. Columbus wrote a number of marginal notes in his editions of the books of Ptolemy and Marco Polo, indicating deep interest. Put together, his geographical miscalculations led him to believe that by sailing westward, he could reach Japan in about 3,000 miles. He actually would have had to sail something like 10,500 miles. Thus, when Columbus reached the island of San Salvador in the Caribbean, he was convinced that he was somewhere near Japan.

The first voyage

The Spanish monarchs Ferdinand and Isabella, like other European leaders, were interested in obtaining access to the spice trade. Since the Ottoman Turks had conquered Constantinople in 1453 and made it the seat of their expanding empire, the land route had become too dangerous. The obvious sea route down the coast of Africa was firmly under the control of Spain's rival, Portugal. Yet the Spanish initially hesitated, because what Columbus proposed seemed so impossible. As in other regions, scientific advisors in Spain also advised against the voyages. But in Spain, several factors intervened on Columbus' behalf.

The year 1492 was a critical year in Spain. The king and queen had just completed the *Reconquista* (or reconquest) of Spain, finally defeating the forces of the Moors (North African Muslims) at the city of Granada. Although the Moors had been relatively tolerant of other cultures and beliefs, the Spanish monarchs were not and ordered the remaining Muslims and Jews who had lived in the Muslim territories to convert or depart. They launched the Spanish Inquisition to apprehend anyone who had feigned conversion in order to remain in their homeland. These events meshed with Columbus' proposals in several ways. The Catholic monarchs saw their conquest as part of a crusade to establish Christianity in Spain and were interested in Columbus' aim of bringing Catholicism to Asia. Furthermore, with the expulsion of the Muslims and Jews, they had also expelled a number of scholars such as Abraham Zacuto, the preeminent scholar of astronomy, suggesting that they were less drawn to promoting scientific knowledge than to religious and national aims. In addition, having completed the principal task of their reigns, they were at that moment ready to take interest in other projects, such as the venture proposed by Columbus.

Columbus' plan was a bold one: to sail westward over the open ocean to reach the eastern side of Asia. If his estimates of distance were accepted, it might mean an easier route to Asia. Although a Portuguese voyage had not yet reached Asia, it was clear that this was only a matter of time. However, the great length of the African coastline meant that such a voyage would require a journey of at least a year. It had taken Bartolomeu Dias months merely to sail to the southern tip of Africa. Indeed, when Vasco da Gama finally sailed for India in 1497, the entire journey took two years. On the other hand, Columbus' route promised a much shorter trip. In fact, when Columbus embarked, he only carried provisions for about a month of sailing – the capacity of his ships' stores – believing that he would reach Asia within that time.

Nonetheless, the dangers of Columbus' plan were apparent, and the Crown consequently invested little in the expedition. Part of the funding came from a consortium of Genoese financiers. Columbus was supplied with three smallish, somewhat worn ships. It was very difficult to obtain sailors, and there was an attempt to pardon convicts who would serve as sailors, though few took up the offer. There was only one priest. Those who finally participated were desperate, broke, or convinced by Columbus' plans.

Columbus depended on his navigational skill and on divine assistance, but he was also lucky. Because he ultimately sailed on Spanish ships, he embarked from the Spanish Canary Islands, putting him directly into the westerly currents that pushed him all the way to the Caribbean. As an astute navigator, Columbus knew how to take advantage of the rotational currents of the *volta do mar*, necessary for a return to Europe from the Caribbean. Columbus was also lucky on his return, keeping a good wind behind him.

Columbus recorded the voyage, including his private thoughts, in his journal. He had gambled everything on his success. He did not divulge to the crew that his ships did not have sufficient provisions to retrace their course. Whenever he made measurements during the voyage, he regularly deceived his sailors about the amount of time and distance that they had been sailing in order to avert mutiny, yet nevertheless there were increasing complaints among the sailors about the length of the voyage. Fortunately for Columbus, just as the discontent was about to grow into mutiny, the crew began to spot signs that they were nearing land, such as flocks of shorebirds and floating debris. This was about a month after departing from the Canary Islands. When land still did not appear and the men began to speak of turning back, Columbus reminded them that they did not have sufficient provisions to return. About six weeks after leaving Spain, they made landfall in the Bahamas.

Columbus believed that he had reached Asia, a supposition that he never gave up. He labeled the people he had met "Indios," assuming that he had reached the islands of the East Indies, identified Cuba as "Cipangu" (or Japan), and hoped to make contact with the Great Khan – the Mongol ruler of China. On his return voyage, Columbus was forced to dock at the Portuguese Azores islands for supplies and then at a harbor in Portugal before making his way back to Spain. Upon receiving notice of Columbus' discoveries, the astute King John II of Portugal immediately surmised that Columbus had encountered new lands. Columbus' assertion that he had reached India was not convincing, and the Portuguese also knew that Columbus' estimate of the globe's size was inaccurate.

First contact

Columbus and his crew encountered indigenous people immediately upon landing. The first encounters went peacefully, with the two groups exchanging goods, and Columbus remarked in his journal that the Taíno people that he had met were peaceable and good looking. He described them as simple, without clothing or weapons, and ready to adopt Catholicism. Even in the first days of meeting the "Indians," Columbus described them as potential slaves and also expressed interest in their gold ornaments, repeating a pattern that he had learned in Africa. By his second day, he had taken a number of captives on board his ships, many of whom were later taken to Spain along with a few pieces of gold. These actions set the stage for the next few centuries of European contact with Native Americans.

One of Columbus' first steps was to declare that the Spanish monarchs were the rulers of the "Indies." He described the lands as a kind of paradise, with a pleasant climate, willing workers, and plenty of gold, and immediately set to work building forts and trading centers. Although the native peoples were peaceful, Columbus asserted that they could be easily defeated if they fought the Spaniards. Before he left the Caribbean, the *Santa María* was shipwrecked. Guacanagarí, the most welcoming of the five main Taíno chiefs on Hispaniola, agreed to let Columbus leave the ship's crew on the island of Hispaniola and to build La Navidad, a fort, with the remains of the *Santa María*. After three months in the Caribbean, the voyage back with the two remaining caravels was quick and uneventful; Columbus was highly honored on his return to Spain and made Governor of the Indies. His first report of his voyage, printed almost immediately upon his return in 1493, fascinated readers throughout Europe.

Later voyages

Columbus' second voyage in 1493 comprised a much more imposing fleet of seventeen ships and about 1,000 men. His brother Bartholomew followed in 1494. By then, relationships with the Indians had soured, with a number of aggressive encounters caused by the Spaniards' incessant search for spices, gold, and slaves. Indians were forced to mine gold and provide gold as tribute and were beaten or maimed if they did not provide sufficient amounts. The gold tribute imposed by Columbus was so exorbitant that it resulted in mass suicides. In addition to forced labor and slavery, the Indians were increasingly subject to violence, murder, and rape. Some Indian slaves were shipped back to Spain, where most died. The Spanish Crown, hoping to convert the Indians to Catholicism, showed some hesitation about enslaving them but ultimately acceded to what had already been done. The Taíno were much more vulnerable than the Africans the Spaniards had previously encountered, possessing no metal weapons, and were extremely susceptible to European diseases. They began to die in large numbers, with up to a third of the population gone before 1500.

American natives were seen in an increasingly hostile light as the initially amicable relationship slipped into naked exploitation, which then resulted in armed resistance to the Spaniards. As early as 1493, La Navidad was destroyed and the men killed, supposedly by Indians hostile to both the Spaniards and Guacanagarí. The first organized rebellion against Spanish control broke out as early as 1511, led by Hatuey, a Taíno cacique from Hispaniola who tried to organize resistance to the continuing conquest from the island of Cuba. He was executed by being burned at the stake in 1512, an event which was famously described by Friar Bartolomé de las Casas. Hatuey refused the offer of a last-minute conversion to Christianity because he did not want to associate with Christian Spaniards in the afterlife.

Columbus returned to Spain in 1496 and set out for the Caribbean again in 1498 with a small fleet of three ships. For the first time, he reached the South American mainland. He arrived to find the new Spanish colony in chaos, with both colonists and natives in rebellion. His execution of rebellious Spaniards resulted in his replacement as governor by Francisco de Bobadilla in 1500. Bobadilla arrested Columbus and sent him to Spain in irons. However, Columbus, though initially disgraced, was able to ingratiate himself with the Spanish monarchs one last time, and a small fourth voyage was financed in 1502. Although Columbus completed some exploration, he was also stranded on the island of Jamaica for a year and then returned home with little credibility.

Columbus died sick and embittered in 1506, two years after his return. He was still convinced that he had reached Asia. He had made exploration of the Americas a family concern, bringing over his brothers, Bartholomew and Diego, and his two sons, Fernando and Diego, the latter of whom achieved the post of Governor of the Indies in 1509. His sons spent many years unsuccessfully litigating for a return of Columbus' titles, which had been stripped after his third voyage. The most significant consequence of Columbus' voyages was a pattern of exploitation and conquest for subsequent colonizers from Europe.

The legacy of Columbus

One question to ask ourselves is whether Columbus was essential to the "discovery" of the Americas. Columbus was the first fifteenth-century European to succeed in sailing across the Atlantic because of a combination of boldness, determination, and luck. His assurance about his own divine destiny and his persistence in trying to convince Western monarchs to sponsor his voyage finally paid off. His abilities as a sea captain and navigator enabled him to cross the ocean successfully, and he was lucky in attracting Spanish support, because it enabled him to embark from the Spanish Canary Islands directly into the westerly currents. Nonetheless, even though other European monarchs had turned him down, the venture that he had proposed remained attractive to many of them, because they hoped to gain access to the lucrative Asian spice trade. They had mainly been reluctant to invest because of the difficulty of the voyage. The many legendary and real reports of Atlantic voyages during the previous century had served to whet the appetites of Europeans interested in exploration, and some of these voyages, such as the fishing expeditions by English and Basque sailors on the northern coasts, suggest that such a voyage would have soon been embarked upon. Likewise, the Portuguese had already reached the Azores islands by the mid-fifteenth century. The Azores are almost at the midpoint of the Atlantic Ocean, about 900 miles west of Portugal and 1,200 miles to the southeast of Newfoundland, and could easily have served as a way station for further exploration. By Columbus' time, the new innovations in navigation, shipbuilding, and various other technologies had made long sea voyages possible for the first time. Together, these points suggest that other voyagers would also have eventually tried to develop a westward course to the Indies. Furthermore, because of the circulation of currents in the Atlantic Ocean, there would likely have been accidental contacts, such as the voyage of Pedro Álvares Cabral.

Cabral, like Columbus, was connected to a seafaring family; he was the nephew of Gonçalo Velho Cabral, who was credited with discovering the Azores. Likewise, among his captains were Bartolomeu Dias and

Bartolomeu's brother Diogo Dias, one of the discoverers of the Cape Verde Islands. In 1500, while Cabral was attempting to follow Vasco da Gama's route to India around the coast of Africa, he was accidentally swept all the way to the Brazilian coast. Rather than sailing directly down the coast, he had endeavored to shorten his voyage by crossing open water. He employed the *volta do mar* to swing westward from the Cape Verde Islands, intending to loop down to southern Africa. However, part of his fleet veered too far west and ended up on the coast of present-day Brazil, which they claimed for Portugal according to the Treaty of Tordesillas. Like Columbus, the sailors named the people they encountered there "Indians" but realized relatively quickly that they were in a land as yet unknown to Europeans. If Columbus had not already crossed the ocean eight years earlier, Cabral could have been the "discoverer" of the Americas.

Similarly, in 1496, the Venetian Zuan Chabotto, known to English speakers as John Cabot, sailed from Bristol with English sponsorship, aiming to sail westward through northern latitudes to develop a shorter route to Asia and perhaps also to seek some of the lands that Columbus had discovered. Cabot, like Columbus, was a stateless man and had lived and traveled at various times in Italy, Portugal, Spain, and possibly the Middle East. His first voyage was forced to turn back, but a second voyage in 1497 reached North America, somewhere in the vicinity of Newfoundland. Although knowledge of Columbus' prior crossing influenced Cabot's expedition and perhaps that of Cabral, their voyages – together with the earlier Bristol voyages, Icelandic contacts, Portuguese and Spanish exploration of the Atlantic islands, and continuing incentives for further exploration – suggest that Europeans would soon have arrived across the Atlantic even without Columbus' historic 1492 voyage. Nonetheless, Columbus' voyage shaped the subsequent history of Atlantic interactions, ensuring the early dominance of Spain in the Atlantic and establishing many of the ensuing patterns in relations between Europeans and Native Americans.

Columbus' explorations also became the source of a controversy that still exists. While his voyages were evidence of daring and ingenuity, they also enabled a number of global social changes whose consequences still affect us, including the colonization of the Americas by Europeans, the annihilation of most Native Americans, and the trans-Atlantic slave trade. In addition, the wealth that began pouring across the ocean into Western Europe was crucial to the eventual ability of Europeans to dominate the rest of the world.

Voyages after Columbus

The extent of the new lands revealed by Columbus was not immediately apparent, and they served as a great incentive for further exploration and discovery. In addition to the voyages of Cabral and Cabot, there were soon many other ships and fleets crossing the Atlantic and also continuing to explore the African coastline. The Portuguese, realizing that Columbus had reached new territories, though not comprehending their full extent, insisted on validating their own Atlantic gains, consistent with the Treaty of Alcaçovas. The Spanish pope, not fully to their satisfaction, responded with the 1494 Treaty of Tordesillas, effectively giving Spain most of the new western territories. In the meantime, the Portuguese continued to consolidate control over the eastward route to Asia, sending out Vasco da Gama's expedition in 1497, by which time Columbus had already returned from his second voyage to the Americas.

Da Gama, using the information provided by Bartolomeu Dias and Pedro da Covilhã, and guided from East Africa by Ahmad Ibn Majid, one of the foremost navigators in the Indian Ocean region, sailed to the port of Calicut on the western Indian coast. Once in India, da Gama aimed to engage in trade for spices. However, the Hindu ruler of Calicut was unwilling to trade with da Gama at first, because the city had profitable connections with Arab merchants, and there was little interest in the European trade goods of brass, raw materials, and crude cloth. Nonetheless, da Gama did manage to collect some pepper and cinnamon over a long period and returned to Portugal after a voyage of over two years, during which more than half his men died. He returned a few years later and supported Pedro Álvares Cabral's attempts to negotiate with the ruler of Calicut. In the process, da Gama demonstrated an unparalleled brutality that was striking even for a very brutal era, attacking and torturing unprotected fishermen, civilians, and pilgrims. In order to establish a successful European trade, he used his ships' cannons to defeat a local fleet in front of the city. He succeeded in subduing most of the smaller neighboring cities, though it took more time to bring Calicut to submission. Da Gama's efforts eventually culminated in a series of permanent fortresses and trading centers along the west coast of Asia and the Middle East, the beginning of the exploitation of Asia by European nations.

Columbus' expeditions were also followed by a number of voyages aiming to circumnavigate the globe. The first effort was led by the Portuguese captain Ferdinand Magellan sailing under the Spanish flag from 1519 and completed under the command of Juan Sebastián Elcano in 1522 after losing Magellan, four of five ships, and 182 of 200 sailors. It was followed by a voyage led by the Spanish captain García Jofre de Loaísa which, like the previous attempt, was completed by another. The remnants of Loaísa's fleet limped back under Portuguese custody in 1536 led by Andrés de Urdaneta, eleven years after leaving Spain. Urdaneta later became a friar in Mexico City. These voyages illustrate the European drive to explore and expand and the dangers of ocean exploration in the sixteenth century, while Urdaneta's life also demonstrates the increasingly strong Atlantic connections already forming for Europeans in this period. Thereafter, voyages of circumnavigation were predominantly the purview of the English and the Dutch, with the next voyage commanded by the English captain Francis Drake from 1577 to 1580.

Figure 5.1   An early world map by Peter Apian (1520), one of the first to use the word "America" to describe the new continent. Map reproduction courtesy of the Norman B. Leventhal Map Center at the Boston Public Library.

Florentine banker Amerigo Vespucci also made a contribution of great significance. His description of sailing the South American coast on a Portuguese ship sometime between 1497 and 1502 demonstrated for the first time that Columbus had reached a new continent rather than some scattered Atlantic islands. Vespucci may have been the first to reach the actual continental land masses, preceding both Columbus and Cabot. His findings were published in 1507 by German cartographer Martin Waldseemüller in a widely read book, which included an accompanying world map naming the new continent "America" in honor of Vespucci (see Figure 5.1).

Timeline: early explorations

1402 Spaniards start the conquest of the Canary Islands

1410 Pierre d'Ailly's *Imago Mundi* published

1415 Portuguese capture North African port of Ceuta; Prince Henry begins promoting exploration

1418 Bartolomeu Perestrello, João Gonçalves Zarco, and Tristão Vaz Teixeira discover Porto Santo

1419 Perestrello, Gonçalves, and Vaz discover Madeira

1431 Gonçalo Velho Cabral discovers the Azores

1434 Gil Eanes sails beyond Cape Bojador

1441 Portuguese bring slaves from west African coast

1448 Portuguese establish trading post on Arguin Island

1451 Christopher Columbus born

1453 Ottoman Empire conquers Constantinople

1456 Genoese António de Noli, sailing for Portugal, discovers the Cape Verde Islands

1473 Lopo Gonçalves crosses the equator

1478 Abraham Zacuto publishes tables delineating positions of heavenly bodies

1479 Treaty of Alcáçovas divides the Atlantic between Portugal and Spain

1481 John II ascends Portuguese throne

1482 Portuguese fortress of Elmina built on Gold Coast

1487–92 Pedro da Covilhã travels to Arabia and East Africa

1488 Bartolomeu Dias rounds the Cape of Good Hope

1492–3 First voyage of Columbus

1493–6 Second voyage of Columbus

1494 Treaty of Tordesillas gives Spain control over most Atlantic territories

1497 John Cabot reaches Newfoundland

1497–8 Vasco da Gama sails to India

1498–1500 Second voyage of Columbus; Columbus reaches the continent of South America

1499 Amerigo Vespucci recognizes South America as a large land mass

1500 Pedro Álvares Cabral reaches Brazil

1502–4 Columbus' fourth voyage

1507 Cartographer Martin Waldseemüller names the new lands "America" in honor of Vespucci

1513 Vasco Núñez de Balboa crosses the Isthmus of Panama and sees the Pacific Ocean

1519–22 Ferdinand Magellan's fleet circumnavigates the globe

1525–36 García Jofre de Loaísa's expedition circumnavigates the globe

1534 Jacques Cartier explores the Gulf of Saint Lawrence

1577–80 Francis Drake circumnavigates the globe

6   The Columbian Exchange

By the first quarter of the sixteenth century, the Atlantic world was characterized by continuous motion. In the "Columbian Exchange," not only people but also animals, plants, diseases, raw materials, trade goods, and ideas circulated around the Atlantic basin, leading to profound changes in the societies and ecosystems of both sides of the Atlantic. Three groups of people came into sustained contact: Europeans, primarily as conquerors; Native Americans, primarily as colonized peoples; and Africans, primarily as slaves. In addition, the colonizers brought European livestock and crops to the Americas and took American animals and products back home with them. Unintentionally, the colonizers brought diseases and pests. Eventually, both sides of the Atlantic participated in a vigorous system of trade, which included raw materials and manufactured products, as well as livestock and human beings.

Many of the plants and animals that came across the ocean were brought intentionally by the first Europeans to come to the New World. A number of domesticated animals arrived as early as Columbus' second voyage. Old World livestock varieties were much more plentiful than domesticated animals in the Americas, and several of the former had a major impact on the New World, especially farm animals such as cattle, sheep, goats, pigs, and various fowl, as well as horses which provided rapid and long-distance transport to many indigenous groups. Horses were particularly important to Indians of the North American Great Plains, for whom they facilitated transportation and hunting, as well as changing the balance of power among various tribes and within groups themselves. In addition, Europeans inadvertently brought rats and insect pests such as cockroaches and biting insects like fleas and mosquitoes, including varieties that carried human diseases. The most important animal to make the journey in the opposite direction was the turkey.

The exchange of crop plants was more equal. Europeans brought many crops to the New World, including wheat and various fruits and vegetables, as well as a number of plants that became major plantation-grown products in the Americas, including sugar, rice, and coffee. Cotton, also a plantation product, was cultivated on both sides of the ocean prior to 1492.

On the other hand, many American crops that crossed the Atlantic became worldwide staples, including potatoes, sweet potatoes, tomatoes, peppers, corn (maize), cassava (manioc), most varieties of beans, peanuts, chocolate, and squash, in addition to non-food plant products such as tobacco, rubber, and quinine.

The new crops produced dramatic and unexpected effects. In many cases, they became a major component of human diets throughout the world, often displacing indigenous crops. Tomatoes, peppers, and potatoes became dietary staples all over the world from Italy to India. Maize, sweet potatoes, and peanuts in particular contributed to massive population growth in Asia, especially China, during the early modern period. Likewise, cassava, sweet potatoes, and peanuts became dietary staples in parts of Africa, and European peasant populations began depending on potatoes, which require much less land than wheat as a subsistence crop. Potatoes, like many of the American crops, are full of useful nutrients and contributed to significant population growth in Europe. This was to become a double-edged sword in the nineteenth century. Poor farmers in Ireland, already pushed onto marginal land, subdivided their farms among their children into increasingly tinier plots, an inheritance pattern made possible only by the nutritiousness of potatoes. When a fungal blight struck European potatoes in the 1840s, Irish and Highland Scottish farmers who subsisted entirely on potatoes were hit with a severe famine. Other regions were affected, but over a million people in Ireland and many thousands in the Highlands of Scotland starved. More than 1 million Irish and 1.5 million Scots immigrated as a result of the famine, coupled with long-standing political inequality in their homelands. Although there had been similar immigrants earlier, this was the beginning of a long-term trend of Irish emigration and of an Irish and Scottish diaspora that contributed to population growth in the United States and Canada.

Three major American non-edible crops – tobacco, rubber, and quinine – also had a major impact on world history. Tobacco became a plantation crop in the Americas and is still a widely used drug around the world. Rubber became an important commercial crop even before the process of vulcanization was developed in the nineteenth century and was a major incentive for colonial exploitation in the form of forced labor and resource extraction in Asia and Africa from the late nineteenth century. Quinine, originally a Peruvian folk medicine obtained from the bark of the cinchona tree, was an effective antimalarial drug which enabled Europeans to enter Africa in large numbers during the colonizing frenzy of the late nineteenth century.

Disease and the New World

Infectious diseases were another insidious force crossing the ocean. Europeans and their African slaves inadvertently carried new infectious agents across the ocean on their bodies. So did their animals, including dogs, horses, pigs, chickens, and cattle, as well as the ships' rats and other pests that were brought inadvertently. It was disease that precipitated the sudden destruction of much of the Native American population in the New World.

European and African diseases were probably the most pervasive force shaping the Atlantic encounter. They came in many varieties. The most virulent were smallpox and measles, but the infectious agents also included influenza, typhus, typhoid, plague, yellow fever, malaria, leptospirosis, and mumps. The only disease known to have made the reverse journey is syphilis, which was far more virulent during the sixteenth century when it struck unacclimated Europeans, leading to rapid death, than it is today. However, the consequences in the New World were far more destructive. The newly acquired Old World diseases struck the Native Americans with devastating force. Very few of the Amerindian population carried genes resistant to these diseases. Adults and children died alike, until more than 90% of the native population was killed, reducing the initial Amerindian population of approximately 60 million to 6 million in less than two centuries.

The viruses and bacterial infections that Europeans brought to the New World were endemic in the Old World – Europe, Asia, and Africa. More sustained contact with domestic animals, higher population densities, and a higher overall population (approximately 550 million people as compared to 60 million in the Americas) had led to higher rates of evolution and exchange of disease pathogens over millennia. These diseases had been virulent in the Old World as well. Initially, diseases often struck with overwhelming force, and then their strength leveled off as the population gradually evolved resistance. More susceptible individuals died off while survivors passed their resistance on to their children. By the fifteenth century, some of these illnesses had become primarily childhood illnesses in the Old World. Typically, the diseases would reoccur in limited epidemics every generation, usually with a mortality rate of 15% or less. In the New World, however, the pattern was different. The panoply of epidemics struck simultaneously, preventing Native American populations from recovering easily.

The earliest known outbreak of Old World diseases among Native Americans occurred in 1493 after Columbus' second voyage. By 1542, fifty years after Columbus' initial arrival to the island of Hispaniola, a population of approximately 1 million Taíno had been reduced to less than 1,000. It seemed that they were destined to disappear as a community, mainly wiped out by smallpox but also subjected to famine and ill treatment as a result of the Spaniards' arrival. The only thing that prevented their complete disappearance was the blending of the many peoples that came together on the island in the late fifteenth and early sixteenth centuries. Individuals in the Caribbean who identify themselves today as Taíno or Arawak, as well as much of the general population, are descended from a union of European, African, and Amerindian ancestry.

Despite the tenacious existence of a few survivors, disease rapidly wiped out most Amerindian populations. Europeans and Africans were also susceptible to the diseases that they carried, but they sickened in much smaller numbers and were much more likely to recover. It was to take a period of over 200 years before Amerindian populations could begin to recover as they developed similar levels of immunity. When Native Americans were initially struck by Old World diseases, the blow was much stronger than the initial impact of any particular illness had been on the other side of the ocean, because the Amerindians were not attacked by a single disease but rather successive or simultaneous waves of different infections. In the Americas, these coinciding illnesses resulted in death rates of 50% to 70%, with illness affecting virtually all of the population – much higher rates of death than anything that Europeans had ever experienced. In addition to high mortality, a further consequence was social breakdown, with few people left well enough to cultivate crops, produce food, care for the sick, or govern society, leading to starvation, fear, demoralization, and social collapse. Although stemming from the initial arrival of Europeans, the diseases raced ahead of the conquerors, devastating or wiping out populations before Europeans reached them. Epidemics were the central factors in the collapse of the Aztec (Mexica) and Inca (Quechua) empires and in the inability of other Amerindian societies to resist the invaders. For example, an epidemic decimated the Wampanoag peoples in what would become Massachusetts just prior to their contact with the Puritan settlers from England, greatly reducing their numbers and increasing their weakness when confronted with open warfare a generation later.

There was little or nothing that could be done to treat these illnesses by either the Europeans or the natives, neither of whom possessed adequate knowledge or means of treatment. Only those who were lucky enough to have good health and possess resistant genes could survive. The Spaniards were unaware of how diseases spread, since the germ theory of disease would not be developed until the late nineteenth century. Instead, there were a number of theories that included direct physical contact, imbalances in the humors (bodily fluids), miasma (poisonous vapors in the air), and the will of God. Indeed, the Spanish regretted the population destruction caused by the diseases and made attempts to mitigate it – for instance, by setting up quarantines, sending doctors to native villages, and burning the goods of infected people. There were two reasons for Spanish concern. First, the Spanish had hoped that the natives would serve them as laborers; this was jeopardized by their wide-scale deaths. Second, there was genuine concern for the loss of human souls to death before they had a chance to be saved by converting to Christianity. The Spaniards, as Catholics, believed in spiritual free will – that rather than being spiritually predestined, as Protestants believed, individuals could influence their own destination in the afterlife. Many of the Spanish clergy in particular distinguished Amerindian heathens, unaware of the truth of Christianity, from the infidels of the Old World, who had rejected it. To them, Native American population collapse meant that essentially innocent people were dying before they had had the opportunity to accept Christianity. It is unclear how much such qualms troubled ordinary

Spanish settlers, but they were influential in convincing the Spanish Crown to establish laws mitigating the treatment of the Indians from the 1540s.

Protestants, in contrast, usually viewed the disappearance of the Amerindians as the will of God, clearing the land for Christians. Believing in foreordained predestination of the elect, they saw the natives as already damned. In many cases, unlike the Spanish conquistadors, Protestant settlers like the English and the Dutch aimed to cultivate their lands themselves as small farmers or to employ European servants for larger-scale agriculture rather than utilizing an enslaved workforce. English Puritans in particular were interested in both occupying Amerindian lands and creating a new holy society and saw the Indian population as an obstacle to their aspirations. As a result, many among the English settlers of the seventeenth century and after were pleased with the spread of disease in the Amerindian population. Some saw it as the will of God. By the eighteenth and nineteenth centuries, there were even a few murderous attempts by British and American troops to hasten the demise of North American Indian groups by distributing smallpox-infested blankets. While it is not currently established whether it is possible to transmit the virus in this manner, contact with European populations was sufficient to spread the disease in any case.

The Amerindian population collapse had a number of significant consequences. First, it enabled Europeans to colonize the New World, which would have been much more difficult – perhaps impossible – if they had faced native societies at the full peak of their strength. European control over the new territories and the resources they included was to propel them to domination of the world within a few centuries. In the Americas, the defeat and disappearance of Indian groups led to demoralization and social disruption among the survivors. This took a variety of forms, including placing Native Americans in dependent roles while denigrating native culture. Many cultural values of native societies, including languages, customs, and religious beliefs, were transformed or lost. The deaths caused by disease convinced many that native religious traditions were false and that the god of the Europeans had superseded or defeated indigenous gods, paving the way for wide-scale conversion to Christianity. Further, when plantation agriculture became established in the Americas, Europeans looking for coerced laborers turned to African slaves to replace the disappearing Indian population, bringing the continent of Africa into an Atlantic connection with far-reaching but tremendously unequal effects on the shores of all four Atlantic continents. Thus, more than any other factor, it was European diseases that determined the shape of the Atlantic exchange, establishing political, economic, and social arrangements that are still shaping the world today.

7 Earliest encounters

The Spanish conquest wrought an immense transformation in the Americas, truly creating a New World for all who lived there: Spaniards and other Europeans, Africans, and Native Americans. The blending of previously separated human societies resulted in the creation of new societies that included novel forms of culture, politics, economic dealings, intellectual life, and new kinds of human relationships. After Columbus' first voyage, Spaniards poured into the Americas. Most of the original immigrants were conquistadors and their followers, professional soldiers who hoped to acquire money, fame, and influence through military success in what they saw as a land of opportunity. Many of these men were former soldiers who had gained their military experience in fighting the Muslims in Spain and were at loose ends after the ending of the *Reconquista*. They were characterized by unscrupulousness, toughness, and brutality. Typically, they hoped to return to Spain once they had made their fortunes. Columbus' writings had prompted their hopes for wealth by repeatedly mentioning gold and spices, as well as praising the fertility of the soil and the suitability of the Indians as potential laborers. These endorsements became entangled with European legends about wealthy kingdoms like Atlantis located in mysterious, unexplored realms. Soon, explorers and invaders were roaming the mainland, fruitlessly searching for El Dorado – a fabled golden city, the Seven Cities of Gold, or the Land of Cinnamon. The eventual victories of Hernán Cortés and Francisco Pizarro over wealthy urban areas provided additional fodder to these adventurers, most of whom died during their wanderings. These expeditions were characterized by confusion, violence, and the failure to discover great wealth, but they aided the progress of Spanish imperialism by exploring new areas and by "pacifying" the local natives.

The Spanish had some advantages in their meetings with Native Americans. They possessed horses; swords, armor, and shields made of steel and iron; and guns, all of which were superior to native military technologies. Horses needed to be utilized on flat ground, but they conferred speed and height and devastating force when the rider was carrying a lance and were intimidating. Likewise, guns and cannons had a disproportionate impact because they were frightening and lethal. Battle on these terms meant thousands of

Indian casualties with only a few Spaniards felled. On the other hand, a major disadvantage for the Spaniards was their small numbers relative to the numbers of natives, at least in urban areas. However, this was offset by epidemics of European diseases that typically struck before the Indians were defeated, and which devastated native populations. Even with these benefits, Spanish fighting abilities were typically not enough to carry the day. The pattern of Spanish conquest was to first establish diplomatic relations with the Native American leader and then kidnap him. Often they took advantage of local political and military disputes and established alliances with groups hostile to the faction they were attacking. As each area was defeated, it became a base for the next extension of the conquest. Military expeditions were sometimes funded by prosperous individuals who would either band together or individually employ mercenaries, but often the hired soldiers also invested in the venture and hoped to receive a share of the proceeds. The best profits came from gold, which was melted down and distributed to each soldier according to status, but they also gained silver, food, other goods, and Indian slaves. The wealth accrued on these expeditions could be used by the men to increase their status within Spanish society.

As it became more apparent that gold was not available in abundance, the Spanish focused more on the control of land and Indian laborers and, where it was available, underground silver sources. Although the conquest was nominally under the control of the Spanish Crown, in reality the Crown merely recognized what had been taken in its name. In any case, communication across the ocean was slow, taking weeks or months, so the conquistadors had to make decisions and plan attacks without waiting for approval. The Crown did send officials to serve as administrators, but they themselves were interested in accruing personal wealth and power. Especially in the early decades, there was competition between noblemen, administrators, explorers, and other influential men to control as much land and wealth as possible. The Crown did not inquire about methods of conquest too closely as long as it received the *quinto real*, or king's fifth, of all profits.

The conquest of Mexico

By 1520, Europeans, especially Spaniards, were already in control of most of the islands in the Caribbean and were continuing to arrive to the New World. The Arawak and Taíno populations had dropped to unrecoverably low levels. The rumors of plentiful gold in the New World were continuing to attract conquistadors, who were particularly drawn to the lands of the Mexica (Aztecs) and Quechua (Inca) because of the rumors of the wealth to be found in those powerful urban societies.

Probably the most famous of the conquistadors was Hernán Cortés (1485–1547), who arrived on the island of Hispaniola in 1504 while still in his teens. In 1511, he sailed as part of an expedition to conquer Cuba under the command of Diego Velázquez de Cuéllar, who later became the governor of Cuba. Cortés exemplified the conquistador spirit; although he came from a lesser noble family of relatively modest means in Spain, through his connections with the governor he gained a large *encomienda* – or estate – and twice served as the mayor of Santiago, the capital, and became an influential businessman. However, as he became increasingly prominent, his ambitiousness created a rift with the governor, who may have seen him as a competitor.

When Velázquez decided to send an expedition of conquest to the mainland in 1519, he appointed Cortés as its leader, perhaps hoping to be rid of him for a time. Previous contacts had demonstrated that there was potential for gold and conquest among the wealthy urban populations in the region, including the Maya in the Yucatán Peninsula and unknown cities further inland. Cortés eagerly grasped the opportunity that he had been waiting for, rapidly assembling a force of eleven ships and about 600 men. Although his force was abruptly recalled by the governor, who increasingly doubted his loyalty, Cortés rapidly departed before he could be replaced. Velázquez's distrust was well founded; shortly after arriving, Cortés founded the city of Veracruz on the coast, placing it under the authority of the monarchy, thus circumventing the authority of Cuba's governor. Afterward, he burned his own ships to prevent his men from deserting.

Cortés' expedition fought along the coast, defeating several Maya towns. Almost immediately, Cortés demonstrated the resourcefulness and impressive grasp of diplomatic strategy that would enable his conquest of Mexico, which could never have been defeated by military tactics alone. A key component of Cortés' success was his repeated ability to ally with individuals or groups who assisted Cortés at crucial moments rather than the superior technology with which he has often been credited. Cortés did bring a number of military technologies that Native Americans had not yet encountered, including horses, war dogs trained to kill humans, armor, steel weapons, arquebuses (an early firearm), and a dozen cannons. However, none of these was numerous or very effective – for example, many of the horses were dead before they reached Mexico, the arquebuses were relatively inaccurate, and the cannons were inoperable – certainly not enough weaponry to attack a fortified city of 200,000 people. Instead, Cortés' victories were a combination of luck, strategy, alliances with Indians hostile to the Mexica, and the devastating impact of European diseases.

Soon after Cortés' expedition landed on the coast, they encountered a Franciscan friar, Gerónimo de Aguilar, who had been shipwrecked on the coast in 1511 and enslaved by the Maya; he spoke the Mayan language fluently. A fascinating side note to his story is that he was one of only two survivors of the shipwreck; the other, Gonzalo Guerrero, demonstrated a complete contrast to Aguilar, becoming the first known European to acculturate to native society. Guerrero refused to join the Spaniards with Aguilar. He had accepted Maya culture; adopted Maya clothing, ear piercings, and facial tattoos; married a Maya noblewoman; raised a family; and become a leading general among the Maya. He was killed in the 1530s while battling the Spaniards.

In any case, Geronimo de Aguilar became important to Cortés because of another captive. After his forces defeated the Maya town of Tabasco, Cortés received a tribute of twenty slave women whom he baptized and then gave to his officers. However, one of them, Malinche or Malintzin, called Marina by the Spaniards, became one of the most important members of the Spanish expedition, serving as a translator and liaison between the Spanish and the Mexica. She was a Nahuatl speaker who had been enslaved by the Maya and, with Aguilar as an intermediary, served as an interpreter between Cortés and other Nahua. Marina rapidly learned Spanish, enabling more direct translation, and was so important that the Spaniards soon referred to her as Doña (Lady) Marina as a token of respect. Cortés took her as his mistress, and their son Martín Cortés is sometimes looked upon as the first Mexican. Cortés eventually married a Spanish noblewoman, marrying Marina to one of his officers, who was made an important *encomendero* (or landowner). Martín Cortés was raised in Spain by his father's family.

Even today, the legacy of Doña Marina is controversial in Mexico, because some have seen her as a collaborator who enabled the conquest of the Mexica. Mitigating this perspective, however, is the fact that while ethnically Nahua, she was probably not a member of the Mexica people and likely saw them as enemies. Additionally, it is difficult to determine the amount of agency she possessed as a slave and a captive trying to survive in a hostile environment.

Doña Marina was not the only Nahua who allied with Cortés. Outside of the Triple Alliance, most Nahua speakers were either hostile subjects or enemies of the Mexica and often saw Cortés' arrival as an opportunity to throw off the Mexica yoke. Enemies of the Mexica included the Totonacs, a non-Nahua people who conducted Cortés' forces to the altepetl of Tlaxcala from their capital of Cempoala. The Tlaxcalans, a Nahua group, first fought with and then allied with Cortés. In the initial encounter, both sides were surprised at the other's toughness, but the Tlaxcalans were prevailing. However, some of the Tlaxcalan leaders decided that if they spared the Spaniards, the latter might be useful allies against the Mexica. This alliance, along with others, swelled Cortés' forces by approximately 6,000 troops and provided a safe haven from which to attack Tenochtitlán.

From Tlaxcala, the Spaniards and their thousands of allies marched toward Tenochtitlán. From the beginning, they had had contact with messengers and envoys of the Mexica tlatoani – or leader – Moctezuma, who attempted to deter the Spaniards from coming to the city. However, when they reached Tenochtitlán, Cortés was greeted cordially by Moctezuma, and the two exchanged gifts.

Moctezuma's subsequent behavior still puzzles historians. Rather than sending the Spaniards away, Moctezuma invited Cortés to visit the city of Tenochtitlán with a contingent of his soldiers and provided him with a fortified house inside the city and daily provisions. Moctezuma may have been concerned about Cortés' alliance with the Tlaxcalans or frightened by reports of Spanish technologies. As subsequent events showed, his position on the throne was precarious, and he may have been hoping to co-opt Cortés as an ally. Some later reports claimed that he believed Cortés to be a reincarnation of the god Quetzalcoatl, though this is questioned by modern scholars. Moctezuma may also initially have believed that the Spaniards would not present a serious threat. Tenochtitlán was a fully defensible city, situated on an island in Lake Texcoco, with access only by causeways spanned by retractable bridges. Despite Cortés' large army, the Mexica could easily field more soldiers.

In letters he wrote to Charles V, the king of Spain, Cortés described his astonishment at his first sight of Tenochtitlán, which he described as far larger and more beautiful than any city in Spain. This accorded with the impressions of other Spaniards such as the conquistador and chronicler Bernal Díaz del Castillo. It is also clear from both Spanish and Mexica accounts, such as in the *Historia general de las cosas de la Nueva España* – or *The General History of the Things of New Spain* (referred to as the *Florentine Codex*), a Nahua and Spanish text documenting Nahuatl culture and history – that, in general, the Spaniards and Mexica understood each other well. Both came from formalistic and imperialistic urban societies, and the misunderstandings that occurred in European encounters with other native peoples seem not to have arisen. However, both societies were also accustomed to making war against geographic, economic, and political rivals, and this pattern continued once they had encountered each other.

Once ensconced in the city, the Spaniards were able to take Moctezuma captive, clearly hoping that he would turn over the city to them. However, Cortés received word that Diego Velázquez had dispatched an army of 800 men, led by Pánfilo de Narváez, to apprehend him for treason. Cortés marched to the coast, captured Narváez and, again demonstrating his diplomatic skills, convinced Narváez's soldiers to switch their loyalty to him. In the meantime, he left his second in command, Pedro de Alvarado, behind in Tenochtitlán with about 100 Spanish soldiers. Alvarado arranged the massacre of a large number of unarmed worshippers at one of the city's festivals. His motivations are not entirely clear, but he may have been afraid that the Spaniards would be driven out due to the increasing hostility shown toward them by the Mexica nobility. Many of the dead were important political or military leaders, so it may also have been a preemptive attack.

By the time Cortés arrived, confrontations were escalating. During the course of these events, Moctezuma was killed, either murdered by the Spanish, as the Mexica claimed, or stoned by a crowd when he tried to encourage them to accept the presence of Cortés' forces, as the Spaniards claimed. Once Moctezuma was dead, the surviving Mexica leaders were determined to expel the Spaniards from the city. Moctezuma's younger brother

Cuitláhuac replaced him and rapidly mustered forces against the Spaniards. The Spaniards escaped the city during what they called the *noche triste* (sad night) and fled fifty miles to Tlaxcala, sustaining heavy losses. Almost all of the Spaniards and Tlaxcalans were killed, and all of the survivors, including Cortés, were wounded.

While regrouping in Tlaxcala during the next year, Cortés and the Tlaxcalans arranged to join forces to attack the Mexica, the Spaniards agreeing to give the Tlaxcalans future exemption from tribute, semi-autonomy, and a share of the plunder. The Spanish also established more limited agreements with additional allies. Hatred of the Mexica impelled a number of Indian groups to join the side of the Spanish. Even so, the Mexicas' numerical superiority coupled with the defensibility of Tenochtitlán might have prevailed. However, during this time, the Mexica capital was struck by a smallpox epidemic, brought inadvertently by the Spaniards. Cuitláhuac and his son died, as did up to 50% of the population. When the Spaniards later entered the city, they stepped across the bodies of multitudes of sick and dying people. The *Florentine Codex* related that the survivors of the disease were sickened and weakened, and that after the illness struck, there was no one to provide food, care for the sick, or tend crops. These events created paralysis, despair, and institutional collapse.

Even so, the Mexica fought hard, and a terrible siege of several months' duration was necessary to finally conquer the city. Cortés arrived with an army of approximately 150,000 native allies and moved to cut off the fresh water supply to the city. He built a fleet of brigantines – ships that could be sailed or rowed – to avoid depending on the causeways. Although the city was almost incapacitated by smallpox, the new tlatoani, Cuauhtémoc, was able to hold off the Spaniards for several weeks. Toward the end, even non-combatants such as women and the elderly fought the Spaniards. Cuauhtémoc was captured, tortured, and executed, later becoming a cultural hero for his refusal to show fear before his captors. Most of the Aztec city was destroyed. Cortés became the new ruler of what was named Mexico City. He was awarded a number of titles and died a wealthy man. His conquest of the Mexica established a model for all future conquests and ensured that the richest part of the Americas fell into Spanish hands, even though the conquest of the peripheral areas of Mexico was to take several more decades.

Over the next two centuries, three quarters of a million Spaniards flowed into Latin America. The lands of the Aztecs and other peoples were parceled out in the estates known as *encomiendas*, with resident Indians bound to serfdom, to reward Spanish participants in the conquest. At first, Mexica nobles were treated differently from commoners and were received into Spanish society, but this distinction rapidly disappeared. The conquerors were followed by Catholic missionaries, and Nahua religious practices were forbidden. Indeed, the success of the Spanish conquest convinced many

Amerindians that native religion was inferior to Christianity, because the indigenous gods had been defeated by the Christian deity.

The Tlaxcalans remained allied with the Spaniards for several generations and during that period received special consideration from the conquerors. The city and territory of Tlaxcala remained relatively intact. However, almost from the beginning, their initial expectations were disappointed. They assumed that the Spanish conquest would follow earlier precedents in which a conquering altepetl left its defeated enemies essentially intact and internally autonomous. Instead, the Spaniards came in ever-greater numbers to Mexico and saw "Indios" as social inferiors. They required that the Tlaxcalans and other groups accept their god, which the Mesoamericans would have anticipated, as that was the usual practice during a conquest, but also that they reject their own gods, a new notion in Mesoamerica. The Tlaxcalans were also resented by some altepetl who had also helped the Spaniards but felt that while the former group was singled out for benefits for aiding the conquest, these benefits were denied to other groups who had done likewise.

Spanish victories in other parts of the Americas

Cortés' success in defeating the Aztecs had been due in part to his great abilities as a military strategist but also to his diplomatic skills. His ability to recognize and exploit useful alliances with Moctezuma, Doña Marina, the Tlaxcalans, and other groups was crucial to his victory. Later conquistadors were not as skillful but were aided significantly by European military technologies and the progress of the deadly diseases sweeping through the Americas. Pedro de Alvarado, who had engineered the massacre of the Mexica nobles and instigated the uprising that derailed Cortés' plan to subjugate the Mexica through diplomacy, led the conquest of the Maya in Guatemala. He was aided by Tlaxcalan allies and attempted to repeat Cortés' tactic of allying with one group to defeat another. However, Alvarado treated his allies so cruelly that he alienated them, sparking a rebellion that lasted many years. In the end, the invasion of Guatemala was achieved with great violence and a protracted effort on the part of the Spanish. The defeat of the independent Maya city-states took more than 100 years to accomplish because they had to be defeated one by one. On the frontiers of Mexico, non- and semi-sedentary groups that the Nahua called the Chichimecs prevented Spanish settler encroachment for much of the sixteenth century.

In Peru, the huge Inca Empire was defeated by a small force led by Francisco Pizarro. Illiterate, and initially a poor man, he had made his fortune and reputation in the Indies. Hearing rumors of a wealthy empire in the west, he led a small force of 168 men, including three of his brothers, to Peru, where he encountered the forces of the Inca emperor Atahualpa. The Inca, believing that this small force was not a threat, allowed them to enter his territory undisturbed. However, fortune was on Pizarro's side. The Quechua had been struck by a lethal disease, probably smallpox, which had killed many thousands of people, including the ruler Huayna Cápac and his eldest son, in about 1527. Civil war had broken out between two of the remaining sons who aimed to become the next Inca leader. Atahualpa had just gained the upper hand when he encountered Pizarro in 1533. Like Moctezuma, Atahualpa was disliked by many and only had tenuous control over his domains. With great audacity, Pizarro invited Atahualpa to a diplomatic meeting and then ambushed his entourage, making use of gunfire and a cavalry charge and throwing Atahualpa's much larger forces into confusion. Atahualpa was captured, and over a thousand natives died, with no Spanish deaths. The Spaniards found great wealth among the emperor's personal possessions, but they were unable to effectively take control over the Inca Empire. Pizarro at first attempted to manipulate Atahualpa and then ordered his execution. He established a regime sustained by pillage and noted for its extreme exploitation and violence inflicted against indigenous men and women.

There were some attempts at rebellion. The first major revolt was led by Manco Inca Yupanqui, a younger son of Huayna Cápac, who was initially a pawn maintained on the throne by Pizarro. He led an attempt to restore the Inca Empire from the 1530s until his death in 1544. Although the Quechua experienced a number of victories against the Spanish, ultimately their forces were defeated by a combination of disease and a lack of unity among the Quechua themselves, many of whom had joined factions supporting the Spanish. Manco Inca did succeed in establishing a last stronghold, a small independent state centered on the city of Vilcabamba, although it was sometimes subject to Spanish intrusions. He was succeeded by several of his sons in sequence. The last claimant to the throne, Túpac Amaru, also initiated a brief rebellion but was captured and executed in 1572, finalizing the Spanish conquest. Vilcabamba was destroyed and forgotten.

Individual Spanish conquistadors fared little better. They became embroiled in feuds, which resulted in the deaths of Pizarro, his brother, and many of his entourage. Over the next two decades, most of the original conquistadors died in internecine fighting, leaving the Spanish Crown to take over. Nonetheless, by the 1550s, the Spanish held all of the major populated territories in South and Central America and Mexico. The conquistadors who had initiated the conquest aiming to boost their own fortunes were mostly gone, having been replaced by officials appointed by the central Spanish government.

8 Spanish colonial institutions in New Spain

After the initial conquests in Mexico and Peru, large numbers of Spaniards began to cross the ocean to what they saw as a new land of opportunity. After the first wave of immigrants, there were increasing numbers of family members, including women, and close economic and familial connections were established across the ocean. The Spanish conquest created a new society in the New World, which was based on Iberian norms but which was also strongly influenced by Native American and African customs and values, as well as the legacy of imperialism. Although one might think of a regional society as unified, the realities for an individual varied widely depending on class, race, and gender. A consequence of these intersecting influences was the development of a number of new institutions and social expectations that accommodated the needs of the new society, especially for the upper classes. Nonetheless, all Spanish regions also developed shared social patterns.

The Catholic Church

The Church was one of the most powerful institutions in Spain, where it was closely tied to the Crown, and it continued to take that role in the Spanish colonies. There, the Church was primarily interested in extending its influence over the new Spanish settlements and in territories mainly inhabited by Indians. Indeed, from the beginning, the conversion of the natives was a fundamental aim of both the Spanish Crown and the Church. Nonetheless, a central urge behind all endeavors in the New World, for the governing bodies and most ordinary Spaniards, was material gain. While the Church and the Spanish government did possess a genuine desire to (in their view) save the souls of the Indians, they were also subject to the lure of profit. At times, the two motivations were inextricably intertwined. Spanish success in finding and subduing the Indies seemed to justify the idea that the conquest was God's will. As a result, the Church played a critical role in both furthering and mitigating the conquest.

There was only one priest on Columbus' initial expedition, but the first wave of conquistadors was followed by large numbers of Spanish clergy, mainly friars. Ordinary Spaniards mostly conformed to orthodox Catholicism but probably did not trouble themselves with theology or worrying about the fate of the natives' souls. However, the clergy arriving to the New World were eager to serve as missionaries. They soon established parishes based on the original native jurisdictions and supported themselves through native labor and tribute. Churches were built on the ruins of temples and were constructed by native builders. In Mexico, massive temples were replaced by great cathedrals, while smaller churches were built in other areas. In less settled areas with more transient populations, Catholic clergy built missions around which settlements arose. Sometimes different orders within the Church, such as the Franciscan and Dominican friars, clashed about spheres of influence.

The friars worked vigorously to gain souls for the Church. They distanced themselves from the brutality of the conquistadors and presented themselves as protectors of the downtrodden. In contrast to most early settlers, the friars often promoted a positive view of the Indians as being intelligent and capable, though some also criticized them as being lazy and impious. The friars saw themselves as soldiers for God, wiping out idolatry and saving the souls of millions of people. Most of them deplored the violence of the conquistadors but also approved of conversion by force. They presented the god of Christianity as one who harshly punished sinners but was also forgiving of those who repented and accepted him.

Many of the friars learned native customs and languages and compiled religious texts, such as catechisms, in native languages using the Latin alphabet while at the same time encouraging the destruction of precolonial religious manuscripts. One of the most famous manuscripts was the *Florentine Codex*, sponsored by Friar Bernardino de Sahagún, who studied Nahuatl language and culture. The text was known by that name because it was discovered in an archive in Florence. It was written by Nahua informants working under the friar's supervision and contained a Nahua text and Spanish translation. Although compiled a generation after the conquest, this work included an insider's account of the defeat of the Aztec Empire, and it is considered one of the best sources for native perspectives on these events.

In Mesoamerica and the Inca regions, the transition to Christianity was less difficult than might be expected, because the populations were accustomed to both state-controlled religions and conquests. However, the Spanish takeover was different from earlier invasions, because while previously the new gods of conquerors had been added to a preexisting pantheon, the Spanish demanded that the Indians adopt monotheism. In addition, they insisted that some religious practices, such as the sacrifice of animals and humans, be prohibited. Yet Catholicism also had a long history of tolerance for divergent rituals as long as they did not impact the central tenets of doctrine. In the New World, this went further through a process of syncretism (or the blending of belief systems). After the conquest, overtly religious practice became Catholic in form, while many of the more visible indigenous sacred rituals were abandoned. In some cases, the essence of traditional beliefs continued to be adhered to, sometimes clandestinely or under a cloak of conforming to Catholicism. Often there were opportunities for convergence between Catholicism and native religion, as in the replacement of central temples with churches. Churches in Mexico often evoked aspects of native practices or belief, such as an outdoor patio with a sacred platform similar to what had prevailed in precolonial times, although surmounted with a cross to symbolize Christian worship rather than as a stage for sacrifices. The churches themselves were built on the same location as the preconquest temples using the same stone blocks. Just as had previously occurred in early medieval Europe, native deities were identified with Catholic saints based on the similarity of their attributes or on how well the timing of traditional dates of celebration for the deities corresponded with Catholic saints' feast days. Older beliefs gradually faded away during the colonial period, but traces of them can be seen even today in Latin America, particularly in more isolated areas.

Catholicism took powerful root, especially in the urban preconquest areas. Natives could not become clergy at first, but nobles continued to affiliate themselves with official religion by becoming lay church officials. Natives of lower rank participated in confraternities, church festivals, and official religious rituals. There were many shades of belief, especially at first, ranging from deliberate attempts to continue worshipping the old gods under the guise of acquiescing to the new Christian god, to belief in both religious traditions simultaneously, to unconditional acceptance of Christianity. Likewise, rituals of worship for the former native deities ranged from concealed rituals involving traditional dancing or other activities to rites that conformed exactly to orthodox Church practices. The most famous example of such blending occurred in the image of the Virgin of Guadalupe, who appeared as a native speaking in Nahuatl to a poor Indian peasant in 1531 near a shrine to the Nahua mother goddess Tonantzin. Today, she is the patron saint of Mexico and an important national symbol; her image was carried on banners during the Mexican independence movement of the early nineteenth century.

Outside the urban areas, it took longer for Christianity to take hold. Since the Indians did not congregate in large populations, they had to be forced to concentrate themselves into a parish and follow a state-imposed religious system. In the early days, some among the Christian clergy questioned the degree to which Christianity had penetrated the native spirit, even in the urban areas, and were skeptical that true conversion could occur. Sahagún, for example, worried about the destructiveness of the conquest and doubted the thoroughness of the natives' spiritual orthodoxy.

Acceptance of Christianity was not just a passive response on the part of the Indians. Instead, they shaped how much and what aspects of Christianity they accepted. In addition, in some cases, parts of the new Christian doctrine were misunderstood, especially at first. It was to take many generations for conventional Christianity to take hold. The greatest resistance came from clergy and practitioners of the old religion. They often attempted to uphold the traditional gods and maintain their own sacred status in secret. This was sometimes successful for a time but usually died out within a few generations after the conquest. Both native priests and the Spaniards claimed to be right and that their followers would be rewarded while their enemies would be thwarted. For example, they pronounced their own interpretations of the destruction of the native population by disease; native religious practitioners argued that Christianity was deadly, while the Spanish asserted that the diseases were God's punishment for long-standing sin among the Indians. Ultimately, the death toll was so high that the argument of the dominant group – the Spanish – prevailed.

The Spanish debate on tolerance

Most Spanish colonists did not worry much about the rights of the indigenous peoples, but from the beginning, some clergymen advocated for native rights. The Spanish Crown's justification for taking over the West Indies from the outset had been that it would promote Catholic Christianity. In part, this had helped get the sanction of the papacy and international legitimacy, but the Crown also took its religious charge seriously. During the first decade of conquest, Pope Alexander VI pronounced that the Spanish monarchs had absolute authority in the Americas, and an advisory council of Spanish clergymen contended that Spain had the right to subjugate and even enslave the Indians. All of these assertions were based on the claim that Spain was spreading Christianity in the colonies and that Native Americans would be treated lawfully. Yet in the early days of the conquest, and often later as well, these latter provisions were often ignored. Instead, the conquest of the Americas was characterized by aggression, rapaciousness, and brutality.

By the following decade, however, some members of the clergy were becoming increasingly concerned that Christianity was not being propagated and that the Indians were being abused. In 1511, the Dominican clergy on the island of Hispaniola collaborated on a fiery sermon delivered by Friar Antonio de Montesinos, who asked about the Indians "Are these not men? Have they not rational souls? Are you not bound to love them as you love yourselves?" He contended that the Spanish conquerors were in mortal sin because of their cruelty in keeping the Indians "in horrible servitude."[1]

Although Montesinos' sermon only served to anger his audience of conquistadors, many of the Dominican friars began to withhold communion from the Spaniards on the island, and the Crown revisited the issue. The result was the Laws of Burgos of 1512, which instituted Spanish law in the West Indies, recognized slavery, and established the encomienda system but also mandated that the native peoples were to be converted but not maltreated. The laws had little effect because there was little enforcement of natives' rights. Most Spaniards in the New World considered the Indians to be foolish, impious, and lazy, with an inferior culture. They fixated on exaggerated stories of human sacrifice, cannibalism, and unpleasant cultural characteristics, which justified the forced imposition of Christianity and European values.

In addition, not all of the clergy agreed that a more humanitarian conquest was called for. Indeed, the treatment of the Indians continued to be debated among theologians. There were a number of points of contention, including whether the papacy had the authority to hand the New World territories to Spain, whether Spain had the right to seize Indian territories, and whether the Spaniards had the right to enslave the Indians. Some clergy agonized that the Indians were heathens, or non-Christians, innocent in comparison to those they considered infidels who had rejected the faith, such as Muslims and Jews in the Old World. The Indians were being decimated, they argued, before they had a chance to encounter and accept Christianity. In the meantime, the Spanish Crown's primary interest lay in establishing and maintaining justification for its authority over the land, resources, and peoples of the New World.

Increasingly, clergy on both sides of these questions debated the rights of the Indians. Those arguing that Indians were inherently inferior – "natural slaves," some argued, using a category devised from the works of the ancient Greek thinker Aristotle – included Juan López de Palacios Rubios, Francisco López de Gómara, and Juan Ginés de Sepúlveda. On the other hand, proponents for better treatment of the Indians included Montesinos, Francisco de Vitoria, and Bartolomé de las Casas. This latter group argued that Indians were fully human children of God, endowed with natural rights and the facility of reason, and that it was mortal sin to mistreat them. In between these viewpoints was Toribio de Benavente Motolinia, who protected the Indians from ill treatment but accepted the encomienda system and believed that conversion was the most important goal.

Both sides became influential in the Crown's policies. Palacios Rubios was the author of a 1513 document known as the "Requerimiento," which was to be read when conquistadors landed. It warned Indian populations to willingly submit to the Spanish Crown and the Catholic Church or they would be treated as enemies. This ultimatum was often derided because it was typically read in untranslated Latin or Spanish, in some cases without bothering to find native people within earshot to hear it. Las Casas famously stated that he couldn't decide whether it should make him laugh or cry. However, las Casas was also influential. In the 1550s, he and Sepúlveda took part in a debate in Spain about the appropriate treatment of the Indians. Sepúlveda contended that Spain could make "just war" upon the Indians because they were uncivilized, but las Casas argued that their standards of civilization were equal to those of Spain, and the only legitimate role for Spaniards in the New World was to promote Christianity.

Las Casas was a particularly interesting figure, because he had been one of the earliest Spanish settlers, had initially protested Montesinos' famous sermon, and had been awarded an encomienda for his role in the conquest of the West Indies. Yet he had become more and more disgusted at the cruelties that he observed and eventually became the most vehement critic of the Spanish presence in the Americas. In his writings, he argued that the Spanish conquest had been an atrocity and that the natives should be considered full subjects of the Spanish Crown, able to govern themselves. He briefly proposed African slavery as an alternative to Indian slavery but soon became one of the few Europeans to reject slavery of any kind. Ultimately, he argued that the Spaniards, with the exception of clergy, should leave the Indies. He was influential in developing and promoting the New Laws of 1542, which further regulated the encomiendas, though in the end they were not fully effective because of widespread resistance. Las Casas was a controversial and often reviled figure, and his scathing disclosure of Spanish injustice and cruelty, *A Short Account of the Destruction of the Indies* (1552), created a basis for the "Black Legend" propagated by other colonial powers who rivaled Spain in the sixteenth century, enabling them to claim that the Spaniards were unfit to govern in the New World while disregarding the behavior of their own countrymen. Yet one of his greatest legacies was to initiate a debate about human rights that was a forerunner of Enlightenment ideals.

New ethnicities and identities

Although the Spanish in the Americas usually aimed to replicate the standards of Spanish society, life in New Spain and the rest of the Americas was necessarily different. The society that arose was a blended one, a melting pot in which the cultures of Spaniards, natives, and soon Africans interacted and created a society of new norms and practices. For many of the Spaniards, the Americas offered a place to make their fortunes. Those who came first were typically marginal figures for whom there were few opportunities in Spain – adventurers, lesser nobles, and veterans from the Reconquista, in addition to clergy. If immigrants succeeded in making their fortunes in the colonies, they could rise to much higher social and economic levels than they would have attained in Spain. This was especially true in the early days of the conquest, when large areas of land were available to conquistadors. These early migrants were soon followed by others who either served as lower-ranking soldiers or emigrated in order to take advantage of new economic opportunities in the new territories. Engaging in trade within the colonies or across the Atlantic was risky but offered substantial opportunities for economic growth to entrepreneurs from the middle and lower classes. Yet as the Spaniards became more established in the Americas, they began to reestablish the class distinctions that had been common in Spain, although with several differences. Many individuals and families had risen to a high status that they would not have enjoyed in Spain, and Spaniards were automatically of higher status than Africans or indigenous people. Peasants in the country-side were overwhelmingly natives. Distinctions existed among the Spaniards based upon whether they were *peninsulares*, born in Spain, or *criollos* (creoles), born in the Americas. Although the former group was of higher status in the early days of the conquest, within a few generations creoles became the dominant social group. As the creole population increased, women also began to emigrate from Spain, usually to join family members or to marry previously established men.

Among the natives, many tried to accommodate themselves to the conquest. The Spanish were more likely to accept Indian nobility, who were often able to achieve somewhat privileged access to Spanish society and thus assimilate faster. *Ladinos*, those natives who absorbed Spanish norms such as language, culture, and religion, were more likely to advance in Spanish-ruled society. Ordinary individuals were more likely to interact with the Spanish at a subordinate level through the encomienda or as miners, domestics, or in other forms of labor. Native women often acculturated to Spanish society through domestic service, which could offer economic opportunities but also the possibility for sexual encounters. These were often exploitative but also encompassed voluntary cohabitation and marriage. In Spain and Portugal, unlike much of Western Europe, it was not unusual for men to have informal – but also, to some degree, publicly acknowledged – sexual relationships with women of lower status prior to marrying a woman of their own class. The illegitimate children of such liaisons would be accepted into the father's family, though they did not displace legitimate heirs. This pattern was transplanted to the New World. Most of the Spanish in the sixteenth century had been young single men, and voluntary or forced inter-marriage with Amerindian women resulted in a large population of people of mixed heritage, which the Spanish termed *mestizos*. This group generally gained a higher position in the new society than the indigenous peoples.

In addition to Native Americans and Spaniards, there were increasing numbers of Africans, mainly brought to the Americas as slaves. As a result of encounters between Spaniards, Indians, and Africans, there was an expanding population of people with mixed ethnic backgrounds. The blending of African, native, and European culture especially occurred in regions where there were large numbers of native or enslaved women and few free women. In such areas, including Spanish, French, and Portuguese territories to which relatively small numbers of European women traveled during the first few centuries of colonization, and in which the Catholic Church sanctioned the marriages of whites with non-whites, there arose substantial populations of people of mixed ethnicity – white, black, and Indian – including both enslaved and free individuals. As this population expanded in Latin American regions, increasing anxiety about determining the proportion of white ancestry that an individual possessed gave rise to the system of *castas*. People, whether free or enslaved, were classified according to their degree of white, native, or black ancestry into an increasingly complex set of categories that could stretch back several generations. In practice, these categories were not of much real official use, as individuals tended to assume the identity of the highest status that was possible given their complexion. Whiteness was an indication of belonging to the dominant group, especially in cases where an individual's ancestry was undocumented.

Gender relations in Iberian territories also involved a blending of Iberian and native gender patterns. Men were the dominant sex in both pre-conquest societies, but in both, family connections were central shaping forces in society. The importance of extended families meant that women possessed some economic freedoms, including retaining ownership of property, so that they could support the interests of their birth families within the marriage. For example, ties of kinship allowed trans-Atlantic firms to operate – in some cases, the principal business partner was a woman. This was in contrast to the more patriarchal expectations of other European nationalities, such as the English, among whose colonists women had limited or no rights to own property or to act as a legally independent agent. Nonetheless, men everywhere retained significantly more social mobility, more political and economic opportunity, and more independence than women.

Voices of dissent

There were few who actively decried the inequalities within Spanish-American society. Most people were preoccupied with the struggle to survive or to maintain and improve their social standing. However, there were a few who voiced discontent through literary means, expressing social criticisms in their writing. Often, just as today, such appraisals came from people at the margins of society.

Two sustained critiques came from men of Native American descent from the former Inca territories. In 1615, a Quechua noble, Felipe Guaman Poma de Ayala, a clerk and translator for the Spanish government who had become discouraged after many attempts at filing protests against corruption and inequity, completed a 2,000-page chronicle of Inca history that criticized Spanish authority and pressed for a return to native rule (although in accordance with Spanish law and Christian morality). Although it had little effect at the time, it has been useful to historians. Similarly, Garcilaso de la Vega, the son of an Inca concubine of noble descent and a Spanish conquistador, praised Inca society and critiqued Spanish rule, in several works describing Inca history and legends published in the first two decades of the seventeenth century. Like Guaman Poma, he accepted many Spanish norms but also went further, envisioning a society in which blended Spanish and Inca elites governed over ordinary Native Americans. In his own life, he moved freely between Spanish and Quechua society, spending much time in Spain, but always felt disconnected from both. His sympathetic account of Túpac Amaru's death led to his work being banned by the Spanish government.

Another Spanish-American who broke out of the strictures of social norms was the creole nun and intellectual Sor Juana Inés de la Cruz (1651–95), who lived her life in Mexico. A child prodigy who spoke many languages, read and wrote literature, and investigated science and philosophy, she entered a nunnery, the only way for a woman of moderate means to continue her studies. Unusually for her time, she demonstrated feminist ideals, arguing for women's education and questioning the status of women in Spanish society. However, criticism of her writings mounted within the religious hierarchy, and in later years she gave up her intellectual work. She died in her nunnery caring for the sick during an epidemic.

New social patterns

From the beginning, the Spaniards expected to find others to labor for them in the New World. Although slavery was not a common institution in Spain in 1492, Spanish explorers and conquerors were familiar with Portuguese slavery and with slavery in the Spanish-owned Canary Islands, and they were prepared to use coerced labor in the New World. By his second voyage, Columbus was enslaving the Taíno, and the Spanish were soon raiding nearby islands for slaves. They were ready to regard the local inhabitants of the Americas as inferiors, a perspective aided by the Spanish concept of *limpieza de sangre*, or purity of blood. In the fifteenth century, this was an ideology particularly associated with Spain that had been developed in the context of the Reconquista. The Spanish, as a result of their long struggle against the North African Muslims (Moors), some of whom were dark skinned, had developed an ideology of innate superiority toward non-whites and non-Christians that was easily transposed to their experience in the New World.

Initially, many of the Spanish conquistadors seem to have assumed that they could easily enslave the natives, but there were several impediments to this. First, there were some ethical problems, including doubts from the Crown, which saw the Indians as subjects, maintained a sense of obligation toward them, and questioned outright enslavement. In addition, a number of friars, like Bartolomé de las Casas, maintained that American Indians should be treated with lenience, as they were non-Christian heathens who had never before encountered Christianity rather than infidels or refusers of the faith such as Muslims. Consequently, the Indians had a right to good treatment and to be offered conversion. Another compelling reason against enslavement was the widespread devastation caused by European diseases, which sickened and killed such a significant percentage of the native population that they were perceived as too weak to withstand the rigors of slavery and in any case were too reduced in numbers to serve as a reliable labor force.

Nonetheless, Spaniards did not give up the idea of forced Indian labor and devised institutions that, while not quite as dehumanizing as outright slavery, were still coercive and unjust. They also continued to enslave Indians, especially on the frontier areas of settlement. In the more central areas, the Spanish turned to the *encomienda*, which was similar to the serfdom of medieval Europe but was also comparable to the altepetl arrangement that had existed in Mexico. Natives continued to live within their communities, which then provided labor or tribute to a landlord – or *encomendero* – who had been granted the encomienda by the Crown. Some of the labor and tribute would be used to build a church and support a priest. Unlike feudal lords, encomenderos were usually absentee landlords who lived in Spanish urban areas. In a few cases, they were Indian nobles who had been rewarded by the Crown. As in a conquered altepetl in the past, the indigenous people who lived within the encomienda retained their own cacique, who was in charge of the community and received their labor and tribute. Indians retained certain rights that were not available to slaves – to farm land that was allotted to them, to form households, to marry and have children at will, and to leave the community. The native community was able to continue to engage in some traditional rituals and practices, sometimes shielded by a facade of Christianity. The Crown determined the amount of labor owed by the native community, which limited the landlords' depredations, and oversaw the arrangements through a local official called a *corregidor*, who also collected taxes.

Almost from the beginning, there were problems with this arrangement. It could cause trouble for the Spaniards by enabling traditional leaders such as caciques to lead rebellions more easily because they were still at the head of a community. However, rebellions were rare, while oppression of the Indians was common. Encomiendas were inherently exploitative, and the people within an encomienda could easily be abused by an encomendero or his overseers. The encomienda system was a greater drain on native communities than the altepetl had been because natives still had to support caciques and local nobles but now were also expected to pay labor and tribute to the encomendero and the Spanish Crown as well. The burden became still worse as native populations continued to decline from disease. The Spanish insisted on tribute in specific crops and eventually in money, forcing encomienda communities to produce desired European goods and later to sell goods on the market in order to obtain currency for their tribute. Furthermore, the system caused disputes among Spaniards, especially when newly arriving immigrants were unable to obtain native labor because the native communities had all already been handed over to encomenderos.

The Crown typically tried to present itself as the champion of the Indians against exploitative creole Spaniards in the colonies. There was a kernel of truth to this, and the Crown did attempt to mitigate some of the conquistadors' excesses, especially in regard to the encomienda, in the Laws of Burgos of 1512, the New Laws of 1542, and subsequent legislation, but in practice the laws only made small provisions for better treatment of Indians, and enforcement was lax or non-existent in most areas. The reality was that while the Spanish Crown was interested in conversion and in retaining the

Indians as subjects, it was far more interested in obtaining the wealth of the Indies and lacked the will to make serious changes.

From the mid-seventeenth century, a new labor institution, the *repartimiento*, gradually replaced the encomienda with the Crown's support. Under this arrangement, the Crown allotted groups of Indians to specific Spaniards for a temporary period, usually of a few months, sometimes on an annual basis, in an arrangement similar to the Inca mita system. This policy also favored the interests of the Crown, which mainly collected taxes directly from native communities. Adoption of the repartimiento system spread outward from Mexico, but it too was superseded by more modern direct wage–labor arrangements by the mid-seventeenth century. The encomienda and then the repartimiento persisted centuries longer in more peripheral areas.

Another institution that lasted into modern times was the *hacienda* (or great estate) that was directly controlled by the landowner. While these existed from the early sixteenth century on, they became more common in the seventeenth century. The hacienda could be combined with an encomienda, controlling the native labor from a preexisting community, or the repartimiento system, in which groups of natives toiled on the land for set periods of time, but eventually forms of labor ranged between semi-feudal peasant labor, sharecropping, slavery, and low-paid wage labor. While haciendas were usually plantations or self-sufficient farms, they could also include factories or mines.

Silver mining

The repartimiento system was also wholly suited to mining, because it centered on groups of people who could be transferred from one district to another rather than employing a settled community at a specific location. In the early days of colonization, mining was by far the most profitable enterprise for the Spanish. From Columbus' first voyage, the Spaniards had been convinced that the New World contained ample amounts of precious metals, especially gold. Although they only obtained limited amounts of gold, they were eventually able to develop very lucrative silver mines in Mexico and at Potosí, the most famous silver mine, located in Bolivia, which was originally a part of the Viceroyalty of Peru.

Mines generated a tremendous amount of income for the new Spanish Empire. They produced a liquid commodity – money – that was both portable and desirable around the world. Once mining was under way, a Spanish silver convoy crossed the Atlantic twice yearly, bringing the precious metal to Spain and returning to the colonies carrying goods and immigrants. Silver enriched the coffers of the Spanish Crown, which received the *quinto* (or king's fifth), enabling it to purchase luxury goods from as far away as Asia and take a more dominant role in European affairs. Indeed, it ushered in a period of about a century and a half in which Spain was the major political and military force in Europe, controlling Portugal and its empire from 1580, most of Germany and the Netherlands, and parts of France, mainly under the Spanish Habsburg dynasty. Spain also succeeded in colonizing the lion's share of the Americas and the Spanish East Indies in Asia during this period. More than anything else, it was the existence of the silver mines that led to increased Spanish immigration into the Americas, and the resultant wealth increased trade and created vast fortunes on both sides of the Atlantic. Spanish silver also affected the economy of Europe as a whole, providing an increased supply of monetary metals, which led to both inflation and an increased convenience of money.

Silver mines were worked by Indian and African slaves, as well as temporary forced laborers and free laborers. Indian forced labor was supplied though the repartimiento or rented from encomenderos, often still referred to by the original Incan designation of mita. Mita laborers and slaves did the hardest and most dangerous labor, such as tunneling, excavating, and hauling, whereas more skilled labor, such as refining the ore, was usually done by free workers. Settlements grew up around the mines, bringing in continuous streams of workers to substitute for others in mita rotations or to replace the dead. Mortality was high because of exhausting labor, disease, and dangerous conditions, including contact with the mercury required to extract the ore. In addition, the temporary or permanent absence of miners from their original communities resulted in impoverishment, famine, and often death for their families.

Timeline: early encounters

c.1000 Leif Erikson reaches Newfoundland

1492 Columbus reaches the Caribbean and builds La Navidad

1493 Columbus and his men force the Indians to provide gold tribute; Indians destroy La Navidad; first outbreak of European diseases in America

1497 John Cabot reaches North America

1500 One third of Taíno population dead from European diseases

1500 Pedro Álvares Cabral arrives in Brazil

1511 Hatuey leads rebellion against the Spaniards; Antonio de Montesinos defends Indians in his sermon

1512 Hatuey burned at the stake; Laws of Burgos

1513 Juan López de Palacios Rubios authors the "Requerimiento"

1519–21 Cortés conquers Mexico

1521 Viceroyalty of New Spain created

1523 Martín Cortés born

1524 Council of the Indies created to administer Spain's American possessions

1529–32 Inca Civil War

1531 First appearance of Virgin of Guadalupe

1533 Francisco Pizarro defeats Atahualpa in Peru

1539 Manco Inca founds Vilcabamba

1542 Most Taíno dead from European diseases; Viceroyalty of Peru established; New Laws

1545 Potosí founded

1545–90 Bernardino de Sahagún produces *The General History of the Things of New Spain*

1550 Valladolid debate between Bartolomé de las Casas and Juan Ginés de Sepúlveda

1552 Las Casas publishes *A Short Account of the Destruction of the Indies*

1556 Frenchman Jean de Léry arrives in Brazil and befriends the Tupinamba

1572 Túpac Amaru rebellion

1605 Garcilaso de la Vega publishes his first work on the Incas

1615 Felipe Guaman Poma de Ayala finishes his chronicle of Inca history

1620 Quechua population reduced by 90% due to European diseases

Trade and the economy in Spanish America

Silver was the foundation of Spanish trade in the Americas, and the need to transport it to Spain shaped commercial networks. Trade routes grew up along the roads leading from the mines to the local cities, continuing to the seaports. From there, silver and other American goods were shipped to Seville, which was at first the only city authorized to receive American trade goods. Spanish silver flowed from Seville into the rest of Spain and into Europe and Asia. In Asia, Spanish silver represented increased wealth, but in Europe it took on a much more significant role, replenishing the supply of monetary metals in a region that had previously had an insufficient supply and enabling the growth of a more developed money economy. Back in the colonies, the areas along the trade routes prospered and were tied into long-range trade networks that not only delivered goods from Spanish

America but also received people from Europe and Africa, as well as manufactured products from Europe and Asia.

Products from Europe were highly desirable in the colonies but were not always affordable or available. The colonies did produce some products for domestic consumption, including food, much of which was perishable, and textiles. Where possible, the Spanish continued to utilize traditional native systems of manufacture, such as the household production of cloth by native women. Cloth produced domestically in the colonies was cheaper and was made both in homes, where it might be used for tribute, and in mills and factories run by Spaniards. The latter were particularly suited to producing relatively cheap clothing that imitated European styles. In addition, there was a need for artisans and small businesses, especially in urban areas, which sometimes provided opportunities for poor Spaniards, non-Europeans, or persons of mixed ancestry to make a modest profit.

The decline of Spain

Although immensely profitable, economically the silver mines turned out to be a double-edged sword. Spain's reliance on the direct extraction of monetary metal resulted in economic backwardness just as other Europeans were experiencing greater economic dynamism and experimenting with early forms of capitalism in the form of banking, insurance, stock exchanges, long-range investment, and lending. In addition, Spain had imposed a trade monopoly mandating its colonies to engage in commerce only with the mother country, thereby hoping to profit by direct and cheaper access to goods and through taxation. This was an important principle of the economic theory of mercantilism, then dominant in Europe, which mandated control over all aspects of trade. However, the unintended effect of this was to incentivize black market trading. Colonial merchants evaded high Spanish tariffs whenever they could, and eventually clandestine trade was many times more prevalent and more profitable than legitimate commerce. This boosted the economies of the colonies and the shipping of other European countries and colonies at the expense of Spain. Mercantilist monopolies were implemented by other imperial European states as well, but since non-Spanish traders were heavily involved in underground trading with Spanish colonies, unlicensed commerce affected government tax revenues but not the general flow of independent capital within the economies of other European states. In addition to exacerbating economic inefficiency, the wealth the mines produced did not last forever. Most of them were tapped out by the eighteenth century, leading to Spain's inability to repay its debts in the newly monetized economy and resulting in bankruptcy. This was aggravated by Spain's debasing of its currency and its general inability to cope with inflation. Thus, in the end, a failure to develop economically, together with a limitation on Spain's sources of wealth, led to impoverishment and depopulation.

As Spanish economic might diminished in the mid-seventeenth century, Spain also began to show military weakness. The Habsburg dynasty became increasingly unable to pay for its military expenditures, especially during the exhausting Thirty Years' War (1618–48). The result was a reorganization of powers in the Atlantic. Portugal, which had been conquered by the Spanish in 1580, rebelled against Spanish rule beginning in 1640, achieving independence by 1668. The Spanish were forced to acknowledge the freedom of the rebellious Dutch Republic in 1648 and the end of the Thirty Years' War that same year, weakening the Habsburg dynasty. In 1659, the Spanish Crown conceded the Pyrenees to France. In the West Indies, the English took Jamaica from Spain in 1655, and the French began to encroach on Hispaniola from 1659. The gradual culmination of these events was the fading away of Spain as a world power.

Contact with the New World had made Spain a major European power. However, the same forces that bolstered Spain's influence eventually undermined it. By the early nineteenth century, political events in both Europe and the Americas impelled Spain's former colonies to rebel, resulting in the destruction of Spain's Atlantic empire and the development of newly independent states in Latin America.

Note

1 Montesinos' sermon in Lewis Hanke, ed., *The Spanish Struggle for Justice in the Conquest of America* (Philadelphia: University of Pennsylvania Press, 1949), 17.

9 The colonization of Brazil

After its accidental discovery by Pedro Álvares Cabral, Brazil at first remained a low priority for the Portuguese, and they were initially much slower than the Spaniards in settling the new lands. At the time, Portugal's involvement in trade with Asia and Africa was extremely lucrative, while Brazil was merely an unexplored region that might not prove to be very productive. A series of forts and small settlements were established along the coast and settled by marginal individuals or, often, convicts, called *degredados*, who were deported to the region. In order to settle the interior, extensive land grants called donatary captaincies were provided to lesser nobles, who were given almost unlimited power to rule them. However, the Portuguese government moved to take more direct control in the mid-sixteenth century as it became increasingly concerned about Spanish and French (and eventually Dutch) encroachment and also became more interested in the potential resources of its new colony. After initially searching for precious metals, the Portuguese realized the value of brazilwood trees, which produced a valuable red dye and were already sold in an extensive black market trade by the ships of other countries. In addition, sugar, already produced on Portugal's African islands, also became a valuable crop and eventually became the basis of Brazil's economy. Sugar was ultimately more profitable than dye wood because it could be produced on plantations and was much cheaper to transport. As sugar production grew, European settlement increased, and capital flowed into the colony. Cities developed in the northeast coastal region, near most of the *engenhos* (or combined sugar works and plantations), which both harvested and processed their crop. The interior of Brazil remained relatively unpopulated.

Brazil's society developed along lines quite different from Spanish America. The encomienda system that pervaded Spanish territories never developed in Brazil. Unlike most of the Amerindians encountered by the Spanish, the indigenous Tupi peoples of Brazil were mainly semi-sedentary, subsisting through hunting, fishing, gathering, and intermittent agriculture. Although they engaged in regular warfare with their neighbors and indeed practiced cannibalism, they were not imperialistic like the Aztecs or Incas and had no preexisting system of centralized political administration such as the altepetl. The peoples of the Amazon basin were even less sedentary. The native population was also much smaller than it had been in the urban areas settled by the Spanish. In addition, the Portuguese did not have a tradition of distributing lands and communities among conquerors like the Spaniards had developed during the Reconquista. Instead, they were accustomed to enslaving Africans. These factors shaped the Portuguese encounter with the Amerindians of Brazil, resulting in pervasive Indian slavery. By the early seventeenth century, organized slaving expeditions called *bandeiras* were roaming the interior, attacking Indian villages. Yet at the same time, the native population was already in sharp decline due to mistreatment and especially due to the spread of European diseases. Brazilians were already turning to extensive African slavery, although they continued to exploit Native American slaves, who were cheaper to obtain than Africans.

As in Spanish territories, Catholic clergy tried to mitigate the treatment of Indians. Jesuits strove to convert the indigenous peoples but also to protect them against the depredations of slavery. They established a network of missions and converted entire communities to Catholicism. Yet their efforts did not lead to long-term gains for the Indians because of the devastation caused by disease. Initially, there were few Europeans, and Brazilian natives were able to maintain cultural coherency. For example, in the interior of central and southern Brazil, European men often controlled polygamous households with several Indian wives and servants. Although such relationships were unequal and exploitative, a sparse European population typically adapted to indigenous society, and these households were often heavily influenced by Native American cultural practices. Once Brazilians turned to the extensive enslavement of Africans, African cultural norms were woven deeply into Brazilian society, while indigenous peoples and their customs diminished or perished.

As sugar became the central industry in Brazil, huge numbers of enslaved Africans began to arrive to work not only in the plantations but also as artisans and in markets and factories. At first, Africans took intermediary roles as supervisors and skilled craftspeople, but as the native population diminished, Africans worked in the positions requiring the hardest labor as well. This large African presence had a significant effect on Brazilian society and continues to influence it today.

10 Colonial settlements in northern America and the Caribbean

In the northern parts of the North American continent, the settlement patterns of the French, English, and Dutch took a somewhat different shape than Spanish and Portuguese continental settlements as a consequence of delayed colonization, awareness of the previous Spanish experience, and the result of settling in colder climate zones with diverse native populations. This was in contrast to colonies in the Caribbean islands and along the Caribbean coast, where the settlement patterns were similar for various European nations.

With the exception of Chabotto (Cabot)'s explorations under the English flag, the Spanish were the first to arrive in the northern parts of North America, and for a time they possessed the greatest span of territory in the Americas. Spain succeeded in ruling most of South America, with the exception of Brazil and the Guianas, and it also controlled Central America, though it lost Belize to the British in the nineteenth century. In addition, it controlled the largest islands in the Caribbean, including Cuba, Hispaniola until the French gained the western half in the late seventeenth century, Jamaica, and Puerto Rico. In North America, Spain colonized Mexico, Florida, and the region that would become the western United States. Spanish explorers were the first to reach most of these territories, including Vasco Núñez de Balboa, who was the first European to cross the Isthmus of Panama and see the Pacific Ocean in 1513; Juan Ponce de León, who explored Florida the same year; and Álvar Núñez Cabeza de Vaca, who traveled through the future southwestern United States in the 1530s, possibly getting as far west as Arizona.

The Portuguese also gained a significant part of the Americas with their acquisition of Brazil and briefly attempted to claim parts of Newfoundland according to the Treaty of Tordesillas after Cabot's voyages. However, they were also preoccupied with building their African and Asian trade routes at this time, which promised in the short term to be more lucrative and to which they had papal sanction. In the end, the Portuguese empire was to focus on control over significant portions of Africa, Asia, and Brazil.

Other Western European states also evinced interest in Atlantic exploration after hearing about Columbus' initial voyage, as shown by Henry VII's sponsorship of Cabot to search for a northwest passage (and perhaps new lands) in 1497. However, they were slow to begin serious exploration and established their American colonies much later than the Spanish and Portuguese. There were a number of reasons for this. Initially, the Treaty of Tordesillas seemed to give papal sanction for Spanish control over the newly found lands. In addition, the northern coastal countries lagged behind Spain and Portugal in maritime abilities, and England and France were still recovering economically and demographically from the Hundred Years' War and repeated waves of bubonic plague. England was particularly poor, and the royal succession was unstable during the sixteenth century, decreasing the ability of rulers to engage in expensive exploratory or colonizing ventures. In addition, perhaps the most important reason for the lag in Atlantic colonization by northern European powers was that after 1517, the northern part of the European continent became preoccupied with the Protestant Reformation and then the resulting continental wars.

Nonetheless, during the late sixteenth century, England, France, and the Netherlands began to compete for control over the remaining North American territories. There were a number of incentives for colonization. The perception of tremendous overseas wealth was a major factor, resulting in national competition to acquire new territories that would continue to persist in later imperial rivalries. In addition, the Spanish refused to allow the subjects of other countries to trade directly with Spanish overseas territories. In reality, they were unable to prevent a very considerable clandestine trade. However, this also served as an impetus for European countries to establish their own territories. The new territories also promised other sorts of wealth, including early plantation products such as tobacco and sugar; natural resources such as furs or logwood (a Central American tree that yielded red dye); and the most desired resource: precious metals. In addition, there was readily available land in the Americas, which was scarce in Europe and made the Americas attractive to a wide variety of settlers and their sponsors, including farmers; poor laborers; capitalist entrepreneurs; dissident religious groups; and even governments seeking to expel what they saw as undesirable populations of indigents, vagrants, criminals, and rebels.

French colonization

While the French began settling the New World before the English, they ultimately controlled far less territory. As early as 1524, the French Crown sent Giovanni da Verrazano, an Italian explorer, to scout the North American coast, and a Frenchman, Jacques Cartier, to the Gulf of Saint Lawrence. Soon there was a series of small settlements primarily concerned with fishing and fur trading along the northern coastline. In the 1560s, French Huguenots tried to establish a foothold in Florida but were swiftly ousted by the Spanish. Northern settlements were more fortunate. The explorer Samuel de Champlain established the colony of New France along the Saint Lawrence River in 1608, including the settlements of Canada, which included the cities of Quebec, Montreal, Acadia and, very briefly, Newfoundland. In addition, in the 1660s and 1670s, the explorer Robert de La Salle claimed a wide swath of territory along the Mississippi River, reaching as far south as Louisiana, for France. The Company of New France offered free land to immigrants, but the far northern land was uninviting, while much of the continental interior remained unsettled. The Thirty Years' War (1618–48) meant that France had little attention to spend on its colonies. Meanwhile, the English were taking as much land in North America as possible. Much territory in what is now Canada changed hands several times. The colony of New France, though geographically large, was sparsely settled, and by the mid-seventeenth century there were only about 2,000 French settlers in New France in comparison with 40,000 in New England at the same time. In addition to colonizing, the French engaged in black market trade with Spanish settlers in the Caribbean and South America and in harassing Spanish and Portuguese ships along the trade routes.

Like English colonies, French colonies were financed by joint-stock companies, but unlike the former, they mainly focused on trade with the Native Americans rather than large-scale settlement by farm families. The fur trade required relative little outlay – primarily the establishment of small trading forts staffed by single men – and depended on maintaining good relations with the Indians. The furs, especially beaver pelts, which were used in making felt hats, were worth considerable sums in Europe. In exchange, the natives received metal tools and cookware, cloth, and guns. Although this trade was initially beneficial to both sides, it ultimately had negative consequences. As the numbers of fur-bearing animals began to be depleted, conflict over control of hunting territories exacerbated conflict between the Huron and Iroquois peoples and between the English and the French, which was to lead to full-fledged warfare by the seventeenth century.

Other French settlements in the north included Port-Royal in Acadia, which was a colony of small farmers. It was founded in the wake of the French Wars of Religion (1562–98) and attracted many Huguenots – French Protestants – who hoped to escape religious persecution of a much more acute level than what the English Puritans were to suffer in England. Port-Royal was attacked in 1627 by the Scottish settlement of Nova Scotia, and two years later the English defeated New France, but the resulting treaty allowed France to control most of eastern Canada. The French also settled some Caribbean islands, which proved to be more lucrative for them, taking the western part of Hispaniola from the Spanish in 1664 and founding the colony of Saint-Domingue, which became one of the wealthiest sugar colonies in the Americas, as well as colonizing much of the Lesser Antilles, including Guadeloupe and other islands. In the eighteenth century, the French also established settlements in what would be the southern United States in the region of Louisiana. In 1624, the French began settling in French Guiana, and they also began colonizing parts of Asia and small portions of Africa during the seventeenth century.

In 1556, a group of French settlers, including Huguenots, attempted to found a colony in Brazil. The colony did not ultimately succeed, but it did have a significant impact on Atlantic history. Jean de Léry, a young Protestant minister in training among the settlers, published an open-minded and sympathetic account of his encounter with the cannibalistic Tupinamba people whom he met in Brazil in which he evaluated their society favorably in comparison with the inequalities that existed in Europe. De Léry was unable to convert the Tupinamba to Christianity, but he developed a strong personal connection with them, saying poignantly in his book that he deeply missed living among them, and praising the justice and honesty he found in their society. His book, *History of a Voyage to the Land of Brazil* (1578), became an important source for the famous essay by French skeptical philosopher Michel de Montaigne, "Of the Cannibals," which also influenced Shakespeare's *The Tempest* but even more significantly supplied a foundation for the Enlightenment ideals of toleration and human rights.

In some ways, de Léry's outlook was representative of French relations with the Indians as a whole. Because the early economic basis of the northern French colonies depended on mutually beneficial trade rather than on the extensive settlement of land or the production of plantation products through the use of forced labor, and also because Catholicism encouraged the conversion of the "heathen," French relations with the Indians were more peaceful than those of the Spanish or English. There were so few French women in French territories that many French men formed relationships with Native American women. While this was also the pattern in early Spanish territories and in the Caribbean, the French government, faced with a small population of subjects in North America, aimed to incorporate the Indians as subjects within a French polity and actively encouraged mixed marriages, while the English discouraged them and the Spanish and Portuguese merely tolerated them.

Almost from the beginning, French immigrants had included substantial numbers of Jesuit missionaries among their number. This order dedicated its energies to the cause of spreading the Catholic faith, and its members devoted their lives to propagating Catholicism overseas from Canada to China. Much as in Iberian territories, these missionaries, imbued with the Catholic Church's tradition of toleration of indigenous customs, drew attention to similarities in religious beliefs as a means of incorporating Indians into the Church, including native beliefs in a supreme being and in an eternal human spirit. This was in contrast to the English Puritan demand that Indians reject their past beliefs and adopt Protestant Christianity wholesale. Consequently, French Jesuits were able to convert many among the powerful Huron and Algonquian, while English Protestant missionaries found success among weaker groups. The alliances that developed in this period also shaped native tribes' allegiances when warfare broke out between the British and the French in the eighteenth century. Yet ultimately, in a series of intermittent wars, the English were successful in wresting most of North

America from the French, though the French consolidated their control over the French Caribbean islands. In the end, there were negative consequences for the Native Americans. The Huron, decimated by European diseases, were defeated and dispersed by their traditional enemies, the Iroquois, who mainly supported the English side.

Early English colonies

Although many countries established colonies in the north, it was the English, who were somewhat insulated from much of the continental warfare of the late sixteenth and seventeenth centuries, who managed to sweep to the fore. Indeed, English colonization efforts were increased during the Interregnum period of the 1650s following the wars of the previous decade. By the mid-seventeenth century, the English government was willing to invest in colonization because their navigational technology had caught up to Iberian standards, and the economic advantages of overseas imperialism were more obvious than they had been during the previous century.

As with the Portuguese experience in the coastal African islands, the English could look back at a precedent for imperialism in the colonization of Ulster in Ireland. This had begun in the twelfth century but had gained a new impetus during the sixteenth century. In fact, many of the leaders of "plantation" in Ireland then became colonizers or promoters of colonizing the New World in the late sixteenth century. In addition, the popular travel and geographical writer Richard Hakluyt repeatedly urged English colonization in the Americas in a theme taken up by two early promoters of English colonialism who were also half-brothers, Sir Humphrey Gilbert, an explorer on the Newfoundland coast who advocated establishing a northern colony near the cod fisheries, and Sir Walter Raleigh, who promoted the colonization of Virginia and engaged in exploration of the coast of South America.

During the late sixteenth century, there were a number of small-scale expeditions that aimed to explore or claim land, including Martin Frobisher's explorations of the Canadian coast in the 1570s, Francis Drake's circumnavigation of the globe in the same decade, and attempts to sponsor colonization in the 1580s and 1590s in Guiana and the Caribbean by Walter Raleigh and Humphrey Gilbert. The latter also laid English claim to Newfoundland based on John Cabot's initial landing there in the fifteenth century. At the same time on the other side of the globe, the East India Company was establishing trading posts on the Indian coast – the beginnings of extensive British colonization in Asia.

In the meantime, after some abortive efforts during the previous half decade, the first English colony in North America was founded at Roanoke, Virginia, in 1586, although it disappeared soon after. Jamestown, founded in 1607 in Virginia, was the first permanent settlement on the North American mainland, followed rapidly by others during the seventeenth century.

Many of these settlements started out as refuges for religious dissenters: Plymouth for Puritans; Maryland for Catholics; Pennsylvania for Quakers; and Rhode Island, which promoted religious tolerance more generally. In 1664, the British took over the Dutch colony of New Netherland, renaming it New York. By the end of the seventeenth century, there were colonies dotting the North American coastline, primarily English owned but sprinkled with some French or Dutch territories.

The English also colonized a number of Caribbean islands, including Barbados, in the first three decades of the seventeenth century and captured Jamaica, then under Spanish control, in 1655, moving into the Bahamas in the 1660s. Despite early seventeenth-century attempts to seize land in Guiana, the colony of British Guyana was not established until 1796 as an acquisition from the Dutch during the French Revolutionary Wars. Likewise, in Central America, Belize was originally a Spanish territory, but during the seventeenth century, the Baymen, who were essentially English buccaneers, gradually took over and established "British Honduras" as a source for the logwood trade and as a base for attacking Spanish shipping.

There were significant differences between English and Spanish colonies. The first Spanish conquistadors had arrived to townships in the Caribbean or densely settled urban areas in Mexico and Peru. These early Spanish settlers were mainly single men hoping to make their fortunes and return home, and they initially sought to enslave the Native Americans and use their labor to cultivate the land, mine for metals, and obtain other raw materials. The English, however, arrived to less densely settled areas, where the native populations had already been struck by disease. They knew that extensive native slavery was not feasible, and thus English settlers consisted not only of single men but also of families with servants that hoped to acquire their own farmland. Although these settlers hoped for gold and plentiful crops, most of the territories that they colonized possessed few precious metals, and much of their land did not possess a climate suitable for bountiful crop production. Exceptions to the latter included the southern colonies such as Virginia, the Caribbean, British Guiana (Guyana), and Belize. In addition, English colonies tended to rigidly separate whites from blacks or natives, whereas in the Spanish, Portuguese, and French territories, intermarriage was comparatively disregarded.

As in French territories, most of the early English settlements were sponsored by noble patrons or underwritten by joint-stock companies with multiple investors who did not personally immigrate, including the Virginia Company; its subsidiary, the London Company; the Massachusetts Bay Company; and, in the Caribbean, the Somers Isles (Bermuda) Company. For shareholders, this meant shared dividends when successful, shared risk when not. For the settlers, it represented funds for immigration, tools, seed, and equipment. The state legitimized the enterprise with a royal charter, and capitalist investors who had advanced larger sums sat on the boards of directors and attempted to determine the direction of the colonies. In order for the venture to be successful, individual settlers were needed to sign on to the undertaking, and companies published pamphlets promoting the healthiness, wealth, and agricultural productivity of the new lands. They provided further legitimacy by claiming that the main reason for overseas endeavors was conversion of the Indians. In reality, however, English colonies expended little effort in conversion, though some individuals did attempt to convert native populations. Instead, the religious impetus went toward creating a new religious society far away from the corruption of Europe or the governance of the Anglican Church – a "city on a hill" as Puritan leader John Winthrop proclaimed in 1630.

Because the English colonies were so wide-ranging and showed many disparate settlement patterns, there were very significant differences between them. The earliest North American colony was Virginia, founded at Jamestown by the Virginia Company in 1607. Governance was split between an executive council led by a governor appointed by company directors in London and a colonial assembly composed of shareholders, one of the earliest experiments with democracy in the New World. Shareholders were either those investors who had sponsored at least one settler or settlers who had immigrated with family and servants. Both types of shareholders received land and could elect members to the assembly. Nonetheless, the early days of the colony were difficult. During the first few years, most colonists died from disease or starvation caused by inability to properly cultivate the land and because the settlers had neglected agriculture in a futile search for gold. Hostility between the settlers and the Powhatan Confederation of local Native American tribes dissuaded the natives from helping or trading with the colonists. The Virginia Company eventually went bankrupt, and its control reverted to the Crown. However, in due course, the cultivation of tobacco led to the colony's economic success. In order to do so, tobacco growers had to develop a product that could compete with Spanish Caribbean tobacco and overcome the prevailing perception that smoking tobacco was decadent, but they were helped by the habit's immense popularity in England. King James I exemplified the contradiction; he had written a treatise against tobacco entitled "The Counter-Blast to Tobacco," but he agreed to give Virginia a monopoly on the sale of tobacco, and the English state profited from taxes on it. Virginia tobacco was grown on plantations worked at first by indentured servants – people who traveled under an agreement of temporary servitude, usually four years – but this rapidly switched to slave labor, thus establishing English participation in the African slave trade. The colony continued to be troubled in early years, going through a 1676 rebellion led by disgruntled planter Nathaniel Bacon that aimed to expel Indians from Virginia and reorganize economic structures. Nonetheless, tobacco eventually made Virginia the wealthiest mainland colony.

New England, on the other hand, showed a very different settlement pattern. The earliest settlers were the Puritan "Pilgrims" who had lived for some time in Leiden in the Netherlands in order to escape conforming to the

Anglican Church. While in England, they had been subject to fines, imprisonment, and various forms of discrimination, relatively mild by the standards of the seventeenth century, but still galling. However, they feared losing their identity in the tolerant Netherlands and aimed to create new devout Puritan lives in the New World. The society that they founded was extremely austere, not allowing political differences or religious opposition and inspiring the growth of breakaway colonies such as Rhode Island, which was founded by religious leader Roger Williams and populated by those who had been driven away for refusal to conform, such as Anne Hutchinson and her followers.

Puritans mainly came from the middle level of society and believed in the redemptive value of hard work, so they had some money to invest. However, they required a partnership with the London Company, which underwrote their expenses in exchange for their eventual profits. When they arrived in 1620, the heads of household signed the "Mayflower Compact," named after their ship, one of the earliest instances of an agreement to democratic governance (among adult free men) on non-religious matters. Although the Pilgrims were more industrious than the Virginia settlers and initially established relatively amicable relations with the local Wampanoag Indians, they also experienced a period of starvation at first, exacerbated by their inexperience with farming and the poor quality of the soil and climate. Through hard work, they began to sell food supplies to other colonies as well as wooden barrel staves, a necessity for shipping, plus fish and furs until the latter were depleted. They were able to purchase the Company's interest in their colony and establish themselves as the Massachusetts Bay Colony. The colony also increasingly flourished as it began to receive higher levels of Puritan immigration from the 1630s as the English state increasingly promoted Anglicanism in the prelude to the English Civil War.

In the meantime, as more Puritans arrived, the conflict over land grew sharper, and the relationship with the neighboring Indian tribes worsened. Both sides had hoped to use the other to their benefit. Initially, the Puritans hoped to remain safe from attack and learn local methods of cultivation. The Wampanoag had recently been decimated by European diseases, and their sachem Massasoit hoped that the English settlers would act as allies to boost their numbers against the tribe's Narragansett rivals. In addition, Squanto, a man who had been previously enslaved as a youth, had spent several years in England, and supported the colonists as a guide and translator, may have been aiming for greater political influence among the Wampanoag. In the end, the peace between the two peoples lasted only a generation, with large numbers of English settlers, both Puritans and non-Puritans, pouring into New England, while Native American numbers dwindled until the latter were hugely outnumbered by the new arrivals. War broke out when Massasoit's son, Metacomet, also known as King Philip, led his people in reprisals against English hostilities. King Philip's War (1675–8) raged through New England with great violence, with thousands killed on both sides, until fighting began to diminish with Metacomet's death in late 1676. Many captured

Native Americans, including Metacomet's wife and young son, were sold into slavery in the Caribbean.

While in French, Portuguese, and Spanish territories, there was considerable blending between native peoples and Europeans, this was less likely to occur in English colonies. This was due to both the preponderance of single men in the former territories in contrast to English settler families, and to religious differences. The Catholic French and Spanish believed in spiritual free will, thus encouraging the conversion of Native Americans to bring them into the Church and thereby the settler community. In contrast, Protestants, especially Calvinists, believed that spiritual grace came solely as God's gift and could not be influenced by human will or actions. There was little purpose, then, in pursuing widespread conversions or in incorporating Indians into the Christian community. In general, although there were some attempts at converting natives, most of the Puritans spent little energy on it and were more likely to dispossess Indians from their lands or enslave them. What conversions did occur tended to take place among small, weak groups that were discouraged by fighting the English and suffering sharp population declines from disease. These "Praying Indians" were congregated in "praying towns" where they accepted Christianity and English cultural norms but also retained some self-governance. The praying towns began to disappear after English warfare with the Indians broke out in the 1670s.

Many of the other northern colonies followed the pattern of the New England or Virginian settlements, with some regional variations. The main exception was Pennsylvania, which changed hands a number of times between the English and the Dutch but eventually fell into English hands and was then deeded to William Penn by Charles II in 1681 in repayment for a debt. Penn, a Quaker, established a colony founded on religious toleration and democratic assembly, much like Rhode Island. He made sustained attempts to create amicable relations with the Lenni Lenape Indians, also known as the Delaware, but his efforts were undermined by increasing population pressure caused by growing immigration from England. After Penn's death, his heirs colluded to dispossess the Delaware of their lands, inspiring the tribe's long-standing resentment against the British. On the other hand, the more southern British colonies, Belize and Guiana, followed patterns similar to mainland plantation colonies of other countries, such as Brazil, establishing plantation economies based on slavery, harvesting logwood, and producing sugar, while the sparsely populated northern colony of Newfoundland subsisted on its plentiful cod fishery.

Much like the Spanish, the English imposed a monopoly on trade between their colonies and ships with other nationalities. Again, as in the Spanish example, it was not successful, and this policy instigated a series of Anglo-Dutch Wars during the seventeenth century as the two countries jostled for control over land and trade routes in the Americas. The conflict eased after the accession of William of Orange, *stadtholder* (or executive officer) of much of the Dutch Republic, to the English throne in 1688 at a time when the British were on their way to becoming the dominant force in the Caribbean and soon throughout the Atlantic basin.

Dutch and other European colonies

The Dutch were relative latecomers to America. In addition to some of the impediments facing other northern European countries, the Netherlands were still part of the Holy Roman Empire until they were able to effectively throw off Spanish rule by 1581 during the Dutch Revolt. When they did begin to colonize in the Atlantic, they were equally focused on founding colonies in other parts of the world. Most of the Dutch settlements in the Atlantic were relatively small and focused more on trade than on settlement. Dutch colonization in the Atlantic was backed by the Dutch West India Company, which found a major source of revenue in engaging in trade with existing colonies of other nations and also in harassing Spanish shipping. The Dutch were successful in seizing the entire Spanish silver fleet in 1628, and with their large merchant fleet, they dominated the Atlantic trade routes through most of the seventeenth century, especially the lucrative sugar and slave trades, despite the trade monopolies imposed by the governments of other countries.

During the early seventeenth century, the Dutch settled a number of regions in the Atlantic. On the North American coast, they founded the colony of New Netherland, which included New Amsterdam, the settlement that was to become New York City. This was a relatively small community that primarily subsisted on trading in furs with the Algonquian Indians. This region was to become an issue of contention in the Anglo-Dutch Wars until it was finally taken by the English in 1673. In the Caribbean, the Dutch had a brief presence on some of the smaller islands and retained the Netherlands Antilles. On the South American coast, Dutch colonies included Dutch Guiana (Suriname) as well as a brief presence in Brazil and Chile. Suriname became a plantation colony producing sugar, coffee, and cocoa and, like other plantation regions, was noted for its brutal regime of slavery.

In addition to Spanish, Portuguese, English, Dutch, and French settlements, other northern European regimes briefly sustained territorial ambitions in the Atlantic. There were some small German settlements in South America and the Caribbean that were eventually incorporated into the colonies of other nations. Denmark established colonies in Greenland and the Caribbean. The latter were sold to the United States in the early twentieth century, becoming the U.S. Virgin Islands, by which time the islands were occupied mainly by people of African and English descent. Sweden also possessed the short-lived colony of New Sweden (1638–55) on the North American mainland, which was taken over by the Dutch, and very briefly held some Caribbean territories as well.

Piracy

One consequence of monopolies and competition was the growth of piracy. It was very difficult for governments to control colonial trade, resulting in a burgeoning black market, and the appearance of independent contractors in slaves and colonial products. In addition, early modern governments regularly licensed privateers, called buccaneers in the Caribbean, to raid the vessels of other countries, especially during wartime. For instance, Captain Henry Morgan made his fortune in semi-legitimate attacks against Spanish colonies, was knighted, and rose to Lieutenant Governor of Jamaica. In practice, however, privateers were indistinguishable from pirates from the point of view of those they attacked. Privateers were inherently difficult to control, and privateering was only a small step from plundering ships of all nations indiscriminately. The growth of piracy, especially by English buccaneers, became a growing problem, and the English government took increasing measures to curb it, essentially succeeding during the early eighteenth century as the size of the British naval fleet greatly increased. Nonetheless, there were resurgences of piracy into the nineteenth century, especially during wartime while national militaries were preoccupied, and privateering reemerged. The age of piracy was definitively ended by the invention of steam-powered ships in the mid-nineteenth century.

Although pirates could be very violent, they lived in an extremely violent age. English Royal Navy vessels functioned as a brutal dictatorship, with crew members flogged or killed for small offenses. In contrast, pirate crews governed themselves through a kind of rough and ready democracy, electing their captains, maintaining equality between crew and officers, and sharing spoils. Turning pirate offered escape to sailors in the Royal Navy who had been impressed – abducted and forced to serve – or who sought to escape from a life of cruelty. On the other hand, pirates' reputation for ferocity was not always fully deserved. While attacking a ship was always violent, many pirates allowed captured sailors to go unharmed. For example, the notorious Edward Teach, known as Blackbeard, preferred to rely on intimidation through his reputation and fierce appearance and rarely resorted to bloodshed. He was an imposing man who would lead attacks with lit fuses smoking in his full beard, and most ships' crews quickly surrendered to him. Although pirates sometimes engaged in slaving, piracy also offered a path to freedom for former African slaves, and many pirates were of African heritage, such as, for example, two thirds of the crew on Blackbeard's ship, *Queen Anne's Revenge*.

Witchcraft panics

Witchcraft had become a major concern in Europe after the Protestant Reformation, especially from 1560 to 1680, the height of the witch panics. The medieval Catholic Church had been skeptical about witchcraft, questioning the ability of the devil to possess physically effective force in the world. The Church maintained that the universe obeyed God's will and that the forces of evil only had the power to sway human minds, not to set aside the laws of nature (for example, by allowing brooms to fly or curses to cause tangible effects). In the Middle Ages, most witchcraft cases were tried by Church courts, and the Church's aim was to bring sinners back to the fold rather than execute them. However, during the early modern period as religious denominations increasingly splintered, a growing sense of instability led to a sense that evil was encroaching on the world. More and more people believed in the reality of witches and demons. At the same time, with the growth of the centralized state, secular courts took over judging cases of witchcraft. Magistrates and juries were more likely to accept that an accused person was a witch than theologians had been. They also believed that they should deal harshly with witches, because many Protestant denominations emphasized the concept of a vengeful God who would be angered by lapses in the community. Witchcraft cases tended to be oriented geographically in regions where there were multiple denominations in close contact and where people were increasingly anxious that the ungodly beliefs and practices of their neighbors would bring God's punishment on them all. While both Catholics and Protestants prosecuted witches, areas that retained traditional Catholicism, such as Ireland and Spain, saw few persecutions of witches.

The individuals who were the subject of initial witchcraft accusations were typically vulnerable and marginal individuals in the community: older widows, orphaned children, or aggressive beggars. In some cases, accusations snowballed until hundreds of individuals were accused together. In Western Europe, women made up about 75% of the approximately 100,000 accused witches, as well as a large percentage of the accusers, while in eastern Europe, accused witches were mainly men. In the West, changing norms of communalism led to hostility toward beggars and the poor. The indigent elderly were more likely to be women than men, both because of women's longer lifespans and the existence of marriages in which husbands were older than their wives and so predeceased them. At the same time, there was growing contestation of women's roles. Women were believed to be morally and intellectually weaker and were increasingly urged, especially by Protestants, to be subordinate to their husbands, yet at the same time they were also gaining greater access to education and urban society. Witchcraft prosecutions began to die down as magistrates became increasingly skeptical toward supernatural claims in the late seventeenth century.

While there were sporadic accusations of witchcraft in the Americas, the most famous was a full-blown witch panic that occurred in Salem Village, Massachusetts, from 1692 to 1693, with 20 people executed and some 150 people prosecuted for witchcraft. In many ways, this event diverged from European precedents. The event occurred in Salem at a point in time when witchcraft accusations had died down in Western Europe. Furthermore, in Europe, a witch's confession was necessary for conviction. Indeed, conviction rates were much higher in areas where magistrates allowed torture to be employed to force confessions, such as in Germany, than in regions where torturing accused witches was illegal, such as in England. However, in Salem, while accused witches were not tortured, it was those among the accused who refused to confess that were executed. When this pattern became apparent, accused individuals began to confess to witchcraft to forestall execution. However, in several ways, the Salem witchcraft trials also exemplified the picture of witchcraft accusations elsewhere. Initially, most of the accused were marginal or friendless women. The villagers in Salem subscribed to a particularly strict and unforgiving version of Protestantism and possessed a pervasive fear of the imminent invasion of the forces of evil because of the continuing Indian attacks on exposed border territories, attacks which had personally affected most of the accusers. Deep-seated jealousies and rivalries over land and economic success delineated which individuals would be grouped among the accused and the accusers. These factors led to political and social instability and convinced frightened magistrates to allow "spectral" or supernatural evidence to convict witches, contrary to the law. Much as in European witch panics, as too many men and prominent persons began to be accused, the prosecutions wound down. More unusually, they were rapidly followed by apologies from jurors and magistrates and even attempts to make restitution by Massachusetts courts, perhaps because the Salem witch panic occurred at the cusp of the major change in intellectual and religious values that occurred during the eighteenth-century Enlightenment.

Colonial economies

In addition to national origin, it is fruitful to look at the economic basis of the American colonies in North America and the Caribbean, because in many ways this is a more accurate way to categorize differences between colonies. In most cases, the initial aim for colonies was not necessarily to establish the livelihoods of individuals but to provide a profit for investors. In the early days, many held naïve beliefs that the Americas were a land of plenty that would produce profits without much hardship. Among the most sought-after commodities were precious metals, but these proved to be scarce, with the exception of the Spanish silver mines. Thereafter, successful colonies, usually after much hardship, developed products that they could sell on the Atlantic market. In addition to direct profits, they produced profits for the state in taxes and also served as markets for manufactured products from Europe. Some seventeenth-century colonies based their livelihoods on selling natural raw materials, such as furs; fish, which was a dietary staple when dried; timber for shipbuilding and barrel staves; and logwood. Others focused on producing plantation products, including the major products of tobacco and sugar, as well as coffee, cocoa, rice, indigo and, after 1800, cotton.

Plantation societies, whether in the Caribbean or on the mainland, all shared similar characteristics. Production of agricultural products was through forced labor, which initially began as Native American labor in Spanish regions and indentured labor in British and some French territories but by the seventeenth century was increasingly supplied by the African slave trade. In plantation areas, the population primarily consisted of black laborers who were kept in check by white supervisors through brutality and deprivation. In non-plantation-based regions, the economy was more diverse, including small farming, artisanal manufacturing, and sometimes the processing of plantation products. By the late eighteenth century, slavery was diminishing in areas with non-plantation-based economies as capitalist efficiency and ideology took hold. Divisions began to appear between three types of regions throughout the Atlantic world: peripheral hinterlands with low populations that were either mainly Native American or creole; plantation regions, which were enormously profitable but politically and economically static and dependent on coerced labor; and new dynamic urban areas and small towns that were developing new ideologies, technologies, and expectations that would challenge global regimes.

Sugar and the Caribbean

Although all Atlantic powers held Caribbean territories at one time, their Caribbean colonies were strikingly similar in economy and governance because of their dependence on plantation products, primarily sugar. Initially, most of the Caribbean islands were under the control of the Spanish, especially the larger ones like Cuba and Hispaniola. English and French colonizers thus concentrated on the smaller islands, in particular those initially inhabited by Caribs, who had often successfully driven off the first wave of Spanish colonization. By then the Spanish had turned to the colonization of the North and South American mainlands. Some of the islands, like Barbados, were depopulated when they were finally colonized – in this case, by the English in 1624, a consequence of Indian populations being kidnapped by or fleeing from Spanish slave-raiding expeditions and the spread of European diseases.

From the first, the Caribbean colonies were reasonably successful, producing plantation products such as tobacco, coffee, cocoa, cotton, and dye, but they became far more prosperous when sugar was introduced in the mid-seventeenth century. Like Brazil, the Caribbean was an ideal place to grow sugar, which requires a great deal of warmth and water. Sugar became the most valuable Atlantic crop, with a value that continuously grew during the colonial period, shaping much of the Atlantic economy and particularly dominating the economies of Brazil and the Caribbean.

Sugar is an extremely labor-intensive crop. Sugarcane can grow to twice a man's height and had to be cut by hand using machetes. Then it would be crushed, boiled, crystallized, and washed. Some of this work was done at night, creating an exhausting regime of labor and punishment that quickly wore slaves out. Sugar plantations were typically large undertakings, because farming sugar requires a significant investment of capital and a sizeable labor force. Within a generation, sugar plantations transformed the Caribbean from a realm of small farms and plantations that produced products such as tobacco and coffee using slave labor to vast tracts of sugar plantations. The population in the mid-seventeenth century went from about two-thirds free whites and one-third enslaved blacks to a ratio of ten slaves to every free white. The rate of the slave trade vastly increased in order to continuously replenish the supply of deceased slaves.

Although sugar seems a commonplace crop today, it was a relatively new one in the early modern period. Prior to the seventeenth century, sugar had been rare and exclusive. Honey and fruits had been the main sweeteners previously. By the seventeenth century, sugar was still expensive but ever more available to people in the middling ranks of society, who were consuming it in increasing quantities, though at first not on a daily basis. For example, from the mid-seventeenth century to the late eighteenth century, sugar consumption increased by twenty-fold in England. The European appetite for sugar appeared unquenchable, and the sugar colonies became the most profitable European outposts in the New World. Thus, Barbados, the main sugar-producing colony of Britain, produced significantly more wealth than any other British colony. The most profitable sugar colony of all was the French colony of Saint-Domingue on the island of Hispaniola.

The economic influence of sugar was much greater than it might seem. In addition to the end product of sugar itself, it was central to a complex and lucrative exchange of products tied to slave labor circulating throughout the Atlantic world, including sugar-containing consumables such as molasses, jam, chocolate, tea, coffee, and rum; containers and serving implements, including glassware, porcelain, metal utensils, and barrels; agricultural and transportation equipment, including tools, parts for sugar mills, nautical equipment, fertilizer, livestock and carts used for rendering and transporting sugar, and slave food and clothing; and instruments of punishment and restraint utilized in slavery such as whips, chains, and shackles. Each of these products were further connected to others and to a human network of investors, manufacturers, suppliers, shippers, laborers, and consumers, tying the Atlantic together in a pervasive web of sugar consumption and production.

As sugar became more omnipresent in Europe, it had an increasingly significant effect on the economies of European countries and on ordinary people's lives around the Atlantic world. Anthropologist Sidney Mintz, who has written extensively about the history of sugar, has named sugar one of the "proletarian hunger-killers," which also included coffee, tea, rum, and tobacco – all plantation products produced by slave labor.[1] These are all stimulants or drug-like food substitutes which provide empty or no calories but enabled capitalist expansion during the Industrial Revolution by allowing workers to work longer with less food. Thus, sugar, like cotton, tied slave labor in the colonies with capitalist production in industrialized areas in Western Europe, the United States, Canada, and parts of Latin America. Sugar produced a greater amount of human misery than any other product in the Atlantic, a combination of the fact that it was the most important slave-produced crop in the Atlantic and that the sugar plantations featured the harshest conditions for slaves. Even when slavery was officially ended in the Atlantic, sugar cultivation continued to take its toll on human lives as the labor force on sugar plantations shifted to indentured laborers from Asia, whose lives were little different from those of slaves.

Note

1 Sidney Mintz, "The Caribbean as a Socio-Cultural Area." *Cahiers d'Histoire Mondiale [Journal of World History]*, Vol. 9, No. 4 (1966), 916–941.

Part III
Connections, journeys, and war

11 Atlantic trade and empire

The discovery of the Americas had a profound effect on the world economy. Once Europeans became established as the dominant force in the Atlantic, regular conduits of trade and transportation developed across the ocean. This period saw a transformation of global commerce that was reoriented from centers in the Mediterranean and the Indian Ocean to the Atlantic. This change had significantly different effects depending on the nature of various continental societies' involvement. For Europe, the Atlantic became a source of wealth, a zone of territorial expansion, and a place to absorb surplus population. For western African states, the Atlantic produced both riches and misery. States involved in the slave trade realized an increased flow of wealth due to participation in world markets, but for the 12 to 20 million people who were enslaved, it meant dislocation and suffering. For Native Americans, the Atlantic encounter brought depopulation and displacement. European influence also extended with European colonization. As new societies arose in the Americas, they were dominated by the descendants of European colonizers, though they also incorporated the cultural values of Africans and Native Americans.

One of the first major consequences of Atlantic trade was the influx of silver from Spanish silver mines, which created a huge increase in the availability of monetary metals. This incurred significant consequences to the European economy as a whole, in some cases augmenting changes that had already begun to occur in the pre-Columbian period. Money rather than barter increasingly became the basis of exchange in Europe; the real value of agricultural rents, which were not adjusted for inflation, decreased, thus reducing the incomes and influence of the nobility while boosting the peasantry. Meanwhile, middling-level merchant capitalists and entrepreneurs prospered through Atlantic commerce, leading to a growing and increasingly wealthy middle class with interests that often clashed with the ideals of aristocratic society. The new availability of money-based taxes led to an increase in state incomes and the rise of the centralized state. Urban areas grew, while commerce, investment, banking, and lending flourished, enabling the development of more complex global markets and supply chains.

Well-established trade routes, often termed the triangle trade, developed in the Atlantic. In the most basic form of this trade, manufactured products from Europe, especially guns and textiles, were exchanged for slaves in Africa, who were then sold in the Americas, from whence slave-produced plantation goods such as sugar, rum, tobacco, rice, and cotton traveled to Europe. In addition, Europeans produced manufactured goods such as metal wares, trinkets, and cloth for both the colonists and Africans; the colonists traded in raw materials such as furs and fish and sold liquor to both Europeans and Africans; and Africans sold cloth to European merchants. Rather than encompassing the whole Atlantic with their voyages, individual merchants and their ships typically plied one or two legs of the triangle.

Dominance in Atlantic trade was initially the preserve of the Spanish. As the enormous potential for wealth became clear, control over Atlantic trade became a source of contention among European nations. It was successively taken over by the Portuguese, the Dutch, the French, and then the British from the late eighteenth century, in the end financing Britain's rise to the dominant world power of the nineteenth century. Atlantic trade fundamentally altered global economic systems, and the relationships of world societies as international trade routes shifted to the Atlantic from the Mediterranean and the Indian Ocean. In addition to national focuses of Atlantic trade, intercontinental networks developed between groups of immigrants and their family members and associates on the eastern side of the ocean, including religious dissenters, refugees, and minority communities. These connections often provided the basis for commercial firms that developed great wealth and influence. Atlantic port towns such as Boston, Massachusetts, provided nodes for the transmission of vast of amounts of wealth. By the end of the eighteenth century, Europe had become the center of a worldwide system of wealth, military power, and technological innovation. In Africa, on the other hand, the slave trade led to depopulation, political instability, and dependency. Thus, from the beginning, European growth was inextricably tied to African underdevelopment.

The slave trade was coupled with control over Atlantic shipping; while first initiated by the Spanish and Portuguese, it was taken over by the Dutch in the seventeenth century and then the British from the late eighteenth century. European Atlantic empires profited from both the slave trade itself and from the plantation economy in agricultural products produced by slave labor. By the early nineteenth century, the United States, Brazil, and Cuba (though still a Spanish colony) had become active in the slave trade, while the French and especially the British had grown into the main European participants in Atlantic trade. The United States and Britain both ended their official participation in the slave trade (but not slavery) by 1807, but ships from both nations continued to take part in the trade clandestinely.

The Spanish Empire in the eighteenth century

Although diminishing in its strength as an Atlantic power, the Spanish Empire in the eighteenth century remained the largest political and military entity in the Atlantic. However, it continued to weaken during the course of the century. With the death of Charles II, the last of the Spanish Habsburg dynasty, in 1700, the heir was Philip of Anjou of the French Bourbon dynasty, raising the prospect of uniting the French and Spanish Crowns and resulting in the War of the Spanish Succession (1701–13) as European rivals united to prevent this possibility. In the 1713 Treaty of Utrecht, England took over Spain's monopoly in the slave trade, and Spain lost some European and American territories. Spain still retained most of its vast empire but was further weakened by this defeat. An unanticipated consequence of this conflict was that the Dutch, although on the winning side, had drained their treasury and gave way to Britain as the new rising power in the Atlantic.

Within Spain, the new dynasty aimed to modernize, establishing the Bourbon Reforms, a series of laws intended to improve the institutions of the Spanish Empire and more strongly consolidate royal power in the Spanish colonies. The reforms included secularization of political administration, agricultural improvements, modernization of trade policies, the replacement of corrupt colonial administrators with Spanish officials more loyal to the Crown, the institution of more efficient tax collection, and the establishment of colonial militias. Meanwhile, Spanish clergy ranged through the North American continent, setting up missions and converting Indian populations, sometimes by force. Spain still controlled the largest amount of territory in the western Atlantic. Its Atlantic empire encompassed three times the population of about 3 million inhabitants within British North America and contained most of the large cities in the Americas. It had also acquired the vast Louisiana territory from France, comprising the land west of the Mississippi River up to Canada, in the Seven Years' War (1756–63). However, Spain's power was already in decline, as its reduced nautical and fiscal power made it unable to resist the actions of other powers. In 1800, Napoleon's government forced the Spanish to return the eastern portion of the Louisiana territory, while the rest of Spain's territories in continental North America were lost at Mexico's declaration of independence in 1821. Meanwhile, Spain was also to lose its South American territories in the Latin American independence movements of the second decade of the nineteenth century.

The rise of the British Empire

Many European empires competed for control in the Atlantic, including the Spanish, Portuguese, British, French, and Dutch Empires. Even Sweden and Denmark were involved in territorial conflicts concerning their small Caribbean territories. In the end, however, the realm that was to benefit most from the wealth of the Atlantic and become the world's first superpower was Great Britain. Britain was, in fact, a latecomer to Atlantic ventures which, as we have seen, were initially led by the Portuguese and Spaniards. The country of England first began to realize economic gain from its colonies with its Caribbean sugar plantations, which were expanded significantly with the settlement of Barbados in 1627 and the seizure of Jamaica from Spain in 1655. England's success in the Anglo-Dutch Wars which took place during much of the seventeenth century further established its dominance in the Atlantic. Although Spain was already weakening in this era, England, the Dutch, and the Portuguese continued to jostle for influence in both the Americas and Asia during the seventeenth century. England's union with Scotland in 1707 established Great Britain, consolidating the state, which was also strengthened by the dearth of warfare on the island of Britain after the English Civil Wars of the mid-seventeenth century. Economically, the rise of the English middle classes, who had made their fortunes from the wealth of the Atlantic, established a stable commercial basis for the expansion of trade and industry. The British constitutional monarchy, governing alongside Parliament, created a political system that was more responsive and flexible than those of continental governments.

In the meantime, Britain kept on acquiring colonies as a result of its effective involvement in European wars. Through the eighteenth century, Britain was involved in a series of European confrontations that spiraled much wider than merely the colonies in the Americas, including disputes between dynasties on the European continent and struggles for control over colonies in other parts of the world, especially Asia. Britain gained territory in almost every conflict that it took part in. An important early struggle was the War of the Spanish Succession (1701–14), fought to prevent the unification of the French and Spanish dynasties. The Treaty of Utrecht at its closing resulted in the British acquisition of Newfoundland and Nova Scotia from France; control over Gibraltar, which was the conduit between the Mediterranean and the Atlantic; and access to the Spanish slave trade.

Britain continued to gain from later eighteenth-century wars. From 1739 to 1748, Britain fought Spain in the picturesquely named War of Jenkins' Ear, which was initiated when British sea captain Robert Jenkins' ear was severed by Spanish naval forces; wielding his embalmed ear before Parliament, Jenkins demanded retribution, though the underlying impetus of the war was actually commercial competition over the slave trade within Spanish territories. This conflict was also entangled with the War of the Austrian Succession (1740–8), a dynastic conflict over the Habsburg succession that embroiled most of Europe, while in the American theater of King George's War (1744–8), Britain and France fought over American territories. The concurrent Carnatic Wars (1746–63) extended British control over French colonies in India. The net effect of these wars was to weaken continental European powers while consolidating British power in the Atlantic, the Mediterranean, and Asia.

Among the most wide-ranging of such conflicts was the Seven Years' War (1756–63). Referred to as the French and Indian War in the United States, it was truly a worldwide conflict. The Treaty of Paris, which ended it in 1763, led to a considerable extension of British territory in North America, with Britain gaining almost all of New France, including Canada and parts of Louisiana. In addition, Britain gained control of French colonies in India and West Africa. From that point, Britain was the dominant naval power in the Atlantic. Nonetheless, it suffered its only eighteenth-century defeat a few years later in the American Revolution (1775–83), another global conflict, as Britain's recently defeated enemies – the French and Spanish – rushed to aid the American colonists. As the United States began to establish itself on the North American continent, Britain continued to maintain its global dominance but gradually turned to an emphasis on expanding its empire eastward into Africa, Asia, and Australia rather than in the western Atlantic.

Indentured servants

Trade and slavery were the two main props of imperial wealth. In British-controlled areas, African slaves were preceded by European indentured servants, who comprised about two thirds of all British immigrants. The majority of these were indigent youths and young adults who had pledged their labor for a period of years. In some cases, these included unwilling individuals abducted or "Barbadosed" by "spirits" or professional kidnappers, as well as convicts, vagrants, and prisoners of war sent by the British government. In the mid-seventeenth century, a number of Irish servants were sent to the Caribbean by the British government after the quelling of the Irish Rebellion of the 1640s and 1650s. Yet by far, most servants were English, and most servants, whether English, Irish, or Scottish, had signed an indenture contract of their own volition. An approximate figure comprises some 330,000 English servants, 30,000 Irish, 7,000 Scots, and fewer continental Europeans. Upon arriving in the colonies, servants' contracts could be sold, with the price declining depending on the amount of time left to serve. Young men generally served a four-year term of servitude, but women, children, and unwilling servants, who had a reduced market value, could serve for longer periods, usually seven years. Upon finishing their contracts, voluntary servants, and even some involuntarily indentured persons, received "freedom dues" of money, land, clothing, or tools.

Servants were often treated brutally, and many did not survive their contracts, but although they could be legally beaten, they also had important basic legal protections that were not available to slaves. They could not lawfully be maimed, killed, starved, raped, left without clothing or shelter, deprived of their freedom dues, or kept past the term of their contracts. However, although these protections were legally recognized, it was often difficult for dependent servants to prosecute a violent or neglectful master or mistress. Women servants were particularly vulnerable to sexual exploitation, as most served as domestic servants with little recourse for resisting their masters. Women who bore children while under contract usually had their contracts extended; in some cases, the father's contract, if he was a servant, was lengthened, unless a servant could manage to prove that her master or another free man was the father of the child, in which case he was responsible for its monetary support, and the servant herself might be freed or placed with another master or mistress. The children of women servants were usually indentured until the age of 21, but they did not inherit a permanent condition of servitude as the children of slave women did.

Although indentured servants comprised the vast majority of Britons crossing the ocean in the seventeenth and eighteenth centuries, their ability to supply the labor needs of the colonies was deemed insufficient because of the limitations of their contracts and because their numbers were not great enough. Furthermore, indentured servants were difficult to control – for example, there was considerable difficulty in recruiting them to work in certain areas, such as the Caribbean. On the other hand, they helped provide a model for the transportation, recruitment, and investment in slaves, and as the colonies' labor preferences altered, shippers of servants moved seamlessly from shipping servants to shipping slaves.

Native American struggle and accommodation

Throughout the Americas, Native Americans faced a continuing question of whether to confront or adapt to European colonizers. Native populations were still being stricken by waves of epidemic diseases, but their numbers had begun to stabilize by the seventeenth century in Latin America and by the eighteenth century in the north. Nonetheless, by that time they had been reduced to a small percentage of their former population, and Europeans had already taken possession of most Native American lands or were in the process of laying claim to them. Yet native peoples strove in various ways to retain their cultural values, control their territories, or simply stay alive. In many cases, Indians blended into the dominant culture, either as part of an underclass, like much of the mestizo population in Latin America, or sometimes as individuals who assimilated into the European population. Many native populations retained cultural distinctiveness by living in separate communities from whites but increasingly found it difficult to maintain economic security or defend themselves from further encroachment.

From the beginning of the conquest, Native Americans attempted to rebel against their new colonizers. In Spanish America, these revolts became fiercer after Amerindians began to acquire some biological resistance to European diseases in the mid-seventeenth century and as their numbers began to increase. Some areas remained fractious and hard for the colonizers to control. Even from the beginning, the Spanish conquest of the Maya in the Yucatán, which lasted 170 years from 1527 to 1697, was particularly protracted and bloody, involving a number of temporary victories for the Maya. Unlike much of the rest of Mexico, the Maya cities were relatively independent and had to be conquered on a piecemeal basis. There continued to be major revolts among the Maya, including a year-long rebellion by more than twenty towns that erupted in Chiapas in 1712. The rebels were participants in a sect that believed their cause to be supported by the Virgin Mary, thus appropriating Spanish religious values to reject Spanish rule. Territories that had been previously conquered sometimes rose up as well. In the Pueblo Revolt of 1680, the Pueblo Indians temporarily ousted the Spanish in what was to become the U.S. state of New Mexico. In 1751–2, Luis Oacpicagigua led the Pima in an unsuccessful rebellion against the Spanish in Arizona.

One of the biggest uprisings occurred in the Andes, where oppressive government and inequitable revenue collection had created widespread discontent. The rebellion, which involved several thousand supporters, was led by Túpac Amaru II, who claimed to be of the Inca royal dynasty but who also endeavored to create a broader coalition of the disenfranchised, including Indians, mestizos, blacks, and whites. The rebellion broke out in 1780, shortly after the American Revolution and perhaps inspired by it. In 1781, the rebellion was defeated at Cuzco by Spanish forces, who executed Túpac Amaru; his wife, Micaela Bastidas Puyucahua, who had been a co-leader of the rebellion; and the rest of his family with great brutality. In the same year, another leader, Túpac Katari, and his wife, Bartolina Sisa, led a brief further revolt but were also captured, tortured, and executed by the Spanish. After these deaths, the Spanish government increased efforts to wipe out Quechua culture, and the rift between the indigenous people and upper-class Spanish creoles widened. Nonetheless, thousands of natives came to revere the sites where the body parts of the executed leaders were displayed by the Spaniards, and these leaders were commemorated long after their deaths.

Northern Amerindian groups likewise engaged in repeated attempts to challenge European power and authority. In Virginia, the Powhatan Confederation launched attacks against British settlers in 1622 and 1644. From 1675 to 1678, Native American attacks during King Philip's War terrified Puritan colonists in New England. In the Tuscarora War of 1711–15, the Tuscarora attempted to drive European settlers out of North Carolina. After their defeat, they traveled north, becoming the sixth nation of the Iroquois Confederacy. Likewise, in the Yamasee War of 1715–17, a number of tribes united in an attempt to drive British settlers out of South Carolina. Pontiac's War, named after the Ottawa war leader Pontiac, one of the primary leaders, took place in 1763 in the aftermath of the Seven Years' War when a coalition of Native American tribes aimed to drive the British out of the Great Lakes region. In addition, there were many smaller conflicts with similar aims – to prevent the encroachment of European settlers and to preserve Native American territorial power.

During the seventeenth and eighteenth centuries, Native Americans frequently became involved with one or both sides of wider conflicts that involved European colonial powers. For example, in the Pequot War of 1634–8 in Massachusetts, a conflict between the Pequot and their rivals, the Mohegan, spiraled wider as the two groups developed alliances with the Dutch and the English, who were at odds over control of local trade. The Beaver Wars, a series of sporadic conflicts in the Great Lakes region, began in the 1630s and lasted until 1701, pitting the Iroquois Confederation and their English and Dutch allies against the Algonquian and the French. Native Americans also participated, often on both sides, in King William's War, known as the Nine Years' War in Europe (1688–97); Queen Anne's War, the American theater of the War of the Spanish Succession in Europe (1702–13); Father Rale's War (1722–5); King George's War or the War of the Austrian Succession (1744–8); Father Le Loutre's War (1749–55); the French and Indian War or Seven Years' War (1754–63); and the American Revolution (1775–83). In the Northwest Indian War (1785–95), a coalition of Indian nations, with British help, attempted to prevent the young United States from expanding into the Northwest Territories to the northwest of the Ohio River. Although these conflicts often threatened and inflicted damage on European settlers, for Native Americans the result was often disastrous, with severe repercussions, including many deaths and the loss of native land. The Pequots, for instance, were mostly killed or sold into slavery in the West Indies by the victorious English in 1638.

12 Slavery

Slavery was one of the most important and troubling aspects of the Atlantic world system. It was made possible, above all, by the lack of a principle of human rights during the period in which it took form. While it had roots in the ancient world, slavery as it developed in the Atlantic took on a new and forceful role that was both created by the conditions of a modernizing world and also helped sustain economic modernity. The wealth of the new Atlantic colonies was sustained by enslaved African labor, and slavery came to underpin the Atlantic world system.

Slavery had existed in many areas of the world since ancient times. In Europe before the fifteenth century, most slaves were from eastern Europe rather than Africa; hence, the English term "slave" derived from "Slav." However, slaves were relatively rare in Europe during the Middle Ages. Although slave labor had been common in the ancient world, in northern and Western Europe it had mainly been transmuted to serfdom, a form of bound labor in which agricultural laborers were bound to the land or to powerful landlords who could force them to work but typically could not sell them and who also had some social responsibilities toward them. Serfdom and debt bondage were essentially permanent situations that ranged from systems of mutual obligation between serf and landlord in Western Europe, though they always remained oppressive, to extremely exploitative forms of subjugation in parts of Asia and eastern Europe. In Western Europe, serfdom had begun to die out by the fourteenth century, when it was gradually replaced by wage labor. In eastern Europe, serfdom persisted until the nineteenth century. Yet outright slavery that permitted human beings to be bought and sold at market was not common outside of Asia and the Middle East during the Middle Ages. In the Middle East and North Africa, there were large numbers of both European and African slaves, as in Asia, where forms of serfdom also prevailed. Slavery also existed in sub-Saharan and West Africa, mainly as a form of debt or military bondage that in some cases was similar to serfdom.

In Africa, most slaves were household slaves who had come to enslavement as war captives or criminals or who had been sold by family members or themselves as a result of poverty. In many cases, slaves in both Africa and the Middle East possessed some rights and avenues for rising in society, while their children did not necessarily retain their slave status, although some African kingdoms did engage in the practice of sacrificing human slaves. Slaves within Africa, if male, fulfilled a wide variety of roles, including in agricultural work, mining, construction, and artisanal work and as household servants and porters, though they could also serve as soldiers or even government officials, even at high levels of governance. Women typically served as agricultural workers, artisans, servants, or concubines.

Wide-scale plantation slavery as it developed in the Atlantic was a new phenomenon that arose in response to the growth of a number of preconditions in the Atlantic world. These included the increasingly international orientation of countries along the Atlantic rim, the demand for raw materials and manufactured products on opposite sides of the ocean, and the need for labor in order to produce raw materials. The growth of capitalism augmented the possibility of large-scale investment in agricultural production and promoted the commodification of human beings in order to increase production for new global commodity markets for slave-produced products such as sugar, rum, tobacco, rice and, eventually, cotton. New markets for Atlantic raw materials necessitated an increasing labor force to produce them, leading to the rise of what has been termed the "plantation complex" as described by historian Philip Curtin in *The Rise and Fall of the Plantation Complex* (1990), a new mode of organizing labor that increasingly shaped the economic relations of the Atlantic world.

In the 1940s, historian Eric Williams argued in *Capitalism and Slavery* (1944) that the Atlantic economy, resting upon the base of slavery, was instrumental in developing modern capitalism, which arose in tandem with the increase in global trade and commodity production. The triangle trade, in which manufactured goods from Europe were exchanged for raw materials from the Americas and human beings from Africa, generated enormous wealth for merchants, contractors, and investors. In order for agricultural products such as tobacco, sugar, and cotton in particular to be profitable, they required plantation agriculture, sustained by grueling, unremitting, and cheap labor. The desire to make an ample profit necessitated a large labor source.

The shape of this economic system arose as the result of a number of factors. It received its initial impulse as early as the first encounter of 1492, when Columbus arrived in the Americas and began immediately speculating about the possibility of employing slave labor. There were particular reasons that Atlantic slavery turned to the exploitation of Africans. Although the Spanish initially hoped to enslave Native Americans, it soon became apparent that after the devastation of disease had taken its toll, Native American populations were not sufficient to supply the new colonies' desire for cheap labor. In some areas, their population had dropped to very low numbers. Until native populations began to develop genetic resistance to

Old World diseases, they continued to appear too susceptible to make up a reliable source of labor. As this became evident, the Spanish began to resort to new sources of labor, though they continued to employ Native American slaves and forced laborers through the encomienda and repartimiento systems. Instead, they turned to importing African slaves. The Portuguese had already pioneered the employment of African slaves in the sugar plantations of Madeira. Columbus had had personal experiences with African slavery while working with Portuguese shippers and sugar producers, and Spaniards began bringing African slaves to the Americas by 1502. The friar Bartolomé de las Casas, who arrived in Hispaniola with the first shipment of African slaves across the Atlantic and who was known for devoting himself to the cause of defending the Indians, initially advocated importing African slaves as one way to spare the natives. Although las Casas later retreated from this idea and became a critic of African slavery, his initial promotion of it is indicative of the way in which Africans were perceived even by a relatively humane European. In addition, preexisting markets selling slaves already existed along the African coast, with African coastal states willingly engaging in the trade as an economic benefit to their regions.

Non-Spanish areas followed the Spanish precedent of not relying on Native American labor. In any case, Native American populations were relatively sparse outside of Peru and Mexico, even before disease struck. Portuguese and French areas moved rapidly from an initial reliance on Indian slaves to Africans, while the Dutch and British areas utilized a combination of African and Indian slaves and various forms of bound and free labor in their settlements in North America, South America, and the Caribbean. Although slavery existed throughout the Atlantic, it took much stronger hold in the warmer zones of the Caribbean, South America, and the American South, where wide-scale plantation farming was possible.

New forms of slavery

By the seventeenth century, African slaves began to replace the other types of forced and free laborers, including indentured servants, as the main source of labor in the Atlantic. There were a number of reasons why this change took place. In addition to the limitations on the numbers of available Indians and Europeans discussed previously, there were other justifications for using Africans. First, there was an elastic supply of African slaves available for purchase to European shippers. In addition, the precedent for African slavery had already been set on the Portuguese sugar islands, and business contacts were already established at African ports. Second, in European eyes, there were important status differences between European and African laborers. In the early period, this was not due to perceptions about racial differences but because African blacks were not Christians. Often a perfunctory baptism of slaves was performed before sailing from the African coast, which justified the claim that slavery was actually beneficial because it saved slaves' souls. Further, in contrast to the curbs on the authority of masters found in various other forms of both free and unfree labor, masters had absolute power over slaves. Finally, it became apparent that the monetary value of the labor of a slave was greater than that of a servant, because slaves could be worked harder and were kept in bondage longer. The ruthless logic of slavery also revealed that there were few economic reasons to treat slaves well; slaves could toil without being well cared for, and the costs of importing a healthy adult slave were less than those of raising a child to adulthood. Thus, slaves were worked to death and replaced with fresh slaves when they were worn out. The prior experiences of African slavery on the Portuguese islands, Native American slavery in Spanish territories, and white indentured servitude provided the models for the African slave trade.

The slave trade comprised the largest forced migration of human beings in history. By the ending of the slave trade, approximately 12 million slaves had crossed the Atlantic, with about 2 million going to Spanish America, 4 million to Brazil, 600,000 to the English mainland territories that would become the United States, and most of the rest to the Caribbean. The numbers of slaves continued to increase until the height of the slave trade in the late eighteenth century, when about 85,000 slaves were crossing the Atlantic yearly; they were mainly young adults, and about two thirds of them were men. Historians have further projected that about 50% of all slaves initially captured in Africa died during capture, imprisonment, or transportation to the coast or while sailing across the ocean in the Middle Passage before they ever reached the western side of the Atlantic.

The slave trade in Africa

The vast majority of slaves were procured by contractors and middlemen in West Africa, especially Guinea, Senegal, Angola, Mozambique, and Congo. African merchants had sold slaves for a long time but had mainly sold war captives and criminals on a small scale. However, with the increasing demand for slaves in the Atlantic, two new major sources emerged. From the mid-sixteenth century on, most slaves were kidnapped by raiders. In addition, some African kingdoms began to engage in warfare with the objective of acquiring slaves from neighboring regions. The aggressors often became much more powerful within their regions as a result of the slave trade, because the most important trade good obtained from the Europeans was guns, which were then employed in the capture of further slaves. By the mid-eighteenth century, close to 200,000 guns were arriving yearly in Africa. In addition, Africa absorbed other manufactured goods, the same ones that were sold in the Americas, such as cloth; alcohol (including rum, which was produced by slave labor); and metal goods such as weapons and cooking ware.

Although slavery had profoundly negative consequences for Africans and African states, the slave trade itself was not a one-sided enterprise forced on Africans. It was dependent on African participation, and the African states, middlemen, and individual merchants involved saw it as beneficial and productive for their regions. Europeans were unable to force African states into participating and were dependent on maintaining good relations with local rulers, which typically involved obtaining a license to be allowed to engage in trade. Throughout the period of the slave trade, the process of acquiring and selling slaves remained under the control of African governments and entrepreneurs.

The slave trade resulted in enormous social disruption within Africa. Commerce with Europeans became central to the economy of many West African states, which greatly increased their efforts to obtain slaves, either by raiding them from the interior or by attacking neighboring states. For example, the city-state of Loango, in what is today the Republic of the Congo, traded copper and cloth to the Portuguese early in the seventeenth century but greatly expanded its participation in the slave trade by the end of the century, receiving slaves from the interior who were then sold to European merchants (see Figure 12.1). Although Loango profited, the consequences of the slave trade were an increase in both political violence and political disintegration overall. In some cases, eager to maintain levels of income, local rulers even sold their own people, though such instances were rare. Power relations between kingdoms were affected by the presence of European guns. While a number of kingdoms refused to participate in the slave trade or tried to limit their participation, such as the Kongo under Affonso I in the sixteenth century or Angola while ruled by Queen Nzingha Mbande in the seventeenth century, these regions were simply avoided by slave traders and, in some instances, were defeated by stronger territories that were actively engaged in the trade. While some kingdoms, like the Kongo, became increasingly fractured during the era of the slave trade, others, like Dahomey (Benin), prospered – in the latter case under authoritarian and militaristic government.

Slaves came from a number of African ethnic groups and were most frequently represented by the Igbo, Akan, Yoruba, and Bakongo peoples but included many other ethnicities. By the eighteenth century, the largest numbers of slaves originated in West Central Africa, along the coast of Angola and the Congo, and many came from the northern coastal region stretching south and east from the Cape Verde Islands to the sharp southward curvature at the Bight (Bay) of Biafra at present-day Cameroon. So many slaves came from the Bight of Benin, slightly northeast of Biafra, that it became known as the "Slave Coast." Twenty percent of all slaves were shipped from three ports: Luanda in West Central Africa, Whydah in the Bight of Benin, and Bonny in the Bight of Biafra.

Once slaves were captured in the interior, they were sold to middlemen, tied together in "coffles," and forced to walk to the coast. In some cases,

Figure 12.1   The West African city of Loango, a major slave-trading location in the late seventeenth century. © Bettman/Corbis

slaves were forced to march hundreds of miles, with the weakest dying along the way. When they reached the coast, they were examined and sold. They were then branded with the symbol of the merchant who had purchased them and rebranded when they were resold to further brokers, usually acquiring three or more brands. Eventually they would be congregated in coastal "factories" until a slave ship put into harbor to purchase them.

The Middle Passage

Once sold to shippers, slaves would usually be branded again and then loaded onto ships. If the slave ships still had room to carry extra slaves, they would then sail along the coast looking for further purchases, a process that could take weeks. However, conditions were worst when the ships turned toward the ocean for voyages averaging two months or more. Slaves survived or died under dreadful conditions during the voyage. Some captains tried to pack as many slaves into their ships as possible, calculating that the increased mortality from "tight packing" would be offset by the value of the extra bodies on board. Slaves were kept naked, with men usually chained together in the hold, lying down. Typically they were brought onto the deck once a day to prevent excessive deaths due to lack of movement. Conditions in the hold were particularly terrible, with extreme heat, little air circulation, and filthy conditions. Women and children, who might make up one third and one quarter of the cargo, respectively, were often kept on deck unchained, where they were particularly subject to rape. Disease was frequent, and in a typical voyage, 10% of the slaves on board were lost because of illness, brutality, and suicide, but the death toll could be much higher. Slaves were terrified by the prospect of leaving their homelands and of the Europeans who had imprisoned them, whom they often believed to be cannibals. By the time they arrived in the west, usually to the Caribbean, the slaves were often so sick and weak that they had to be treated and cured before they would appeal to buyers.

Slave ship crews' treatment of slaves was shaped by two competing factors: the incentive to keep slaves alive – for which they provided food and water, treated disease, and provided an opportunity to move about deck for more compliant slaves – and the desire to prevent uprisings among the slaves. Revolts, a prospect which terrified ships' crews, were a common occurrence, taking place on about 15% of slave ship voyages. In order to prevent rebellion, crews applied a regime of terror involving public whipping, torture, and execution in response to any form of insubordination. Slaves who tried to commit suicide were beaten or tortured, while those who tried to starve themselves were tortured or force fed. Ships typically carried netting along the sides to prevent slaves from drowning themselves in the ocean.

The treatment of slaves during the Middle Passage, which was far worse than that of indentured servants or criminals, was part of a cold-blooded economic calculation that reduced human beings to merchandise. This was particularly illustrated by the *Zong* incident. In 1781, the British slaver *Zong* ran low on water after a long voyage during which it had gone astray in the ocean. The ship's owners had previously taken out insurance on its cargo of slaves. During the 1781 voyage, the crew threw more than a quarter of the slaves, mainly women and children, into the sea alive, claiming that it was necessary in order to save the lives of the crew and the other slaves. When the ship's owners tried to claim the insurance on the dead slaves, the two subsequent trials hinged on whether insurers could be made to pay in such circumstances, but there was no attempt to prosecute the sailors for the killings, even though some argued that the ship's water supply would have been sufficient. Publication of these events did much to awaken British public opinion against slavery.

When slaves arrived in New World ports, usually to the Caribbean or Brazil, they were typically in poor physical condition. They were subsequently sold at auction and then underwent a period of "seasoning" during which they would be brutalized into submissiveness and trained in specific tasks, taught the slave owners' language, and accustomed to continuous work. Mortality was very high during this period, as the weakened slaves faced violence, despair, exhaustion, poor living conditions, and a new tropical disease environment.

The experience of slavery

The most defining characteristic of slavery is its brutality. Merciless punishments, severe ruthlessness, and harsh constraints were inherent to the system itself in order to force human beings to work for slave owners and to prevent slaves from seeking to obtain their freedom. Exemplary punishments, in which a rebellious slave was killed or tortured in front of others, were common. In a 1785 essay on slavery and the slave trade, abolitionist Thomas Clarkson described the whipping of slaves which "cuts out small portions of the flesh at almost every stroke" and which was applied so frequently that "the smack of it is all day long in the ears of those" who were on the plantations.[1]

A combination of brutality, disease, and despair ensured that the slave population was not self-reproducing in the areas of hardest labor – the plantation colonies – during the earlier centuries of slavery. Although most slaves entered the slave system as fit young adults, most died in less than a decade. The average lifespan for an able-bodied male slave in his twenties was seven years. Children were rarely born because there were far more male than female slaves, and women were usually sterile for years after the Middle Passage, with fertility remaining low afterward as a result of undernourishment. Infant mortality was high, and children could not normally survive to adulthood. In some cases, enslaved mothers killed infants to prevent them from suffering in slavery. In addition, the new climate and disease environment, particularly in the Caribbean, took a steep toll on Europeans but was even more devastating for Africans, who also had to contend with overwork, sleep deprivation (it was common for Caribbean field slaves to have less than five hours of sleep nightly), and malnutrition. Although such conditions undermined slave health, they also limited slaves' capacity to resist and maximized production. As part of this system, individual slaves were seen as expendable, and early slave populations were not expected to be self-sustaining. Thus, for example, after the slave trade – the shipping of slaves from Africa – to Brazil was abolished after 1850, the slave population also rapidly declined.

As the slave trade began to decrease in the early nineteenth century throughout the Atlantic, the lives of slaves became marginally better as slave owners within the plantation complex saw the need for a self-replenishing population. This meant that they became less likely to work a healthy slave to death or to starve or beat a pregnant woman. Still, ruthless treatment of slaves continued, and scenes of murder and severe cruelty remained common. It is notable that some of the brutal portraits of slavery that are available to us today, such as in the autobiography of American abolitionist and escaped slave Frederick Douglass, *Narrative of the Life of Frederick Douglass, An American Slave* (1845), come from the later period during which conditions were actually better than previously.

Slavery affected every aspect of slaves' lives. Most importantly, the institution dehumanized slaves, who were treated according to law and custom as a form of property, even though there was always a tacit acknowledgement that slave ownership did not fit with other forms of holding property. In most circumstances, slaves had few or no rights in law. Thus, they had no right to an education, to marriage, to family ties, or even to the necessities that sustain life – all of this was obtainable only at the whim of the master. While masters normally had an economic interest in keeping slaves alive and healthy, this could easily be superseded by sadism, anger, the desire to intimidate slaves, or financial considerations such as a rush to generate products by a deadline. Slavery itself encouraged ferocious and violent behavior in masters. In his life history, Frederick Douglass described numerous instances of slaves, including children, who had been severely abused or maimed by their masters for small infractions. English abolitionist Thomas Clarkson wrote that slaves were treated very differently from other forms of chattel – the same masters that would "torture, mutilate, [and] murder" their slaves would never mistreat their livestock. He believed that slavery in itself "begets a turn for wanton cruelty."[2]

The day-to-day lives of slaves varied considerably according to their situation. The majority of slaves worked within the plantation complex, producing plantation products such as rice, tobacco, sugar, or cotton. Field slavery was extremely grueling, with quotas enforced through severe discipline. However, plantation slaves were often left to their own devices during the evening, and in some cases this permitted a tiny amount of personal freedom. Domestic slaves, who toiled in the household, were likely to have better food and clothing but were constantly under the eyes of their masters, often slept on the floor near or in the bedroom, and were always subject to work, day or night.

As with female servants, female slaves were particularly vulnerable to both physical abuse and sexual exploitation by their masters but without the few protections that servants possessed, as described in the autobiographies of former slaves, such as Harriet Jacobs' *Incidents in the Life of a Slave Girl* (1861) or Mary Prince's *The History of Mary Prince* (1831). Any child born to a slave woman was considered her master's property, even if he or she was the child of the master. While some masters made special provisions for their own slave children – such as placing them in positions requiring lighter labor or greater responsibility or, rarely, manumitting them – many did not.

In general, slavery was extremely damaging to family life. Although many slaves did form family relationships, they could never count on stability, and families only remained together at the whim of their masters. The separation of husbands from wives and children from parents was an everyday affair, and children, or even infants, were readily sold. Enslaved children were viewed as a commodity and were put to work as soon as possible, both to earn their keep and to accustom them to the labor regimen. The threat of splitting up a family by sale was also a constant form of intimidation used by masters to enforce compliance among slaves.

Legal status of slavery

When slavery initially began in the Atlantic world, the legal status of slaves was unclear, mainly because slavery had not been a significant source of labor previously. In English areas, for example, the earliest imported Africans were treated as indentured servants and were released after working through their contracts. However, as the number of slaves increased, their legal position as slaves was solidified, and most of the imperial powers drafted slave codes – legislation that clarified the status – and, to some degree, the treatment – of slaves.

The most protective legislation existed in Spanish, French, Portuguese, and Dutch areas, all of which had some provisions against badly mistreating slaves, even if they were often discounted in principle. For example, Spanish slaves had a right to manumission if they could find the wherewithal to purchase themselves. For the former three regions, strong central governments; the protection of the Catholic Church, which saw slaves as redeemable souls; and the tradition of Roman law offered some protections for slaves. However, even in these areas, legislation aimed for the regulation of slaves and the mitigation of slavery. For example, in the French *Code Noir* of 1685, slave owners were enjoined to avoid murder and torture, to support their slaves materially, and to avoid splitting up families, but slaves were restricted from resisting their masters, marrying without permission, gathering in groups, or trading on their own. In addition, the reality of slave life differed greatly between urban areas and the rural hinterlands, including the plantation areas where most slaves were consigned. The latter possessed far larger enslaved populations and epitomized the viciousness of slavery.

Likewise, in English areas where there was a strong centralized religious leadership, such as that of the Puritans in New England or the Quakers in Pennsylvania, treatment of slaves was typically less brutal, and slaves might be allowed to assemble in groups, join the local church, marry at will, and obtain an education. However, in English colonies, legislation regarding slavery was a piecemeal tapestry developed by local colonial administrations. Plantation colonies avoided imposing restrictions on masters' rights in drafting legislation. The *Barbados Slave Code* of 1661, while claiming to protect slaves, in actual fact allowed masters unlimited dominion over them, even allowing the murder or torture of slaves, unlike the *Code Noir*. It served as a model for slave codes in other British plantation colonies, such as Virginia, which adopted similar provisions in 1662. Such laws defined slaves as property, and as time passed, subsequent laws included more detailed provisions, such as forbidding slaves to leave their masters' property while fining whites who educated slaves or gave them weapons. In some cases, the codes included small provisions nominally protecting slaves – for instance, forbidding the murder of slaves unless they were perceived to have committed an infraction, which in effect still allowed masters to kill slaves with impunity, or mandating that they were to receive one suit of clothing yearly. Since these provisions were not enforced, they were essentially meaningless. None of the laws in British plantation colonies directed masters not to harm their slaves or to feed and care for them according to any standard. In general, slave codes throughout the Atlantic defined slaves as legal chattel and gave masters almost unlimited power, in some cases adding relatively minor restrictions on masters' behavior, with weak and usually unenforced penalties for breaking the rules.

Regional variations

Slavery varied considerably according to region. Paradoxically, the regions with the worst forms of slavery – plantation societies – also saw the greatest influence of African culture on both slave and white society. This was because these were the regions in which the percentage of people with African heritage was highest.

Almost one half of all slaves arriving in the Americas were destined to work in the sugar colonies of the Caribbean, which included the Spanish, English, French, and Dutch Caribbean islands, as well as the colonies of Brazil and the Guianas around the Caribbean rim, which received another third of the total slave population. These colonies shared many similar characteristics. Most of them were dependent on sugar produced through plantation slavery, and the majority of their inhabitants – about 80% of the population – were enslaved. Often plantations were administered by managers standing in for absentee owners. These plantations were characterized by large profits, high ratios of slaves to whites, and extreme brutality toward slaves. Most new slaves only survived a few years after arriving in the Caribbean, succumbing to overwork, disease, and violence.

The brutality of these colonies was dictated by an essential logic based on profitability: fulfilling the twin goals of sustaining high rates of production and maintaining submissiveness among the slave population. Severe levels of violence were aimed at preventing slave uprisings, though rebellions nonetheless occurred with increasing frequency. In this system, individual slaves were expendable, and indeed the occasional murder of slaves was desirable as a form of exemplary punishment to intimidate those who might otherwise rebel. With mortality rates much higher than birth rates, fresh shipments of slaves were necessary to maintain slave populations. Indeed, Caribbean slavery was the motor of the slave trade system.

In much of Latin America, outside of sugar colonies, slave populations constituted much smaller percentages of settler populations. The largest African populations in Spanish territories were in the central, more urban areas. There were fewer slaves in less populous rural areas, except in some regions where there were only a small number of remaining Native Americans due to the depredations of disease. Since the Spanish territories were the first to use slavery, they saw a significant change in the way slaves were employed over time. During the initial conquest of native societies, African slaves supported Spanish military endeavors, often functioning as Spanish soldiers. A number of slaves as well as free people of African or partially African descent fought on the Spanish side during the Inca conquest, for example. In some cases, slaves were promised freedom for fighting, and some succeeded in integrating into Spanish society afterward. The early situation was similar in Portuguese territories during the first century of slavery, except that Brazil became a major sugar producer and developed a plantation complex similar to that of the Caribbean, which consumed the lives of more Africans than anywhere outside of the Caribbean.

During the following century of colonization, slaves were utilized mainly as servants and skilled workers, much as had been the case in the Mediterranean during the Middle Ages. Africans, and people of partially African, partially European ancestry, called *mulattos* in Spanish territories, ended up as intermediaries between the Europeans and Native Americans based on their familiarity with European language, skills, and society. They served as artisans, managers, traders, and carriers. Enslaved African women were involved in the marketing of goods. Native Americans occupied a place below African slaves, especially in the early days after the conquest, with some exceptions made for those of noble blood.

As time passed, Africans were increasingly utilized as unskilled laborers on plantations, especially in the sugar industry in Brazil and the Caribbean, which boomed after 1600, though they also sometimes continued to occupy the middle role of intermediaries. However, after the first century or so, that role was mainly taken by the increasing numbers of poorer Spanish and Portuguese immigrants or creoles, natives, and *mestizos*, especially after the native population had adapted to European culture and had become more resistant to the Old World diseases. At the same time, the numbers of Africans imported to Latin American territories began to decrease, except in the plantation areas of the Caribbean, especially Cuba and Brazil, which were increasingly receiving many thousands of slaves yearly. In most areas, African slaves eventually merged into a mixed ethnic population of natives, blacks, and whites. Anxiety about ethnicity gave rise to the system of *castas*, though, as discussed previously, in practice individuals were often able to evade the expectations imposed by the complicated delineation of ethnic ancestry.

Another small source of slaves was individuals of Muslim descent, *Moriscos*, who had been enslaved in Spain during the Reconquista. Unlike other groups of slaves, women "Moriscas" greatly outnumbered men and served as domestic servants and concubines for Spanish men until large numbers of Spanish women began to arrive in the later sixteenth century, at which point most of the Morisca women blended into Spanish society as freed Spaniards. In general, slave women were often more integrated into white society than men because of their contact with white families as domestic servants, nursemaids, and concubines.

The Northern American colonies experienced their own patterns of slavery. The first African captives to arrive in British territory came to Virginia in a Dutch ship in 1619; they became indentured servants. They were soon followed by slaves brought into Dutch New Amsterdam by 1626. The Puritans in New England were engaging in the slave trade, buying and selling both Indians and Africans by the 1630s, and by 1641 had enacted legislation that referenced biblical justifications for slavery. In Virginia, the status of Africans and European indentured servants had diverged by the 1650s, with the former counted as slaves, a condition which was reinforced in the 1662 Virginia slave code.

In British and Dutch Atlantic colonies, the treatment of slaves depended on the economic basis of the colony. Thus, slaves were often better treated in what was to become the U.S. North or in short-lived New Amsterdam than in the plantation colonies like the U.S. South or Suriname and Curaçao. In the northern British mainland colonies, most slaves lived in urban settings or small farms. In addition to farm labor, they worked as artisans, domestic servants, dock laborers, and builders and at other tasks. Nonetheless, as slaves, they were considered chattel and subject to the whims of their masters; thus, slaves in non-plantation areas also frequently experienced extremes of cruelty and subjugation.

In English territories, which were mainly Protestant, anxieties about "miscegenation" or intermarrying between white and non-white populations led to increasingly restrictive regulations against its occurrence. The English government tried to equalize the gender ratio of whites by attempts to send poor white women to the colonies, especially the Caribbean, as eligible wives. In some cases, such plans went awry as transported women criminals and prostitutes continued to ply their trades in the colonies. However, in practice, interracial sexual relations continued to occur, especially in areas with large populations of slaves, with relative impunity for masters, such as in the British Caribbean or the American South, where considerable mixed-race populations developed. This was less common in mainland English colonies, where white women accompanied white men from the beginning of settlement.

In the new United States, the majority of slaves were at first primarily found cultivating rice and tobacco on southern plantations. While lucrative crops, the market for these was insufficient as the basis for the economy of the entire southern region. Cotton was a potentially lucrative crop, but removing the seeds was a laborious and time-consuming process that effectively limited the value of large-scale cotton production. As a result, slavery actually began to dwindle in the southern United States until about 1800. However, a number of inventions during the Industrial Revolution greatly increased the rapidity and efficiency of cloth production and, vitally for southern slavery, the ease of processing cotton. In the 1790s, northern inventor Eli Whitney invented the cotton gin, a labor-saving device that made this process rapid and easy. Cotton was transformed into a tremendously profitable crop, essential to the newly industrialized cloth factories in New England and Great Britain, which gave southern slavery a new lease on life; indeed, it became dependent primarily on the cultivation of "King Cotton."

Manumission and freedom

Those individuals who were most acculturated into white society were more likely to be freed and to prosper. Even freedom, however, did not mean a good life. Freed Africans were viewed with suspicion and prejudice throughout the Atlantic world and were vulnerable to illegal reenslavement and discriminatory laws. They constituted a permanent lower order of society that had to remain deferential to social elites. Manumission was highly regulated. In contrast to slaves' legal right to manumission in Spanish territories, some of the British mainland colonies made it officially impossible.

Manumission could be achieved by gift of the owner, either during the owner's lifetime or in a will, as occurred in the case of the first American president George Washington, who freed his slaves in his last testament. In some cases, slaves managed to earn enough money to purchase their own freedom, especially if they worked independently in trade or as artisans. Enslaved women involved in sexual relationships with white men, and the children resulting from such liaisons, were more likely to be freed than male slaves, especially in Catholic areas where there was less stigma toward acknowledging such relationships or in marrying non-white freedwomen. Thomas Jefferson, the third American president, freed or facilitated the freedom of his children with Sally Hemings, his enslaved mistress, who was left to live informally as a free woman after his death.

Free people of African and partially African descent were an increasing, though always small, group in the Caribbean, Brazil, and mainland Spanish cities throughout the last few centuries of slavery. In many areas, they formed associations that supported their interests in trade or legal issues. There were many variations in how free people of African ancestry managed to exist in white-dominated society. Although most existed at the lowest levels of society, some prospered. Some attempted to help runaway slaves. Others became slave owners. Especially in Spanish areas or Brazil, a few opened successful businesses or contracted themselves out as skilled laborers. Sometimes they married into white society, with their children or grandchildren blending into the dominant culture.

Cultural resistance

One alternative to slavery was resistance, but organized resistance was usually met with vicious retaliation. Nonetheless, it was effective in demonstrating the slaves' determination to continue to oppose slavery and perhaps in building slaves' sense of self-worth. Large-scale resistance such as slave revolts and the runaway slave societies formed in the Caribbean and South America will be discussed later in the section on abolition. Yet in addition to rebellions by organized groups, very rarely a person might establish better treatment for himself or herself through an individual act of overt resistance, such as in Frederick Douglass' famous fight with his master, Edward Covey.[3] In most cases, the punishment for such a confrontation would have been ferocious. In Douglass' case, his deed did not meet with reprisals because of Covey's fear of losing his reputation as a breaker of slaves. Suicide was also a form of defiance, one that was more common among slaves who had been born in freedom in Africa. For most slaves, resistance had to be accomplished by less violent means. Disguised forms of opposition, such as complying with orders slowly, feigning stupidity, or secretly destroying property, were more common and less likely to incur retaliation.

Slaves also struggled to retain the cultures of their homelands, and in areas where they outnumbered Europeans, they were able to exert a permanent influence on colonial societies. In areas with large African populations, such as plantation societies, Africans were often in contact with others who possessed the same languages or cultural norms. Many clung to the heritage of their African ancestry, sometimes in secret. More slaves went to Brazil than to any other place in the Americas and, as a result, the African imprint was especially strong there, as also in the Caribbean, where African influences left their mark on cuisine, music, language, dance, clothing, and other customs.

Perhaps the most important tradition influenced by African heritage was religion. Spirituality proved to be one of the most powerful means of retaining African culture, unifying slave society, and providing comfort. Slaves sometimes could improve or give meaning to their lives by engaging in social practices or spirituality that were outside of the control or knowledge of their white masters. Some slaves accepted European Christianity, with its respect for the humble and its message of salvation. Especially in Catholic areas, which promoted the idea that human free will enabled salvation, the state tended to encourage conversion. The Catholic Church presented a mixed message on slavery. On one hand, it encouraged better treatment of slaves, but on the other hand it owned and sold slaves and invested in the slave trade. Indeed, there was always indecision in slave-owning societies about whether or not to encourage religion among slaves. Masters feared that conversion to Christianity would make slaves more likely to demand fair treatment or were concerned about their right to retain Christians in slavery. However, some also argued that Christian values would make slaves more compliant. When slaves did accept Christianity, however, they were selective about their spirituality, emphasizing elements that encouraged equality and resilience, promoted self-worth, and advocated deliverance from injustice. In urban areas in Brazil, some slaves maintained Islamic beliefs that they had brought from Africa.

In some regions, slaves developed new faiths through syncretism – the blending of religious beliefs – including African spirituality transported in the course of the African diaspora, European Christian, and sometimes Native American spiritual traditions. Among the most widespread of these new religions were Brazilian Candomblé, Haitian Vodou, Cuban Santería, and Caribbean Obeah, all of which continue to be vital today. In general, they share a belief in a powerful but aloof creator god and multiple lesser gods or spirits that are associated with forces of nature and who regularly intervene in human affairs. These are derived from West African spirituality, but the lesser gods, termed *orishas* in Brazil and Cuba and *loas* in Haiti, are also often associated with Catholic saints. Often, African languages, such as Yoruba from West Africa, are employed as the language of ritual. These religions also feature male and female practitioners who engage in healing and communication with the gods through spirit possession and a complex series of rituals. They are empowering to worshippers who desire control over their fate and who seek recognition of their innate value as human beings.

During the time of slavery, these religions offered meaning, spiritual empowerment, and the promise of righting wrongs. It was difficult for masters to restrict activities which carried a veneer of Christianity. The Christian framework thus offered some self-sufficiency of identity in worship, whether the slaves were members of the Catholic Church, new syncretic religions, or North American evangelical churches. In celebrating Christian festivals or joining religiously oriented organizations such as Catholic confraternities, slaves could temporarily escape the drudgery and violence of their lives.

Consequences of the slave trade

The slave trade caused dramatic changes in African society. In addition to altering the political dynamic between African states and making systemic violence a central aspect of the political interactions on the west coast of Africa, it had significant demographic effects on both Africa and the Americas. In Africa, the slave trade caused a major loss of population due to the departure of 12 million people and the deaths of approximately the same number during the course of the slave trade. This was exacerbated by a concurrent slave trade to the Middle East that encompassed roughly the same numbers of people as the Atlantic slave trade. Thus, while the populations of Europe, Asia, and the Americas grew during and after the slave trade, the population of Africa remained stagnant and actually decreased in the most severely affected areas. Although African kingdoms had willingly participated in the slave trade, the loss of productive potential was tremendous and brought Africa into world trade systems in a dependent position.

On the other hand, the slave trade increased the population of the Americas, with slaves making up three quarters of the migrants across the ocean before the nineteenth century, with the labor they provided bolstering the productive capability of the Americas. The slave trade was so lucrative that nations quarreled over claims to segments of the African coast. Slavery and the slave trade were thus major factors in the economic rise of Europe, particularly in increasing the availability of wealth, leisure time, and liquid capital that made the innovations necessary for the successive developments of the Scientific Revolution, the Enlightenment, and the Industrial Revolution possible.

The slave trade had pervasive social effects as well. In the early days of slavery, there had been little justification needed for enslaving human beings. There was no overarching conception of human rights or human freedom, and Africans were enslaved simply because of their geographic proximity to the Atlantic and because they were vulnerable. If any validation was needed, it could be found in the widely held perception that European culture and religion were superior to African culture. Because most Africans were not Christians, there was a belief that they therefore ought to be brought into contact with Christianity and would even benefit from this. Later justifications based on the idea of biologically fixed races did not exist, and Europeans even speculated that a few generations of living in a warmer or colder climate would change skin color for both whites and blacks.

Ironically, it was the growth of conceptions of human rights and of scientific attitudes that changed these perceptions. Once Enlightenment ideals of tolerance and skepticism toward religion began to take hold, religious rationalizations were no longer adequate for justifying slavery. At the same time, the conception of human rights and of universal human reason began to gain wider acceptance. However, this posed a problem, because these doctrines would seem to condemn slavery. Yet the new middle classes that were most involved in the intellectual and cultural changes taking place were also the same group – as planters, merchants, middlemen, and investors – that profited the most from the wealth generated by slave-based Atlantic trade. They were not ready to abandon their sources of capital and so found a new justification for slavery in the new sciences of biology and anthropology, which from the late seventeenth century increasingly began to classify Africans as innately different from whites. The new ideology of racism was based on the knowledge that human physiological appearance was not rapidly changeable and the further claim that this was evidence of innate differences between human populations. Black skins became physical evidence of biological inferiority – the creation of modern racism. Although it was the attitudes of wealthy middle-class elites that mattered most in perpetuating racism, it was also often accepted by lower ranks of society, whose poverty in the new capitalist society was deemed evidence of personal failure. Racism created a category of people who were inherently beneath even the most wretched of whites. Many Enlightenment philosophers never accepted racist ideas and, in the end, Enlightenment ideals and science would promote and defend the ideal of human equality. However, some who initially participated in the Enlightenment paradoxically defended an economic system based on human exploitation and initiated a legacy that the world is still grappling with today in terms of global racism, underdevelopment in Africa, and discrimination and inequality in Europe and the Americas.

Notes

1 Thomas Clarkson, *An Essay on the Slavery and Commerce of the Human Species* (London: J. Phillips, 1788), 7.
2 Clarkson, 107, 111.
3 Frederick Douglass, *Narrative of the Life of Frederick Douglass, An American Slave* (Boston: Anti-Slavery Office, 1845).

Part IV
The age of ideas

13 The Enlightenment

The Atlantic encounter contributed to immense cultural shifts in Europe in the early modern period. These ranged from embracing new ideas and values to fearful reactions against change and transformed ideas in the realms of religion, politics, and economics. Europe was already in the grips of change prior to 1492 as a result of a number of significant events. These included the expansion of the Ottoman Empire and its defeat of Constantinople in 1453, which created pressure on the eastern flank of Europe and pushed European expansion westward; increasing contact with Muslim science and the works of ancient classical authors after the Crusades, inspiring the flow of new ideas exemplified by the Renaissance; the growth of nautical technology and contact with Asia and Africa, best exemplified in the Portuguese voyages of discovery; new developments in military technology; and, perhaps most importantly, the invention of the printing press in the 1450s, which allowed international contact between scholars and scientists and the rapid dissemination of ideas around Europe. The Atlantic connection furthered this ferment of development in many ways, including stimulating contact with entirely new societies and geographical regions; providing an outlet for restless adventurers and for overpopulation generally; and making available an enormous new source of wealth for Europe. By the eighteenth century, these disparate forces had paved the way for significant developments in the technology and economy of Europe and for the major transformation in intellectual and cultural life called the Enlightenment.

The Enlightenment was the result of a number of societal changes. Major changes in scientific understanding, often termed the Scientific Revolution, led to the questioning of previously accepted norms, at first in understanding the natural world but gradually extending to religion and politics. In addition, society became more complex and religiously diverse. The Protestant Reformation and the Catholic response to it had provided a template for criticism of a national government by religious dissenters. Economically, the slow transition to capitalism created competing interests among various social ranks that were difficult to accommodate according to the traditional structure of society. There was also an increased desire for political representation that originated both from religious dissent and from the new experiments with self-governance in the Atlantic colonies. These political issues were exacerbated by growing popular discontent and poverty caused by environmental pressures, especially an exceptionally cold period of several decades that decreased agricultural production which occurred at the same time as a surge in population growth.

Religion

The year 1492 had a profound effect on European religion and religious devotion. The earliest consequences were felt almost immediately in the Protestant Reformation. While issues such as religious discontent and increased literacy were at the root of the Reformation, an additional catalyst was the earthshaking reassessment of the world occasioned by the discovery of the Americas, which contributed to an atmosphere of change and uncertainty. In 1507, soon after Columbus' voyages became the topic of scholarly and popular discussion, Martin Waldseemüller published the Latin translation of Amerigo Vespucci's book arguing that the Americas were an entirely new region of the world. Ten years later, Martin Luther, another German, initiated the Protestant Reformation. The discovery that there were vast unknown territories inhabited by previously unfamiliar peoples acted to subtly undermine the Catholic Church's claim of encompassing important human knowledge.

Almost immediately, Protestantism fragmented into a series of dissenting movements and sects, from strict Calvinism and Presbyterianism to radical and egalitarian Quakers and Anabaptists, while the Catholic Church responded with the Counter-Reformation, a period of institutional reform and increased spirituality. In the meantime, Europe was convulsed by a series of vicious religious wars and widespread panics against witches, as religious dissension coupled with social and political changes fostered a period of divisiveness and social anxiety. By the end of the seventeenth century, repressive religious fervor was mainly spent, in part due to exhaustion and disgust toward the religious wars and in part because of a widespread and increasing turn toward rationalism. Many enlightened thinkers became increasingly skeptical toward religion and turned toward science and human reason as ways of making sense of the world.

At the same time, a countercurrent arose in the shape of a new approach to religion, one that was more fervent and emotional: Protestant Evangelicalism. Abandoning Calvinist emphasis on predestination, Evangelicals believed in adult baptism that symbolized a rebirth in Christian faith, which could be achieved by acceptance of God. This was a theology that had the power to reach many ordinary people, who felt disheartened by the Calvinist insistence on restrained behavior without guarantee of salvation. Evangelicalism was the driving force behind the first Great Awakening, a period of increased religious fervency and emotion in England, Western Europe, and the British colonies in America during the eighteenth and nineteenth centuries. In the early eighteenth century, English Methodists, led by John Wesley, insisted on an individual connection to God, toleration, and human spiritual equality, as well as activism in the worldly sphere, which meshed well with new intellectual and humanitarian concerns emerging from the intellectual sphere. In North America, George Whitefield and Jonathan Edwards preached passionate sermons to huge excited crowds. The latter's 1741 sermon, "Sinners in the Hand of an Angry God," terrified his audience by emphasizing the torments of hell, but Evangelicalism also attracted adherents by emphasizing the forgiveness of God toward those who accepted the Christian faith; it also stressed an individual's personal connection to God. In the American South, many slaves were attracted to Christianity by this movement. In the 1790s, a second Great Awakening began which again revived flagging enthusiasm in an increasingly rational age.

Economics

The year 1492 also had a profound effect on global economies. Europe was already undergoing major economic changes beginning with the Crusades and lasting to the eighteenth century, known collectively as the Commercial Revolution and characterized by the gradual development of banking, investment, recordkeeping, and increasing reliance on money. The Atlantic encounter underlay most of the other economic changes of the period. The accumulation of capital resulting from European control over the Atlantic was crucial in propelling Britain to its domination of the world economy during the Industrial Revolution in the nineteenth century. Long-term investment created new wealth through the flow of liquid capital. Europe displaced the Indian Ocean rim to become the center of a worldwide trade nexus, and many individuals and families rose to great wealth. The rising fortunes of merchants, tradespeople, professionals, and wealthy farmers constituted a new and growing middle class of people who possessed wealth, education, and leisure time and who were thus able to contribute to the new intellectual developments of the seventeenth and eighteenth centuries. In addition, as this group became more prevalent in Western European society, its members also grew increasingly discontented because despite their social influence, they were still excluded from political power and representation because royal administrations clung to the principle of noble blood. The rising middle classes would eventually demand greater equality, instigating major political disruptions beginning in the seventeenth century. At the same time, Europe's rise contributed to African underdevelopment as the loss of many millions of people combined with political and social dislocations produced by the slave trade.

As Europe transitioned to modern capitalism, the change was first described in the writings of the Scot Adam Smith in his 1776 book, *The Wealth of Nations*. Smith challenged the traditional economic theory of mercantilism, which considered wealth to be limited and economic transactions to consist of competition between participants. Smith's theory, in contrast, posited economic exchanges to be mutually profitable and promoted self-interest rather than market regulation as a stabilizer for the economic system. Competition and profit rather than national interests or abstract principles were to determine prices and the value of labor. As an ideology, capitalism fostered individualism and competition and created dynamic potential for growth while also frustrating those who were unable to adapt to the new economy because of inefficiency, lack of opportunity, or poverty. Although Smith postulated that capitalist economics would eventually result in a rising tide of wealth for all, the ideology has been repeatedly criticized by socialists and those on the left for establishing institutionalized inequality.

Intellectual and political changes

The transformation of ideas was the most significant aspect of the Enlightenment. This trend was at first stimulated by the invention of the printing press in the fifteenth century, which allowed ideas from the ancient classic authors, the Arab world, and eventually contemporary European theorists to be disseminated throughout Europe. The existence of printing resulted in increasing opportunities for literacy and education and thus enormously expanded the number of people that could participate in an intellectual public sphere. Likewise, the new wealth of the early modern period, made possible by Atlantic trade and the Commercial Revolution, enabled far more people to engage in intellectual study than in the past. The many new discoveries brought to light by the Atlantic connection contributed to a spirit of inquiry. Beginning in the sixteenth century, a series of important scientific ideas, especially in mathematics, physics, chemistry, astronomy, and biology, overturned accepted views of the natural world in an era that has been termed the Scientific Revolution. This period was characterized by the birth of modern science – a turn toward the use of reason, experiment, and observation rather than traditional authorities such as the Church or ancient authors to explain the world and nature. Scientists such as Nicolaus Copernicus, Galileo Galilei, Isaac Newton, Robert Boyle, William Harvey, Johannes Kepler, Andreas Vesalius, and others demonstrated that the natural world functioned according to natural laws that could be discovered by human reason.

The scientific findings of the seventeenth century contributed to skepticism about previously accepted ideas, particularly about religion, even though most of the seventeenth-century scientists continued to retain conventional religious ideals. Encounters with the Americas and their peoples also led philosophical thinkers such as Jean de Léry, Michel de Montaigne, and Bartolomé de las Casas to consider human beings' inherent rights and to question whether European society could not be improved. These reflections were given increased relevance during the age of religious wars, making Europeans question the very structure of their society. A further factor was increased questioning of the traditional political structure of European society. The English Parliament's defeat and execution of the English king in 1649 during the English Civil War and the successful Dutch revolt against Spanish rule during the sixteenth and seventeenth centuries, both of which are discussed in the following chapters, caused many to query whether monarchy was necessary or whether other forms of government, even democracy, might not be better suited to human needs. Together, these new ideas contributed to the radical cultural, political, and intellectual changes of the eighteenth century known as the Enlightenment.

By the eighteenth century, changing intellectual ideals had spread beyond the isolated laboratories of brilliant individuals. Because of the availability of printing and the rising income levels of people at middling levels of society, more people were able to participate in the exchange of knowledge during the eighteenth century. Middle-class people read newspapers and met in coffee houses and in salons, which were literary, political, and scientific gatherings held in private homes, often hosted by influential women. The Enlightenment was especially strong in France, where its intellectuals were called *philosophes*, but also had a great impact in Germany, England, the Thirteen Colonies, and elsewhere. Increasingly, enlightened individuals such as Denis Diderot, Voltaire, Jean-Jacques Rousseau, Benjamin Franklin, Thomas Jefferson, Mary Wollstonecraft, Thomas Paine, and Immanuel Kant communicated internationally, questioned established ideas such as absolute monarchy, and advocated political reform. They championed the idea that human beings had natural rights which merited a politically representative government, tolerance, liberty, and freedom of expression. A few radicals argued that human rights also encompassed women and people of color. The aim of an enlightened government would be to protect human rights and freedoms and, if it failed to do so, it should be changed through revolution. This philosophy, together with the example of successful pre-Enlightenment revolutions in the Netherlands and England, led to an era of revolution beginning in the eighteenth century and expressed throughout the Atlantic.

In an era of immense social inequality, the promise of the Enlightenment was expressed in complex and sometimes convoluted ways in the Atlantic. Not all Europeans participated in or experienced the Enlightenment, with many groups, such as the poor, non-whites, and most women, left out. In addition, the new perception that all human beings had natural rights led to both humanitarianism and its opposite. Most philosophers were troubled by the unfairness they saw in European society and advocated for democracy to replace authoritarianism. Enlightenment ideals also became an incentive for abolishing slavery on humanitarian grounds. However, these ideas were inherently radical and challenged existing power structures. They were difficult for many to accept, and some groups and individuals resisted them strenuously. Contradictory ideas also emerged in the new marketplace of ideas. As discussed previously, the Enlightenment also contributed to modern racism. Although racial ideas became so engrained in the eighteenth and nineteenth centuries that it is hard to believe that they did not always exist, they actually emerged during the period of the Enlightenment. The paradox arose because the class of people profiting from slavery was identical to the group participating in the Enlightenment. Slavery, though it arose under a precapitalist economic system, was producing tremendous profits for capitalists and entrepreneurs, who found justification for their enslavement of others in pseudo-scientific views derived from Enlightenment science. Many Europeans and Atlantic creoles who did not directly profit from slavery also accepted racism because it created a tiered society in which they were always superior to Africans, even if they were otherwise at the bottom level of an increasingly meritocratic society. Thus, the Enlightenment produced both abolitionists and proponents of slavery, setting the stage for a series of passionate confrontations over the issue during the next century.

14 The age of revolution

The Enlightenment ushered in an age of Atlantic revolutions that was closely linked to the increasing doubt about traditional modes of human society and culture. Beginning in the seventeenth century, traditional political authority was increasingly questioned, a tendency which intensified in the eighteenth century and thereafter in continuing series of revolutions. Although the earliest political revolutions erupted before the Enlightenment took hold, they helped frame the groundwork for the major shifts in political ideals during the eighteenth century. In the seventeenth century, political and religious concerns were contested in the course of a number of bloody wars and insurrections, most violently in the brutal Thirty Years' War (1618–48) in central Europe. These also included uprisings against royal or local governments, mostly unsuccessful, such as the aristocratic Fronde revolt (1648–53) in France. In some cases, they did bring about a moderation of government policy, as in the Swiss peasant revolt of 1653. Revolts and resistance movements also spanned both sides of the Atlantic, including the many Indian wars in the Americas and Nathaniel Bacon's Rebellion of 1676 in Virginia. From a political perspective, among the most important in the seventeenth century were two successful European revolutions in the Netherlands and England, both of which included a strongly religious component. While these initially had mainly local impacts, they undermined the idea of divine royal authority more generally and helped initiate a transformation of ideas about political representation and forms of governance. They also set the scene for the major revolutions in the United States, France, and Haiti at the end of the eighteenth century that were to transform both the Atlantic and the wider world. Revolutionary ideals criss-crossed the Atlantic, with each revolution leading to the next. The result was the evolution of new inclusive forms of politics that allowed and even encouraged the participation of individuals and groups that had previously been seen as unable or unfit to govern themselves.

The Dutch Revolt (1568–1648)

The first revolution spanned the longest time period and initially seemed very unlikely to succeed. Sometimes termed the Eighty Years' War, it arose in the Seventeen Provinces of the Low Countries (today the Netherlands, Belgium, Luxembourg, and a small portion of France). Many in the region that was to become the Netherlands had adopted Protestantism, which meshed well with an economy based on trade that also fostered liberty and toleration. However, there were mounting attempts by the Spanish Crown, which governed the Low Countries, to impose orthodox Catholicism and to increase the authority of the state. This led to vigorous resistance in the Protestant provinces. The religious component was a central aspect of this revolt, as it would be in the English Civil War of the mid-seventeenth century. Deference to authority was a strongly engrained cultural value in the early modern period, and it was hard to convince people to go against the Crown. Religious validation was the most powerful source of justification and unity for rebellion against the state.

After many decades of military struggle, the Dutch had partially succeeded in throwing off Spanish authority by the early 1580s, resulting in a split between Holland and the rest of the Low Countries. However, the new United Provinces of the Netherlands – the Dutch Republic – were not recognized until the end of the Thirty Years' War in 1648. Governance of the new republic was shared between the representative assembly or States General and the *stadtholder*, the chief executive officer, selected from the royal House of Orange-Nassau. This revolt had significant repercussions in Europe and the Atlantic world. Even before the final victory, Dutch political independence had ushered in a period known as the Dutch Golden Age in which the Dutch Republic developed into a major world power and a leader in trade, economic innovation, shipping, and science and into an international political model for its freedom and religious tolerance. Dutch ships dominated Atlantic trade during the early seventeenth century. Dutch military and economic success also demonstrated that the Spanish Crown's claim to divine sanction was false – a precedent which extended to other royal dynasties throughout Europe.

The Civil War and Revolution in England (1642–51 and 1688)

The Dutch were so successful during the seventeenth century that they were both emulated and resented. England was the country that was to profit the most by the Dutch example, overtaking Holland to dominate Atlantic trade during the eighteenth century and eventually taking control over the largest empire in history. English success was, in great measure, based on significant political changes that occurred during the English Civil War of 1642–51 and the English Revolution of 1688.

The Civil War, which Marxist scholars have termed a period of revolution, occurred during a period of political and religious transition in England. It consisted of a series of armed conflicts that were fought at various times in

England, Scotland, and Ireland, with an outcome more radical than that of the Dutch revolt because the English changed their own national government rather than throwing off foreign domination. The conflict developed as a result of underlying political and religious causes, but it was initially set off by the activities of King Charles I, who aimed to rule as an absolutist monarch. England had been Protestant for some time by that point, but the question of which version of Protestantism would be nationally sanctioned had not been fully resolved. Charles attempted to force Presbyterian Scotland to accept his version of highly ceremonial Anglicanism. The Scots revolted, forcing the king to request funds from Parliament to levy taxes to fund an army. However, at this point, long-standing grievances involving religion and governance came to the fore. Many in Parliament were more Calvinist than the king and his royalist supporters and resented the state's high church interpretation of Protestantism. As a result, critics of the Crown sought greater power of governance for Parliament in order to counterbalance the leanings of the Crown. The king's attempts to curb Parliament led to an escalation of hostilities, and eventually both sides formed armies against each other. In the end, the Parliamentarian side associated with Puritanism won and captured the king.

In a wholly unprecedented event, the king was tried in court by Parliament, purged of its more neutral members. The accusation was that he had broken his covenant with the people – an entirely new idea. The king defended himself, accurately, by stating that there had been no covenant and that the court judging him was illegal but nonetheless was executed in 1649. For the next decade, England was ruled first by Parliament and from 1653 by Oliver Cromwell, previously a major leader of Parliamentary military and political policy, as dictator. Upon his death in 1659, a failed attempt to establish Cromwell's son as political leader was followed by the return of King Charles II, the son of the executed king. Although there was once again a royal dynasty on the throne, the past could not be erased. During the Civil War, a number of new ideas about representative government and the role of the people had emerged – many of them too radical even for Parliamentary supporters. Additionally, the state had prospered politically and economically under Parliament and Cromwell. Just as in the Dutch revolt, these events demonstrated that kings were not necessary for effective government and undermined the Crown's claim of divine endorsement.

The Civil War did not complete the political changes, which culminated in an event termed the Glorious Revolution. After returning to the throne, the new king was conciliatory, but his heir James II was less careful politically and publicly espoused Catholicism. In 1688, he produced a male heir who would be raised as a Catholic, displacing his older Protestant daughter from inheriting the throne. Powerful members of Parliament, including those of previously royalist leanings, invited the Dutch stadtholder, William III of Orange-Nassau, who was married to James' daughter Mary, to take the

English throne. William invaded in 1688 but was mainly met with support from the English, though there were attempts to rebel in Scotland and Ireland. He and his wife Mary were made joint monarchs.

These events had enormous consequences in both England and the world. Parliament had now executed one king and dismissed another. In the revolution's aftermath, King William had been compelled to sign the Bill of Rights (1689), guaranteeing a number of rights to Parliament and the people and stating that Parliament possessed the ultimate sovereignty, making England the first constitutional monarchy. The Bill of Rights thus became the founding document for constitutional governments around the world. England was not yet a modern democracy – only one man in five could vote – but it had been set on an evolutionary path toward democratic representation. The political theories of philosopher John Locke, expressed in his *Two Treatises of Government* (1689), established a number of principles central to representative constitutional government in the West, including government by contract with the people and the idea of individual rights. Although the revolution had initially centered on religious issues, it had legitimated political rebellion against unrepresentative government, a principle emphasized in the writings of Locke.

In Britain, the new form of government proved to be both stable and adaptable over the next few centuries, providing a sound foundation for English political, military, and economic growth. England was to enjoy peace until the Napoleonic Wars of the early nineteenth century. In the Netherlands, the Revolution had a more negative effect. Ironically, the accession of William of Orange weakened the Dutch. William established an Anglo-Dutch alliance against France, ostensibly in the interests of the Dutch Republic, but a series of expensive wars against the French significantly weakened the Netherlands, leaving what was by then the United Kingdom of England and Scotland the major naval force in the Atlantic and the world.

The American Revolution (1775–83)

The revolution of the American Thirteen Colonies was, in some ways, a culmination of English events of the previous century. It extended the promise of the two previous European revolutions, applying the ideals previously fought for in specific national contexts more universally to the human condition. American political philosophers like Thomas Jefferson were imbued with the ideas of Locke; thus, Locke's statement in his *Second Treatise of Government* that men had "a power" from "nature" to preserve their "property" in "life, liberty, and estate" was alluded to in the U.S. Declaration of Independence's (1776) pronouncement that "life, liberty, and the pursuit of happiness" were the "inalienable rights" of "all men" or that "all men are created equal." Although the questions of whether the phrase "all men" included women and whether it truly meant all men, including poor men and non-whites, were left unaddressed, the ideals expressed in these statements eventually inspired many people who had not been originally encompassed by them to struggle for freedom and equality. Indeed, the English Revolution itself had been a constitutive element of the Enlightenment's expression of the ideologies of liberty, natural rights, and political representation. Like all revolutions, the American Revolution stemmed from long-term underlying causes but required immediate political events to set it in motion. Unlike the previous pre-Enlightenment revolutions, it no longer required religious justification. In addition, occurring in the context of the Enlightenment, the revolution was able to draw on previously developed political ideologies.

Prior to the conflict, white people living in the Thirteen Colonies saw themselves as British. Just a decade before, they had fought as Britons against France in the Seven Years' War. However, in the several generations since the original settling of the colonies, Americans had begun to subtly draw away from English norms. Many had participated in local civic governments and had experienced far greater social mobility than was possible in Britain because of the availability of cheap land and reduced competition among skilled workers. Among the educated levels of society, Enlightenment ideals promoting representative government were prevalent, and expectations about political participation pervaded society.

The conflict was triggered by the British government's need for money because of its high debts from the Seven Years' War. Previously, Parliament had not taxed the Thirteen Colonies, and it hoped to recoup some of the costs of defending them. Thus, it imposed taxes similar to those that prevailed in Britain on some sales and imports and on printed documents (the Stamp Act). These taxes were not excessively high but were new and unwelcome to the colonists and were seen as an assertion of power by the British government. In addition, further grievances included British attempts to curb the large black market in goods and to protect Indian rights in the Ohio valley against encroachment by colonists and the British army's practice of billeting extra troops in civilian homes.

Although about one fifth of the colonists remained loyal to Britain, many of the colonists felt that their previously held rights were being lost. The issue of taxes was one of the sharpest at first. The colonists argued that they too had paid for the Seven Years' War in both money and lives. Further, they argued that they could not be taxed without their consent or representation in Parliament. This was a new concept which had a strong basis in Enlightenment ideals. British taxes were met with boycotts, riots like the Boston Tea Party (1773) in which a mob disguised as Native Americans dumped British tea into the harbor, and attacks on tax officials and their homes. In retaliation, the British government seized direct control over Massachusetts, but the colonists responded by forming a Continental Congress as a colonial representative assembly. The British government was willing to compromise on the issue of taxes but insisted on the principle of Parliamentary sovereignty. Escalating tensions led to the colonists issuing a Declaration of Independence in 1776 that established the United States of America as a sovereign nation. After six years of conflict, Britain abandoned what had been a costly, difficult, and unpopular war (see Figure 14.1). About 10,000 former slaves and about 60,000 loyalists, known as Tories, left with the British forces, mainly resettling in other British territories in North America, especially in Canada. Commander in chief George Washington was elected the first U.S. president in 1789. Initially, the loss of the Thirteen Colonies created a crisis of confidence in Britain, but the United States and Britain almost immediately renewed their trading partnerships and have maintained a mainly peaceful relationship since then.

One significant reason for the American victory was that the British were fighting an overseas war, but perhaps more important was that, unlike previous revolutions, the American Revolution began as a colonial conflict but spiraled into a wide-ranging global conflict similar to the Seven Years' War. The international aspect of the conflict significantly limited Britain's ability to effectively fight the Americans. France and Spain, rivals of Britain, soon joined the conflict on the American side, sending military and monetary help to the colonies, especially France, which bankrolled most of the weapons and ammunition of the Americans. The entry of these countries into the conflict opened Caribbean and European theaters of war, including conflict in the Mediterranean over Gibraltar and Minorca. This forced the British to divert troops to defend the valuable Caribbean sugar colonies and Gibraltar. British attacks on French territories in India opened an Asian theater of war, further spreading British resources. The Dutch Republic, previously allied to Britain, at first remained neutral, but Dutch merchants' practice of selling arms and supplies to the Americans and French led Britain to declare war against them. The British then commenced attacks against Dutch ports in Europe and Dutch possessions in the Caribbean, Asia, and Africa. The British bolstered their forces somewhat by bringing contingents of German mercenaries to the Thirteen Colonies, but this was not enough to counteract the massive amounts of French aid to the colonists.

The outcome of the revolution was that the colonists established a representative government according to Enlightenment principles – the first modern representative state. After much debate between federalists such as John Adams, James Madison, and Alexander Hamilton, who aimed for a stronger central government, and those who wanted significant autonomy for the states such as Patrick Henry and Mercy Otis Warren, the U.S. Constitution was ratified in 1787 and quickly modified by the 1791 Bill of Rights. Together, these became a template for subsequent constitutional documents around the world, as did the French Declaration of the Rights of Man and Citizen, which was written at the same time. The two documents sprang from connected sources: two of the primary authors, Thomas Jefferson and the Marquis de Lafayette, corresponded by letter across the ocean as they helped frame the two texts.

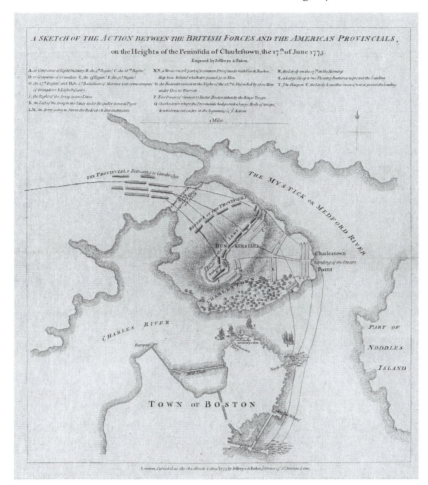

Figure 14.1 "A Sketch of the Action between British Forces and American Provincials on the Heights of the Peninsula of Charlestown, the 17th of
June 1775" by Jefferys and Faden. This image was published in London five days after news of the battle crossed the ocean. The Battle of
Bunker Hill, depicted here, was a British victory, but demonstrated that
the colonial militia was a formidable force. Map reproduction courtesy
of the Norman B. Leventhal Map Center at the Boston Public Library.

Some have argued that the new government established by the colonists
was not fundamentally different from the previous one, resulting in a "conservative revolution." The mandate of a property qualification to vote meant
that elites remained in charge, and only men of means could vote. Women
and non-whites were excluded from voting, and slaves were counted as only
three fifths of a citizen for the purpose of the census and for apportioning

political representation. In addition, there was a fundamental inconsistency in a nation that claimed to be founded on liberty and yet continued to permit the practice of slavery. This discrepancy laid the ground for continuing conflict, culminating in the American Civil War. The double standard was noted by many, including British officials, American revolutionaries, slaves, and even Thomas Jefferson, a major architect of the American revolutionary documents and also a slaveholder, who mentioned his fears of a coming conflict over slavery on several occasions. Indeed, Native Americans and slaves, though they supported both sides, were more likely to support the British in the war.

Yet at the same time, despite all of its limitations, the structure of the new American state was a new political formulation based upon Enlightenment ideals. It was the first true democracy with an elected and representative government. Although the political ideals of the revolution had been mainly framed by elites, they resonated strongly with ordinary people, who were crucial to its success. Many ordinary people, including poor white men, women, Native Americans, and free and enslaved Africans, were formally excluded from political power, but they debated revolutionary ideals and participated in revolutionary activities. Although their contributions were not acknowledged in the drafting of the Constitution, their expectations and ideals persisted and continued to be expressed afterward. One of the advantages of the Constitution as a political document was that it was able to be adapted and modified to match developments in political values; during the centuries that followed, groups and individuals that had been initially left out of political representation fought for and obtained the right to vote and to participate as full citizens of the state. Indeed, the new United States of America became a political model for other nations around the world.

The French Revolution (1789–99)

Of all the Atlantic revolutions, the French Revolution was the most deeply affected by the ideals of the Enlightenment, which strongly influenced its character. The main cause of the revolution was a set of festering long-term grievances, but like the other transformative uprisings described in this chapter, it required a series of catalyzing events in order to occur.

French intellectuals had absorbed Enlightenment ideas about equality, freedom, and democracy and were impressed by the British constitutional monarchy and by the American Revolution. Indeed, some, like the Marquis de Lafayette, had fought in the American Revolution and were closely associated with the new American political leadership. They were critical of the absolute monarchy in France and the constraints imposed by the French state, including the lack of the vote, censorship, and the incredibly high taxes which the newly developing middle classes and the poor paid to support the king and the nobility. The rising middle classes were frustrated because they were excluded from government influence. Many of these ideals were at least partially shared by working people, including laborers, tradespeople, and shopkeepers from urban areas, especially Paris. Peasants in the countryside were also discontented because they bore the brunt of state oppression. They were obliged to do labor duty, called *corvée*, for the state and owed taxes so exorbitant to both nobles and the king that they sometimes starved in years of bad harvests, such as in 1789, the year the French Revolution broke out.

In the meantime, the French state was bankrupt, primarily because of its expenditures in Atlantic affairs such as the Seven Years' War and the American Revolution, as well as from building Versailles, the elaborate palace complex of the French kings. To recoup its expenses, the French Crown decided to levy a new tax which included the aristocracy, as all other social levels were already taxed to the limit, but the tax required the approval of the Estates General, the French representative assembly, which French kings had not called upon for 175 years. Traditionally, when the Estates General met, it met as three groups: the First Estate, or clergy, who were primarily of noble descent; the Second Estate, or nobility; and the Third Estate, which included everyone else. This meant that the two conservative estates outvoted the Third Estate, even though the latter represented far more people. It rapidly became apparent that the king was not interested in the grievances of the Third Estate, so its representatives walked out of the talks on revenue, together with a few nobles and clergy, and formed the National Assembly, a new representative body. Crowds turned out in the streets of Paris to support the new government, storming the Bastille fortress and beginning the French Revolution.

The National Assembly drafted a new constitution, the Declaration of the Rights of Man and Citizen (1789), written in tandem with the American Bill of Rights and containing similar provisions. It was the strongest statement of universal human rights of the time and was to directly influence the text of the United Nations' Universal Declaration of Human Rights (1948). This was the beginning of suffrage (right to vote) movements throughout the world. At first, the French Revolution seemed to be following the path of its predecessors. Civil liberties were recognized, aristocratic privilege was abolished, and a constitutional monarchy was declared, but a distinction was made between "active" and "passive" citizens, and only white male property owners could vote.

However, unlike the American Revolution, the political inclusion of excluded groups quickly became a topic of debate. Constituencies arose to promote the inclusion of women, Protestants, Jews, and free blacks in the state. Citizenship was granted to Protestants and Jews, though the latter continued to experience some discriminatory financial legislation. Free blacks from the French Caribbean colonies also petitioned for citizenship and were granted it in 1791, and there were debates about the legality of slavery which were to become more intense during the Haitian Revolution. Women never became full citizens and eventually were forbidden to protest politically. However, many feminists, including women and a few men, such as Etta Palm d'Aelders and the Marquis de Condorcet, argued for women's rights. Olympe de Gouges protested the exclusion of women from the vote by writing the *Declaration of the Rights of Woman and the Female Citizen* (1791). All of the aforementioned individuals were to lose their lives as a result of their activities criticizing the state. Although the French Revolution did not emancipate women, it was the first time that the question of women's equality had been taken seriously in an extensive public debate, quickly inspiring others, such as the English philosopher Mary Wollstonecraft, who wrote *A Vindication of the Rights of Women* in 1792.

Though the French Revolution is often seen as the starting point of the modern era, in the short term it did not succeed in its original aims of increasing liberty and equality. After its initial radicalism, the revolution began to lose direction as rival political coalitions arose in the National Assembly. At the same time, the political situation rapidly became very dire for the new government as continental European states, all absolute monarchies, joined together to attack France with the support of the French king and some nobles. As a result, a more radical phase of the revolution developed in which the monarchy was ended, the king executed, and a republic declared. The new government established a set of progressive measures, such as doing away with tiers of citizenship and abolishing slavery, but also established a state of emergency known as the Terror, under which it forbade political dissent, including women's organizations; established censorship; limited freedom of speech; and executed opponents of the regime in the thousands. It initially appeared as though France would be defeated militarily, but a brilliant young general, Napoleon Bonaparte, began turning the tide by 1794. In 1799, he seized power as dictator, and his forces proceeded to conquer most of Western Europe.

Napoleonic administrations were repressive by contemporary standards but often less oppressive than the rule of prior absolute monarchs. They exported many elements of the French Revolution, although in diluted form, including the rule of law, representative government, and independent judiciaries, and also bolstered indigenous nationalism. In the Atlantic, Napoleonic rule in Spain and Portugal severely weakened the ties between the mother countries and their Latin American colonies, ushering in an age of revolutions for independence. Napoleon was finally defeated in 1815 by a coalition of continental Europeans and Great Britain. This meant the temporary restoration of monarchy to much of Western Europe, including France, but also meant that Europe, like Latin America, continued to be convulsed by revolutions aiming for greater political liberty and equality during the nineteenth century. Thus, one of the greatest legacies of the French Revolution was the exportation of the ideals of liberty, equality, and revolution to both sides of the Atlantic.

The Haitian Revolution (1791–1804)

The Haitian Revolution, like previous revolutions, occurred as a result of Atlantic events and like the others stemmed from a combination of long-term and immediate catalyzing factors. The revolution occurred in Saint-Domingue, the most important French sugar colony, which took up the western portion of the island of Hispaniola. In 1780, about 450,000 slaves, 40,000 whites, and 28,000 free people of color lived in Saint-Domingue, which was the most lucrative of French possessions. The island was a place of extraordinary brutality for slaves. As in other areas where slaves greatly outnumbered whites, the regime of domination was extremely cruel and violent, and there was a very high mortality rate, necessitating a supply of about 40,000 new slaves yearly from Africa – almost 10% of the slave population. By a twist of fate, a large percentage of these slaves were military captives from the losing side of a civil war in the Kongo and, as historian John Thornton has shown, were not only trained soldiers but had also fought in the past for a more politically representative faction in government.[1] Thus, Saint-Domingue was ripe for a slave revolution.

The French Revolution seemed to indicate that the French administration would be more amenable to the creation of a representative, democratic society in Saint-Domingue. When the National Assembly promulgated the Declaration of the Rights of Man and Citizen in the course of the French Revolution, various groups in Saint-Domingue, including white planters, free people of color, and slaves, expressed hope that the new constitution's provisions would apply to them. The free people of color from the island, who were mostly "mulattos," sent Vincent Ogé as a representative to demand the rights that were apparently given to them by the new French constitution. However, island planters were resistant to the idea of enfranchising the free people of color, although they represented only a tiny segment of the population of the island, because they feared that this would be the first step toward emancipating the slaves. Planters moved to prevent any extensions of freedom, attacking Ogé and his forces when he returned to the island. In 1791, Ogé was captured, tortured, and killed, but shortly afterward the National Assembly agreed to enfranchise the free people of color.

As it became apparent that the planters would prevent any expansion of rights, the free people of color and then the slaves rose up in revolt. Slaves on the island explicitly connected their resistance to the ideals of the French Revolution, stating that they hoped to emulate the poor whites in France who had achieved freedom by killing their masters and by wearing emblems in the revolutionary colors of red, white, and blue. In the meantime, the planters of Saint-Domingue began to open negotiations with Great Britain and Spain, France's enemies. In order to avoid a French military defeat in the Caribbean, Léger-Félicité Sonthonax, the French government's representative in Saint-Domingue and commander of a small contingent of troops on the island, announced the emancipation of the slaves in 1793. By this act, he was hoping that the slaves, who constituted the majority of the population, would thus support the French state in the coming conflict. Emancipation was ratified by the French government, which abolished slavery in France and its dominions in 1794. Toussaint L'Ouverture, the main leader of the rebellion, then agreed to support French interests against Spain and led an invasion of the neighboring Spanish colony of Santo Domingo, endeavoring to free its slaves (see Figure 14.2). When the Napoleonic government was established, however, it attempted to rescind the decree of emancipation in 1802 and succeeded in imprisoning L'Ouverture, but it was unable to defeat the new nation of Haiti. France did succeed in reestablishing slavery in the other smaller French colonies, such as Guadeloupe, until 1848. By 1804, Haiti was the second independent republic in the Atlantic, the first new non-European state in the Americas, and the first society to have effectively abolished slavery.

In many ways, the events in Haiti represented the most radical of all of the revolutions, comprising a total transformation of society in which slaves, the most oppressed members of society, had taken their place as equal citizens. The revolution demonstrated that the ideals of liberty, equality, and justice resonated for all people. Toussaint L'Ouverture himself had been well read in Enlightenment literature and, in a proclamation made in 1793, stated "I want liberty and equality to reign throughout Saint Domingue."[2] Because all of the western Atlantic territories continued to allow slavery at that time, the revolution created tremendous fear that slaves would rebel throughout the Atlantic and provided a beacon of hope for those who were still enslaved. Yet Haiti's underdevelopment was perpetuated, as it was politically isolated from other Atlantic states.

Consequences of a revolutionary era

Despite the far-reaching impact of the revolutions of this period, things changed gradually for many of the lower orders of society, especially in rural or marginal areas. Prejudice against disenfranchised groups continued, and many people were left out of equal social participation. Even in areas where successful revolutions had occurred, they had not been fully realized anywhere. Slavery continued to exist in most of the Atlantic world. Women and even most free men could not vote. These questions were to become the cause of confrontations during the nineteenth and twentieth centuries throughout the Atlantic world, eventually extending the promise of the revolutions to everybody.

The line of continuity between the revolutions described in this section did not end with the Haitian Revolution. The Atlantic revolutions had ushered in a new vision of inclusive politics that demanded democracy and contractual government. Even governments that retained absolutism had to make some concessions to the new expectations. During the nineteenth century, revolutionary fervor continued unabated. Slave revolts increased in

Figure 14.2 Toussaint L'Ouverture and General Thomas Maitland meet to negotiate a treaty between the Saint-Domingue rebels and Britain. Ultimately,
this effort failed. © Corbis

numbers and scope. Spanish America broke away from Spain. In Europe,
a series of revolutions in the nineteenth century led to ever more inclusive
politics. Even in the twentieth and twenty-first centuries, transformative
political ideals continued to spur revolutions against authoritarian states.

Notes

1 John Thornton, " 'I Am the Subject of the King of Congo': African Political Ideology and the Haitian Revolution," *Journal of World History*, Vol. 4, No. 2 (Fall 1993), pp. 181–214.
2 Toussaint L'Ouverture, Proclamation of 29 August, 1793, in *The Haitian Revolution*, Nick Nesbitt, ed. (New York: Verso, 2008), 1–2.

15 New forms of resistance and expansion

The many revolutions described in the previous chapter had forever changed the relationship of the public and of citizens to the state. Nineteenth-century people in Europe and the Americas expected the state to be responsive to the people, even if that was rarely borne out in reality. This was also the age of nationalism, and citizens increasingly felt patriotic toward their nation and experienced a sense of belonging and cohesion among its people. They expected to take part in the life of the state, whether in the public sphere, as a political constituency or electorate, or in defense of the state and its people.

Nineteenth-century Native American resistance

Native Americans, too, continued to insist on their rights in the nineteenth century, inspired by both Enlightenment ideals and their lived experience as colonized peoples. Often, resistance occurred not as revolution but in the form of support or hostility toward one side in a wider war. Just as Native American groups had become involved in various eighteenth-century clashes among European colonizers such as the Seven Years' War and the American Revolution, they continued to participate in conflicts in the nineteenth century such as the American Civil War, taking sides based on geography, the alignment of traditional rivals, or a group's perception that one side promised a greater benefit. In some cases, Indians fought wars against the extension of colonial powers – by the nineteenth century, this primarily meant the expanding United States and Mexico. There were a number of major conflicts as well as many smaller ones. In the Creek War of 1813, rival parties within the Creek people – one side accepting American settlement, the other faction, the Red Sticks, striving to maintain traditional cultural practices and retain their lands in the Gulf Coast region – fought with each other and with American, British, and Spanish allies. For the Creeks, the outcome was a high death toll and the loss of most of their lands to the United States. At the same time, the Shawnee leader Tecumseh united a large confederation of Native American tribes in the hope of establishing an autonomous native territory with British support. These hopes, too, were shattered with Tecumseh's death in Ontario while fighting the U.S. army in 1813. In the three Seminole Wars (1814–19, 1835–42, and 1855–8), the Seminoles – a group whose ancestry comprised Creeks, Native Americans from other tribes, escaped slaves, and free blacks who had fled to Florida – attempted to resist U.S. expansion, sometimes with British and Spanish help. In Canada, there were two attempts by the Métis, a population with mixed Native American and European heritage, to establish an autonomous homeland in the northwest during the 1860s and 1880s.

Meanwhile, in the decades following the American Civil War, there were a number of armed conflicts between the expanding American state and western Indian nations, including the Apache, Cayuse, Cheyenne, Comanche, Nez Perce, Paiute, Sioux, Yuma, and many others. Many confrontations took place in territories that were part of Mexico before they eventually became part of the United States, such as Arizona, California, and Texas. During the late nineteenth century, the Ghost Dance movement in the west arose as a new spiritual belief system that emphasized a return to traditional Native American cultural values and predicted an end to settler encroachment. This form of religious revival offered spiritual comfort during a time of privation and may also have bolstered the will of its followers to resist the U.S. government, but it ultimately became the target of suppression by U.S. military forces. In the fledgling United States, native groups were challenged by the encroachment of settlers on Indian lands, which was supported by the nineteenth-century doctrine of "Manifest Destiny," which asserted that the United States was entitled to expand across the North American continent.

In northern Mexico in the first three decades after Mexican independence from Spain, Native American groups in the north, especially the Apache, Comanche, and Navajo, engaged in many attacks against Mexican settlers and temporarily maintained considerable autonomy in a region that would soon be overrun by American settlers. Meanwhile, in one of the earliest territories encountered by Spaniards, though also the most difficult to conquer, the Maya people of Yucatán revolted in what was termed the Caste War (1847–1901), which lasted sporadically over many decades as warfare broke out in new centers. Even after the war, skirmishes continued for many decades.

In both the north and south, Native Americans strove to retain or retake control over the few areas where they still had some autonomy. Although these movements often succeeded in reducing settler impact for a time, the final outcome was always the victory of the colonizing societies, who had greater resources, including more effectual weaponry, and greater resistance to disease. Many of the later-rebelling groups ended up being relegated to marginal land or in districts that were neglected or suppressed by their governments, trapped in conditions that made them the poorest and most deprived citizens of their nations. Oftentimes, persistent grievances related to resource management, state services, and discrimination resulted in continued tensions, even into the twentieth century.

Even when native groups aimed to adapt to their altered circumstances, there were many barriers to success. For example, after military defeat by British colonists just before the American Revolution, the Cherokees of the southeastern United States adopted many aspects of white American culture, including switching to livelihoods based on agriculture and artisanal trade, adopting new clothing styles, accepting Christianity, developing a constitution and a government modeled on those of the United States, and publishing a Cherokee newspaper. They had a high rate of education, in part because of the development of an alphabet to write the Cherokee language in 1821 devised by the Cherokee silversmith Sequoyah (see Figure 15.1). However, their lands were desirable to American settlers, and a series of government treaties whittled away much of their territory. The Cherokee were soon pushed to move further west, with a number settling in Arkansas and Missouri. A gold rush in Georgia in the late 1820s was soon followed by the Indian Removal Act of 1830. Consequently, even this acculturated group, together with a number of other Indian nations, was forcibly relocated to Oklahoma by means of an arduous journey, the "Trail of Tears," during which many thousands died.

Revolution and independence in Latin America

As in Europe, the Enlightenment was a factor in the revolutionary fervor that swept Latin America in the early nineteenth century. In particular, the American and French Revolutions provided models for the transformation of society. However, unlike some of the other social upheavals of the era, the revolutions of Latin America were also ideologically unstable and were dependent on uneasy coalitions between rich and poor, whites and people of color, and creoles and immigrants. Creoles, or colonial-born whites, had become increasingly resentful of their lack of representation in government, while the poorer levels of society were angry about their lack of equality and lack of access to opportunity and resources, including education. A new sense of local identity was developing in various regions. Yet elites were often hesitant to fully accept Enlightenment ideals of equality and universal civil rights because they were afraid that their privileged status would be undermined if they separated from their founding countries. Nonetheless, it was this group that led revolutions in Latin America. This meant that the central aim of these revolutions was not the adoption of democracy but independence from the colonial powers of Spain and Portugal.

Equally important was the growing incapacity of the colonial powers, Spain and Portugal. Both Iberian states had increasingly weak holds over their empires by the late eighteenth century as they struggled with mounting poverty and depopulation at home. In the Atlantic, they were unable to compete either economically or militarily with the increasingly dominant British Empire. By the early nineteenth century, colonial ties had loosened until most Latin American regions were financially independent from their

SE - OUD - YAH

Figure 15.1   Sequoyah, developer of the Cherokee alphabet. Illustration by John T. Bowen after a painting by Charles Bird King. © Corbis

home countries. During the Napoleonic wars, British blockades of the sea routes between Spain and its colonies helped sever the ties across the Atlantic. This situation was exacerbated by the imposition of Napoleonic governments in Spain and Portugal, which provided already-resistant creoles with a new justification for opposing their colonial overlords. Initially, this meant a wave of new revolutionary governments composed of creole elites in Latin America who still claimed loyalty to Ferdinand VII, the heir to the Spanish throne, but also asserted their independence from the government in Spain ruled by Napoleon's brother, Joseph Bonaparte, from 1808.

The first uprising broke out in Venezuela, led by the wealthy creole military officer Francisco de Miranda, who was particularly inspired by the American Revolution. He envisioned creating a great new unified state throughout Latin America, stretching as far north as the current western United States. By 1810, Venezuela had declared independence from Spain with English and American help, but political division and economic problems undermined

Miranda's credibility, as did a severe earthquake shortly after independence was declared. Spanish forces and clergy declared that the tremors were God's punishment, and Miranda's demoralized forces disintegrated. Miranda was apprehended and soon after died in a Spanish jail.

Miranda's independence efforts were continued by fellow Venezuelan Simón Bolívar, although the two former associates had fallen out and the latter was instrumental in Miranda's arrest. Bolívar, also a military officer and a creole of substantial economic means, was successful in establishing a short-lived Venezuelan republic. Meanwhile, the rest of the Spanish colonies also began revolts against the Spain Crown. In the south of the continent, Argentine general José de San Martín led a fight against Spain which spanned from Argentina to Chile and Peru and led to a number of military victories.

In older colonies such as Mexico and Peru, entrenched elites were especially resistant to sharing power with the lower orders of society, yet at the same time faced more pressure from the poor, especially natives and mestizos, in a sign of the increasing importance of mestizo identities. In Mexico, revolution first emerged in 1810, led by a priest, Miguel Hidalgo, who was imbued with Enlightenment ideals. He led a movement of poor Indians and mestizos against Spanish elites. However, his army was disorganized and lacked training and arms and was relatively easily defeated. Hidalgo's cause was continued by José María Morelos, a priest and a mestizo, but ultimately both were executed. These rebellions demonstrated both class and ethnic consciousness and also demonstrated the growing role of mestizos. Although Mexican creoles aspired to independence, the collectivist nature of these revolts alienated their potential support. Conservative forces were ultimately more successful – a rebellion led by mestizo military officer Augustine de Iturbide was initially successful, though he was deposed and exiled after attempting to take over as dictator in 1823. The next year, Mexico proclaimed itself a democratic republic with a constitution based on that of the United States but the state religion of Roman Catholicism. Likewise, in Peru, elites were initially hesitant to encourage revolution because of their fearful memories of the rebellion of Túpac Amaru II.

However, broader political events conspired to terminate the first phase of Latin American revolutionary fervor. Britain increasingly sought to curb French power and allied with Spanish forces to defeat Napoleon and overthrow French rule in Europe. Ferdinand VII was reestablished as king of Spain and immediately sent forces to defeat the colonial rebellions. Spanish forces were initially successful and by 1815 had reestablished control over most of Spain's former possessions.

Yet Spain's reassertion of power was also transitory, and within ten years, most of Spanish Latin America was independent. Although wealthy creoles had initially been hesitant to support the cause of revolution, they had significant economic interests in independence, and by 1815, they had experienced its benefits. In addition, the continuing inequality and social discontent in their societies convinced the upper classes that taking preemptive action would be necessary to forestall more democratic revolutions.

While Spain had reestablished control over most of its Latin American possessions, it was forced to leave thinly spread troops and simmering discontent. In a second phase of warfare, Spanish weakness was decisive. Spanish troops in Latin America were gradually repelled, while mutinying soldiers in Spain initiated revolution and civil war. Britain and France, meanwhile, supported revolutionary groups in Latin America, resulting in the success of independence movements led by Latin American creoles, especially José de San Martín and Simón Bolívar. Ultimately it was Bolívar who was the principal leader of revolution against Spain and became known as "The Liberator." A further decisive factor in Bolívar's victories was the support of President Alexandre Pétion of Haiti, who provided Bolívar with shelter, arms, and soldiers under the condition that the latter abolish slavery in lands that he controlled.

Bolívar aimed to establish a united Spanish America – the Republic of Colombia, later called Gran Colombia – which was to cover most of northern South America with the exception of Brazil. Nonetheless, Central America and then South America rapidly splintered into several republics that resisted incorporation into a larger entity regardless of Bolívar's final efforts. Despite initial claims of Enlightenment ideals, full democracy was slow to come to these regions, as creole elites struggled to maintain control. Some areas continued to be governed from Spain: Cuba, for example, did not gain independence until 1898 with U.S. support after two previous attempts at gaining liberation. However, this resulted in the first of several periods of U.S. occupation rather than full-fledged Cuban independence. It was in the same period that Puerto Rico, Spain's other remaining colony, became a U.S. possession.

Brazilian independence occurred in a more peaceful fashion. Napoleon's invasion of Portugal in 1807 led the court and government of King Joáo VI to flee in British ships to Brazil. When the king was able to return to Portugal in 1820, he left his son, Pedro I, as Brazilian regent, who established an independent monarchy – unique in the Americas – in Brazil. The latter's son, Pedro II, was deposed in 1889, inaugurating a Brazilian republic.

The expansion of rights

Political ideals continued to evolve in the nineteenth century, focusing increasingly on the creation of a more tolerant state and expanding benefits to a larger percentage of the population. Central issues included the extension of the franchise – the vote – to groups that had been excluded – lower-class men, women, and non-whites – and the abolition of slavery. Centrist liberals exemplified by English political philosopher John Stuart Mill promoted a limited state that would protect its citizens but avoid what they saw as overregulation. The liberals promoted democracy, individualism, capitalism, and equality of opportunity. Radicals such as Karl Marx and Fabian socialists in England defended social equality, state regulation, and control over public property and institutions, including manufacturing and commerce, for the public good and advocated for the existence of social services like education. They arose in part as a response to the terrible conditions for workers during the Industrial Revolution, which will be discussed a little later.

Among the new ideals, the most universal and the most confrontational was the desire for democracy. At the beginning of the nineteenth century, some men and very few women could vote in both Europe and North America, while by the end of the century, significant numbers of men had achieved the franchise, though in most places women were only successful in obtaining it in the aftermath of World War I, despite the fact that both liberals and radicals included the promotion of women's rights in their platforms. In much of Latin America, on the other hand, the transition to democracy was slower and more uneven, with the majority of the population remaining economically and politically disenfranchised. Periods of democracy or partial democracy were interrupted by episodes of authoritarianism.

As countries in the Americas were being transformed into modern societies with more representative governments, parallel developments occurred in Europe. The revolutionary ideal which had begun in Europe and had transformed American societies crossed the ocean again. Europeans, too, were touched by nationalism and yearned for more enlightened societies that provided participatory democracy, increased opportunity, and less corruption. In particular, European men and women fought for the opportunity to vote. Compelling new political ideologies of the nineteenth century promoted democracy and outlined the rights and grievances of the disenfranchised. The path to achieve these values was fraught with struggle, as entrenched elites fought to retain their roles in public life.

The nineteenth century was therefore an era of revolutions in Europe, breaking out soon after the wars of independence in Latin America. In 1830, 1848, and 1870, all of Europe was engulfed by revolution. In 1848, the year of greatest revolutionary activity, more than 50 regions in Europe (some of them small independent states that no longer exist) erupted in uprisings. They called for liberal and progressive reforms such as rights for disenfranchised groups, including the middle classes, workers, and peasants. Inspired by the political ferment of 1848, Karl Marx and Friedrich Engels published *The Communist Manifesto*. The most radical revolt was the Paris Commune of 1871 that aimed to establish a socialist state in France. A notable exception to this spate of revolutions was Great Britain, where political dissatisfaction was expressed by the Chartist movement as well as by other groups but did not progress to the point of rebellion against the authority of the state. The British political system of a constitutional monarchy retained stability because it preserved hopes of the possibility of a parliamentary

solution among reformers. These hopes were indeed realized with the institution of voting rights acts in 1832, 1867, and 1884 championed by John
Stuart Mill, among others, which enfranchised British men. Many of the
revolutions in other countries met with repression; yet, in the end, most
governments did also agree to some liberal reforms. By the end of the nineteenth century, most countries in Europe still had not achieved democracy,
although they had gained more representative societies and governments,
had achieved an end to both aristocratic privileges and serfdom, and the
remaining absolute monarchies had been replaced by constitutional monarchies. Italy and Germany had become unified states, though not democratic
ones. Women and men without property remained disenfranchised until the
end of the century or later.

In the United States, which was nominally a democracy for white men,
the extension of the vote to white men without property was one of the
central political issues of the early nineteenth century. The U.S. Constitution
never clearly defined the right to vote, and many states had instituted property qualifications for participation in the electorate. In the era of "Jackso-
nian democracy" named for the populist seventh U.S. president, Andrew
Jackson, in office from 1829–37, the franchise was expanded to include
almost all white men. Although this was a time of increased civil rights for
some, Jacksonians and their newly formed Democratic Party also promoted
racial inequality and strongly supported the doctrine of Manifest Destiny,
which was to divest Native Americans of their lands. While black men in the
Southern U.S. states theoretically gained the right to vote after the American Civil War, in practice, their ability to exercise this right and others was
limited after the brief period of Reconstruction in the immediate post-war
period when Southern states adopted segregationist legislation.

While men's rights expanded, women's stagnated or grew only slightly.
Women's rights activists saw women's suffrage as the foundation of their
cause, arguing that other rights would follow once women became a voting
constituency. Like men without property, women generally could not vote,
though a few wealthy women were able to vote through proxies in Europe.
Additionally, as newer states were added to the union in the western United
States, some allowed women to vote in federal elections in an effort to aug-
ment their proportion of the electorate. The first major regions to allow
women to vote at the end of the nineteenth century – the British Common-
wealth territory of Australia, Finland, the British Colony of New Zealand,
and Sweden – were far from the Atlantic. In the Atlantic, women's suffrage
was the result of long-fought movements that lasted almost a century. In
Europe, feminists had increasingly campaigned for political equality, especially toward the end of the nineteenth century. In the United States, the Seneca Falls Convention of women's rights, held in New York State in 1848 by
Lucretia Mott and Elizabeth Cady Stanton, inaugurated a sustained effort
to gain women's suffrage.

Women's rights, though controversial in the nineteenth century, were a cause supported by many progressives. Liberal and radical men also supported women's rights: for instance, Frederick Douglass attended the Seneca Falls Convention, while John Stuart Mill advocated strongly for women's right to vote and authored a pamphlet entitled *The Subjection of Women* (1869) in which he promoted women's suffrage and social and political equality. Women's rights were also often closely linked to support for abolitionism. Both causes were promoted by many activists such as Angelina and Sarah Grimké, Harriet Beecher Stowe, and suffragist leader Susan B. Anthony. Likewise, some former slaves who had become antislavery activists, such as Harriet Tubman and Sojourner Truth, believed that their rights were being abridged both as African Americans and as women.

16 The abolition of slavery in the Atlantic

One of the greatest revolutionary processes in the Atlantic was fundamentally social: the abolition of slavery. Although African slavery was a crucial linchpin of the Atlantic economy, from its inception it had encountered criticism. Nonetheless, the struggle to abolish Atlantic slavery was a long, arduous process from its beginnings to the final Brazilian abolition of slavery in 1888. There were three main factors contributing to the abolition of slavery, all of which intertwined to create a compelling force for change. These included the growth of new ideals of human rights stemming from the Enlightenment, which contributed to a sense of moral outrage among both the secular middle classes and religious evangelicals; changes in economic ideologies, including the growth of capitalism, which resulted in the rejection of slavery as a backward and inefficient economic model; and the increasing pressure placed upon slave-owning societies by repeated and sustained slave revolts.

Moral outrage

The Enlightenment brought with it a new sense of human rights as well as a new tradition of public involvement. These ideals penetrated not only secular segments of society, such as middle-class intellectuals, but also helped create a new type of religious conscience, particularly among new or newly flourishing Christian groups, including Quakers, Methodists, and Evangelicals. While these ideals flourished most strongly in England, the United States, and France, they also were somewhat influential in Spanish and Portuguese territories, inspiring philosophers, writers, and political reformers. Slavery was taken on by these groups as a particularly egregious violation of Enlightenment principles.

In Britain, an increasing number of individuals devoted their lives to the cause of abolition during the eighteenth and early nineteenth centuries, including William Wilberforce, Thomas Clarkson, Granville Sharp, and Hannah More. They held meetings, hung posters, organized demonstrations, wrote letters and petitions, and forged ties with U.S. abolitionists. In the late eighteenth century, pottery manufacturer Josiah Wedgwood produced popular medallions showing a chained black man kneeling with the caption "Am I not a man and a brother?" Some of the most compelling arguments came from the writings of former slaves fighting to end the African slave trade and slavery itself, including Olaudah Equiano, Ottobah Cugoano, and Mary Prince. In England, where there were few slaves and most people were distanced from slavery, this cause had enormous emotional resonance. By 1772, English courts had decided in *Somersett's Case* that slavery was illegal in Britain, though it remained legal in British colonies. In 1792, a Parliament vote on the abolition of slavery was passed, although narrowly, by the House of Commons but was stalled in the House of Lords. At the turn of the century, the antislavery cause in Britain suffered a setback because of the increasingly radical progress of the Revolution in France, which many Britons wanted to distance themselves from. Abolitionists were often seen as radicals as well and suffered a reduction in support.

However, after this delay, the British abolitionist movement again gathered strength and momentum in the beginning of the nineteenth century. As a result, the British abolished the slave trade from Africa in 1807 and slavery itself in 1833, thus emancipating the British slaves who were held in the Caribbean – about 700,000 people, or half of the slaves in the Caribbean. Although Caribbean slave owners tried to hold onto their property in slaves by enforcing "apprenticeships" for freed slaves in conditions little better than slavery, this was ended as abolitionists revealed these abuses to the public. In the last few decades of the abolitionist movement, abolitionism became popular among many classes of people from rich to poor and became especially important to middle-class reformers. In Britain, because there had never been many slaves in the British Isles, most people were not directly involved with slavery and did not have emotional reasons to justify it. Island plantation owners, though vocal in their defense of slavery, were seen as provincials who were outsiders to mainstream British society. Progressive reformers saw slavery as one of many related causes in which they were involved. Indeed, a number of women abolitionists would later translate their participation in the movement to emancipate slaves into a movement to obtain the vote for women.

It was the same segment of society that responded to abolitionist arguments in the United States. Indeed, there were close ties between the British and American abolitionist movements. In the seventeenth and early eighteenth centuries, most of the proponents of abolition were Quakers, such as Anthony Benezet and John Woolman, who had ties to their brethren across the ocean. In the later part of the eighteenth century, they gained the support of influential figures such as Benjamin Franklin and Benjamin Rush, although others among the U.S. Founding Fathers, especially Southerners such as George Washington and Thomas Jefferson, remained slave owners. American political leaders also subscribed to Enlightenment ideals, but most American abolitionists were Northerners who were removed from slavery because they and their families were not personally involved in it, though there were thousands of slaves held in the North. In the mid-nineteenth century, American abolitionists included individuals like the statesman Frederick Douglass, who had escaped slavery himself; author Harriet Beecher Stowe (see Figure 16.1); activist Angelina Grimké; and radical newspaper editor William Lloyd Garrison, whose paper, *The Liberator*, denounced slaveholders on ethical grounds. As in Britain, a significant percentage of abolitionist activists were women. Many in the U.S. North – though not the majority – created an abolitionist constituency based upon a strong sense of moral outrage. Slavery was not abolished in the United States, though, until a violent Civil War (1861–5) had torn the country asunder.

What is not widely known, however, is that parts of the early United States became the location of the first emancipation of African slaves. When the Thirteen Colonies rebelled during the American Revolution, many involved on both sides pointed out that while white Americans were fighting for their liberty, black Americans were still in chains. What made the contrast even more striking was the revolutionaries' use of words and phrases such as "freedom," "liberty," and "the consent of the governed" in contrast to "tyranny" and even "slavery" to describe their status under British rule. These ideals penetrated every level of society; in the late eighteenth century, groups of slaves, especially in the Northern colonies, began sending petitions to state legislatures arguing that they had a natural right to liberty. During the Revolutionary War, the British took advantage of these contradictions and issued a proclamation that guaranteed freedom to slaves and indentured servants who escaped their masters and reached the royal forces. Thousands of slaves responded, fleeing to the British during the war.

These events were to lay the seeds of another conflict ninety years later: the American Civil War, which dealt with the big problem that had not been satisfactorily resolved – slavery. The Declaration of Independence's statement that "all men are created equal" was incompatible with the Constitution's acceptance of slavery. Yet prior to the Civil War, the ideals expressed in the American Revolution also set the stage for the first emancipation of African slaves in the Northern states. Abolitionists of the 1770s argued that if British control over the Thirteen Colonies had been unbearable, then slavery was even more intolerable. In the Northern states, these arguments gained wide support, and while all of the colonies had legal slavery in 1776, Northern slaves were gradually freed after the American Revolution by judicial decisions, acts of legislature, and popular vote. The earliest emancipation was in Vermont, where the state constitution of 1777 made slavery illegal, followed soon after by legal and legislative decisions in Massachusetts and Pennsylvania. Many of these emancipations, though implemented in the eighteenth century, proceeded gradually so that there were still slaves in some Northern states during the early decades of the nineteenth century (about 20,000 in 1820). However, by the American Civil War, slavery was gone in the North despite the continuing existence of legal restrictions and prejudice against blacks.

Figure 16.1 Harriet Beecher Stowe. © Pictorial Press Ltd/Alamy

By 1808, abolitionists in the Northern United States were strong enough to push through a federal legislative ban on the African slave trade, though not slavery, for all of the United States. Some opponents of slavery promoted Liberia in West Africa, one the United States' few colonies, as a site for resettling freed slaves. Abolitionists also attempted to restrict slavery through judicial decision, successfully defending the kidnapped Africans who took control over the Spanish slave ship *La Amistad* before the Supreme Court in 1841 but losing in Dred Scott's suit for freedom in 1857 after his master had brought him to reside in a state where slavery was prohibited. Once the British banned slavery in 1833, American abolitionists were able to both demonstrate the economic success of British abolition and point to the moral superiority of the British. However, in the American South, slavery was too lucrative for these arguments to effectively sway public opinion. Furthermore, the abolition of slavery in the British plantations helped convince Southerners that drastic measures might be necessary if American abolitionists gained strength in government. American slavery continued to exist and in fact increased during the first half of the nineteenth century.

In France, eighteenth-century Enlightenment philosophers such as Diderot, Montesquieu, the Abbé Raynal, Rousseau, and Voltaire argued that slavery was incompatible with the Enlightenment ideal of natural human rights. French Enlightenment thinkers were also influenced by the antislavery movements led by American Quakers such as Benezet and British abolitionists like Clarkson. There were far fewer slaves in France than in the American colonies or even in Britain, and Caribbean slave owners represented a smaller percentage among the French than among the British. Abolitionist arguments became gradually more popular without incurring significant controversy, though Caribbean planters remained vehemently opposed to emancipation. In the late eighteenth century, a number of African slaves brought to France by their masters sued for freedom in Paris courts, and many won their cases. On the eve of the French Revolution in 1788, abolitionists and enlightened thinkers founded The Society of the Friends of Blacks, which began to gradually influence public and administrative opinions on slavery. However, emancipation in France and French colonial territories only came about as a consequence of rebellion by the slaves themselves in Haiti. Despite slave rebellions in other French territories, abolition in Guyana, Martinique, and Guadeloupe did not come until 1848 as a result of the efforts of French abolitionist Victor Schœlcher.

Slavery in the Atlantic existed not only in English, American, and French territories but also in Spanish- and Portuguese-controlled areas. As in other places, the influence of Enlightenment ideals was important in developing moral arguments against slavery. Yet in these regions, the criticism of slavery was muted in comparison to the criticism in England, the United States, and France, and most of it stemmed from the colonial territories of Cuba and Brazil. Some, like José Antonio Saco from Cuba, vigorously opposed the slave trade but not slavery itself. Overall, Spanish critics of slavery were not vocal or powerful enough to become a significant factor in abolition, particularly because Spanish America had not yet emancipated itself from European control. Emancipation there was to come about as a part of the independence struggles of the nineteenth century. In Brazil, a fairly vocal abolitionist movement had developed by the last quarter of the nineteenth century, by which time most other regions had already abolished slavery. Thus, in Spanish America and Brazil, emancipationist ideas were less important than other factors in achieving the abolition of slavery.

Slaves themselves, of course, did not need to be convinced that slavery was wrong. They saw and experienced its violence and atrocities first hand, and their feelings about slavery were repeatedly evidenced by their statements about it and their resistance to it in both rebellion and daily life. Slaves throughout the Atlantic also responded to and developed ideological critiques of slavery. During the American, French, and Haitian Revolutions, slaves embraced the premise of liberty and justice but criticized slavery as well as the duplicity of regimes that claimed to offer freedom but then restricted it to a few. Among others, Toussaint L'Ouverture, the first major leader to emerge in the Haitian Revolution, was well read in the works of French Enlightenment philosophers. Slaves also took on religious ideologies that supported the spiritual equality of all humans, as can be seen in the importance of evangelical Christianity in the revolt of Nat Turner in Virginia in 1831, the role of Vodou priest Boukman in rousing the Haitian revolutionaries, and the role of Islam in the Malê Revolt in Bahia in Brazil in 1835. In Haiti, political ideologies from Africa in support of republican government were influential as well. The former soldiers from the losing side of the civil war in Kongo, who had previously fought for a more democratic form of government, became crucial in the struggle of the Haitian Revolution.

Economic causes

Economic arguments particularly resonated with financial and industrial elites. Despite pressure from abolitionists, the British government was reluctant at first to listen to exclusively moral arguments. For politicians, entrepreneurs, and businessmen, one of the most compelling lines of reasoning against slavery was economic. Economic ideologies were undergoing a tremendous change during the eighteenth century, particularly in Britain and the Northern United States, where the Industrial Revolution was in full gear by the early nineteenth century. These regions, as well as parts of France, were experiencing rapid industrial growth and increases in prosperity during the early nineteenth century, which their governments and their societies ascribed to diligence, hard work, and efficiency. Industrial wage labor – factory work – was increasingly seen as the path to national prosperity. Furthermore, in line with the theories of economic theorist Adam Smith, entrepreneurs and industrialists believed that free trade and an unregulated economy were necessary for prosperity. Slavery was seen as economically unsound within this mode of production, which required industrialists and entrepreneurs to rapidly innovate, including the rapid hiring and firing of laborers as well as their relocation, and also required a labor force that would have an incentive – retaining their jobs – to keep valuable industrial machinery running smoothly. They also believed that slavery was an old-fashioned and inefficient system and were committed to a system of free labor.

Adam Smith famously wrote "The experience of all and nations . . . demonstrates that the work done by slaves, though it appears to cost only their maintenance, is in the end the dearest [i.e., the most expensive] of any" because "a person who can acquire no property can have no other interest but . . . to labour as little as possible."[1] This sentiment was echoed by abolitionists such as Olaudah Equiano, believing that it would persuade those who were not convinced by moral arguments against slavery.[2] Smith's argument had an ideological component and was also based on real trends. Thus, on one hand, slavery did not fit well into economic ideologies such as capitalism, and in fact it was diminishing in most areas. On the other hand, it continued to produce tremendous profits – but only in areas where plantation economies still existed, especially the Caribbean islands, the American South, and Brazil.

While such economic arguments resonated in the Northern United States and Britain, where investments in slavery were relatively indirect and where most of the population was not personally involved in slavery, these arguments did not convince political leaders in regions with plantation-based economies where slavery still produced a significant proportion of economic wealth. Even in industrialized regions that depended on wage labor, it took some time for industrialists to reject slavery because they invested in it and profited from it, buying and selling cotton, sugar products, shackles, slave clothing, and the like. Thus, initially they shared an interest with the plantation regions in the perpetuation of slavery. However, as they became increasingly convinced that it was an uneconomical system, they turned against it. Economically based antislavery arguments were powerful incentives, especially in the British Parliament for politicians who were not swayed by appeals focused on the issue of morality alone. Thus, in the end, as historian Eric Williams wrote, the same "vested interests which had been built up by the slave system now turned and destroyed that system."[3]

In addition to the growth of capitalist economic theory, there was a further economic pressure on slave-owning societies. After the British outlawed the slave trade, they went a step further than other nations and made a sustained effort to prevent other regions from engaging in the trade. In addition to diplomatic and financial pressures, the Royal Navy sent patrols to seize ships engaged in the slave trade in both Africa and the Americas. Captured slavers were arrested, their ships were seized, and slaves were released. These efforts were greatly increased after 1833 when the British banned slavery outright. The British were successful in diminishing the trade near the British colony of Sierra Leone and in putting increasing pressure on slavers in general, but many slave traders moved along the coast to less well-guarded regions, and British ships continued to be major participants in illegal slaving until the 1860s. Nonetheless, Royal Navy squadrons made the slave trade much more dangerous and expensive than it would have been otherwise and freed about 150,000 slaves, approximately half of the numbers crossing the Atlantic in the mid-nineteenth century.

Historians have suggested a number of reasons to explain the efforts of the British to end the trade. During the first decade of the nineteenth century, the British still owned most of the slaves in the Caribbean, and thwarting the trade in African slaves would have safeguarded British economic control over the Caribbean sugar trade. After the British abolished slavery in their own Caribbean colonies, the slave economies of Cuba and Brazil in particular offered competition to British colonial production of sugar products. In addition to these economic concerns, moral concern over slavery still remained strong in Britain in this era.

Capitalism played a lesser role in the emancipation of slaves from other regions. In France and the main French locus of slavery, Saint-Domingue, slavery ended during the first decade of the nineteenth century before capitalist ideologies were fully entrenched. In Spanish and Portuguese regions, on the other hand, capitalism lagged behind and did not offer competition to slavery, which was still generating considerable income for Spanish and Brazilian elites. Nonetheless, economic arguments eventually became an effective force for abolitionists, who argued that the increasing decline of Latin American economies was caused by adhering to an antiquated mode of economic production, including slavery.

Slave revolts

The third crucial factor in ending slavery was increasing resistance from the slaves themselves in all regions where slavery existed. Slave revolts had been occurring regularly since the origins of slavery, and even small-scale revolts were a constant source of dread for slave owners.

The Haitian Revolution, previously discussed as one of the many revolutions that occurred in the Atlantic from the sixteenth to the nineteenth centuries, was also a massive slave revolt that resulted in the first independent nation that completely abolished slavery and the formation of the second independent nation in the Americas, one that was governed by former slaves. Yet although the Haitian Revolution represented the only fully successful slave revolt, it was one of many. Its importance stretched far beyond the victory of the slaves of Haiti. Because of its success in 1804, the revolution deeply frightened Atlantic societies that owned slaves but also motivated and inspired slaves to revolt around the Atlantic world, and thereafter slave revolts began increasing in size and frequency. For example, in the 1835

Malê Revolt in Bahia, Brazil, a revolt led by Muslim slaves, participants carried pendants depicting Jean-Jacques Dessalines, the first Haitian president. Concurrently, slave owners were terrified by the implications of the Haitian Revolution. French colonists from the former Saint-Domingue fled to U.S. shores as refugees, bringing tales to frighten American slave owners. In the United States, Southern states suspended the slave trade until 1803, fearing to bring the African-born to American shores. Governments on both sides of the Atlantic responded by ensuring that the new Haitian state was politically isolated for a century. Haiti was forced to pay reparations to France for its loss of property – the former Haitian slaves and territory. These factors contributed significantly to Haiti's subsequent downward economic and political spiral. In the meantime, slavery actually increased in the American South, Cuba, Puerto Rico, and Brazil, as slave-owning societies responded to the continuing demand for slave-produced goods that were no longer available from Haiti, which had been the most productive sugar colony in the Caribbean.

Yet from the beginning of Atlantic slavery, slaves had organized both small- and large-scale conspiracies and revolts intending to escape from slavery and sometimes to seek revenge on their masters. As early as 1675, there was a major slave rebellion in Barbados involving hundreds of slaves, and another major revolt occurred there in 1692. In 1733, a slave insurrection temporarily took control over the island of Saint John; in 1760, hundreds of slaves rose up in Tacky's Rebellion in Jamaica. In 1816, there was a major rebellion in Barbados involving 20,000 slaves. There were also large-scale revolts in Demerara in Guyana in 1823 and Jamaica in 1831–2. In addition to the Malê Revolt, there were almost annual revolts in Bahia and Cuba during the 1820s and 1830s. In the United States, there were a number of slave rebellions, including a revolt involving about 100 slaves in New York City in 1712 and the Stono Rebellion of about 100 slaves in South Carolina in 1739. In 1741, rumors of an insurrection of slaves and Irish servants in New York City led to over 100 arrests and many executions, even though the plot was never definitively shown to be true. Thousands of slaves planned to rebel in 1800 in Virginia, but they were discovered before they were able to begin. There was a rebellion in 1811 in Louisiana of about 500 slaves and another planned revolt led by Denmark Vesey in South Carolina in 1822 that involved hundreds of slaves. In 1831, the mystic Nat Turner led about 100 slaves in a rebellion in Virginia; in the aftermath, hundreds of slaves were killed by Southern militias in a frenzy of retaliation. In 1839, in a widely publicized incident, the Spanish ship *La Amistad* sailed into New York Harbor after the Africans aboard overcame the crew. In 1859, just before the American Civil War, white abolitionist John Brown led a small group in seizing a U.S. arsenal, intending to initiate a slave revolt. In addition to those mentioned herein, there were many other slave revolts throughout the Atlantic world.

Many of these revolts shared considerable similarity: they involved tightly organized plots, thousands of sympathizers, spiritually inspired leaders, and an awareness of other slave rebellions or, in some cases, parallel revolutionary developments in Europe. In the British Caribbean, they often received support from British missionaries. They usually broke out without warning to slave owners, though some were betrayed before they were under way. Most did not result in large-scale violence toward whites (though there were exceptions), but all were met with extremely severe retaliation from the local government, involving torture and exceptionally brutal executions such as the burning and dismemberment of rebellious slaves. Violent punishments reflected the fears of slave owners, but governments in slave societies also deliberately used terror in an attempt to prevent future revolts in populations where slaves outnumbered free people. Nonetheless, rebellions against slavery continued.

Even though most of these revolts were eventually quelled, they helped convince Atlantic societies that slaves would continue to resist their enslavement, thereby fatally weakening the slave system itself. These revolts directly contradicted the rhetoric of slave owners and entrepreneurs investing in the slave system who contended that slavery was a natural or historically sanctified economic system or that slaves were content with their situations. Some slave owners tried to argue that slaves were content to be slaves but that they had been stirred up into rebellion by agitators such as missionaries. Yet abolitionists such as firebrand William Lloyd Garrison criticized these views. Garrison wrote in his Boston paper, *The Liberator*:

> The slaves need no incentives at our hands. They will find them in their stripes, in their emaciated bodies, in their ceaseless toil, in their ignorant minds, in every field, in every valley, on every hill top and mountain, wherever you and your father have fought for liberty – in your speeches, your conversations, your celebrations, your pamphlets, your newspapers – voices in the air, sounds from across the ocean, invitations to resistance, above, below, around them.

Likewise, the revolutionary leader Toussaint L'Ouverture wrote to the French government that if the Haitian rebels "had a thousand lives, they would sacrifice them all rather than to be forced into slavery again."[4] Garrison, like other abolitionists from the United States, Britain, France, and Spanish territories, repeatedly contended that violence was inevitable if slavery continued, writing "red-handed Slaughter his revenge shall feed."[5]

Slave rebellions played a significant role in the ending of slavery, even when they were not successful. In the 1831–2 Jamaican slave rebellion, although the British government eventually reestablished control, 60,000 slaves – about one fifth of the island's slave population – had rebelled, resulting in significant violence and economic destruction. The words of historian Eric Williams again characterize the transition expressively: "in 1833, therefore, the alternatives were clear: emancipation from above or emancipation from below."[6] It had become clear that slave societies had a choice between an inevitable revolution, as had happened in Haiti, where slaves took over a society and its economic assets, or preemptively abolishing slavery themselves. Thus, in the aftermath of the Jamaican rebellion, the British Parliament passed the 1833 law banning slavery, which went into effect the following year.

Maroons

In addition to overt slave rebellions, fugitive slave societies were increasing throughout the Atlantic. In the United States, fugitive slaves often fled to Canada, the U.S. North, or Native American groups, who would shelter them in the South. In Brazil, Surinam, and the Caribbean, however, where there were fewer available borders to flee to, fugitive slaves, called maroons, created their own communities, which were called *quilombos* in Brazil. Such fugitives founded towns – closely guarded and self-sustaining communities that tried to avoid capture or even notice by colonial societies. Palmares, the largest quilombo in Brazil, survived through most of the seventeenth century with a population of between 10,000 and 20,000 people. During the nineteenth century, maroon communities began increasing in numbers and strength. In Jamaica, two wars fought by maroon communities from 1729 to 1739 and from 1795 to 1796 led to treaties in which the British authorities agreed to cede part of Jamaica to maroons. To this day, maroon leaders such as Granny Nanny and Cudjoe are national heroes in Jamaica. Surinam maroons won similar victories. Although maroons did not fight to end slavery as such, in taking control over their own territory and establishing their own freedom and autonomy, they were also rejecting slavery. Their success in resisting the authorities and in carving out their own sphere of influence also suggested the possibility of more wide-ranging revolutions in the slaveholding world.

The American Civil War

Although slavery was abolished by the British in the 1830s, slavery still existed in other parts of the Atlantic. By the mid-nineteenth century, slavery was withering away on its own in non-plantation regions. The economic arguments of the capitalists were somewhat correct – slavery was an inefficient mode of production in comparison with wage labor. However, slavery was actually increasing in three areas, all plantation zones – Brazil and Cuba, which produced sugar, and the American South. Not only was the number of acres being farmed increasing rapidly, but even though the British were vigorously fighting the slave trade in Africa, increasing numbers of ships were evading British cruisers and bringing new slaves to the western side of the Atlantic.

Unlike Britain, where the combination of moral and economic arguments and slave revolts convinced Parliament to ban slavery, in the United States, the abolition of slavery came only after the contradictions created when the American republic was founded resulted in a bitter civil war. There were many abolitionists in the Northern United States who were especially swayed by moral arguments against slavery, but their perspective did not have much resonance in the South, where slavery had become the economic mainstay. Southerners became even more entrenched in their positions in response to what they had seen happen in the British and French Caribbean, where distant national governments had banned slavery over the objections of slave owners in plantation regions. Southern planters were much more influential in the U.S. Congress than Caribbean plantation owners had been in the British Parliament, and the Southerners effectively prevented legal measures intended to diminish slavery from succeeding.

The U.S. Civil War was eventually fought between slaveholding states and non-slaveholding states. The original issue was the addition of free states in the west to the American union, because the slaveholding South feared that slave states would eventually be outnumbered and then outvoted in Congress and that slavery would be abolished. A series of political negotiations on the addition of new states to the union, such as the 1820 Missouri Compromise, had prevented the outbreak of war for a time, but eventually it became apparent that non-slaveholding states and their populations would eventually outnumber slaveholding regions. This led the South to secede in order to protect slavery, which then moved the North to oppose the Southern Confederacy on the principle that the Confederacy had no right to secede from the union.

Like all civil wars, this war was extraordinary bloody and vicious. The North ultimately won in the end because it had adapted to the new capitalist and industrial economy better than the South. It was able to produce all of its own munitions and equipment and also had a much larger population available for enlistment. Meanwhile, a large percentage of the Southern population was enslaved and thus hostile to the Southern war effort. The Confederacy had little industry and had to import what it needed. The basis of the Southern economy was trade in raw materials. Its greatest purchaser was Britain, who used Southern cotton in its new industrial textile factories. The South had initially hoped that Britain would support them in the conflict. However, the British had little desire to engage militarily with the North, and when Northern ships blockaded Southern ports, the British turned to their own new colonial sources for cotton – India and Egypt. By the end of the war, the defeated South had exhausted its resources. Many thousands of slaves had fled to Northern troops (see Figure 16.2), especially after President Abraham Lincoln's Emancipation Proclamation of 1863, which freed all slaves in rebellious states and which also significantly reduced European support for the South. In 1865, with the end of the war and the ratification of the Thirteenth Amendment to the U.S. Constitution,

Figure 16.2   A group of fugitive slaves at Foller's Farm in Cumberland Landing, Virginia, 14 May 1864. © The Art Archive/Alamy

slavery was abolished in the United States. Even today, descendants of former slaves continue to commemorate the date their ancestors obtained their freedom with the Emancipation Day holiday celebrated in some parts of the United States as well as in the British Caribbean. Nonetheless, the war did not fully emancipate blacks in the American South. Under the policy of Reconstruction, which lasted until 1877, the U.S. federal government made significant attempts to ensure that the rights of former slaves were acknowledged, enabling African American men to vote and hold office. However, this policy was strenuously opposed by white Southern conservatives, who promulgated discriminatory segregationist legislation after Reconstruction ended. Consequently, it became difficult or impossible for African Americans to vote or to exercise their rights in the South until the Civil Rights Movement of the twentieth century.

Emancipation in Latin America

By the mid-nineteenth century, the majority of the African slave population in Latin America was located in the Caribbean and Brazil. In most of Latin America, as elsewhere in the Atlantic, slave populations were diminishing in non-plantation regions, while the population of free blacks was increasing. Latin Americans were also more likely to acknowledge relationships or marriages between whites and blacks than in the United States, and the children of these relationships were much more likely to be freed than in North America. Furthermore, the British had redoubled their efforts to end slavery after they had abolished it in British dominions, sending an increasing number of ships to stop slave-trading expeditions in the Atlantic and forcing or paying other countries to stop the slave trade.

Typically, slavery ended in most of Latin America with the independence of the Latin American states from Spain in the early nineteenth century. A critical factor was the personal experience of Simón Bolívar, the great Liberator of South America. In 1815, while in exile, Bolívar took refuge in the new country of Haiti. As mentioned previously, Bolívar attempted to obtain support from Haitian President Alexandre Pétion for his struggle to liberate South America from Spain. Pétion agreed to provide arms and supplies, but in return he stipulated that Bolívar emancipate slaves in any territories that he succeeded in capturing. Bolívar agreed. For him, this decision appears to have been both ideological and expedient. Bolívar had been born into a slave-owning family and raised in part by an enslaved nanny, and he does not seem to have had abolitionist sentiments prior to this time. However, he also seems to have been genuinely convinced by Pétion that slavery was wrong. At the same time, there were also practical advantages to emancipation, especially in regions that were not economically dependent on slavery, like most of South America. Agreeing to end slavery meant continued aid from the Haitians, including even troops, and it also made Bolívar aware of the military opportunities created by enlisting slaves as troops in exchange for their freedom upon completing their service. He strove to ensure that the new constitutions of South American nations included provisions for freeing slaves or for any new children born to be free. Although some of the new Latin American nations reinstated slavery when they became independent, by the late 1840s these provisions were overturned, and slavery was gone in most parts of South America. The involvement of Haiti meant that the first society to completely abolish slavery had also been a major force in the ending of slavery throughout the Americas.

Political leaders like Bolívar and Pétion could not have succeeded in convincing Latin Americans to abolish slavery without the increasing support of Latin American abolitionists. Thus, while the most important factor in the abolition of slavery in Latin America was the existence of independence movements, they occurred in a context where slavery had been abolished or was on its way out elsewhere in the Atlantic, and vocal abolitionists were gradually gaining support for their cause. For instance, slavery continued to exist in Cuba until the Ten Years' War, a failed attempt at breaking away from Spain from 1868 to 1878. Each side in this conflict feared that the other side would convince slaves to fight against them by emancipating them, so both offered slaves their freedom. Although the war was not successful in achieving Cuban freedom from Spain, which was obtained in 1898, it did result in the gradual emancipation of Cuban slaves.

Cuban emancipation meant that Brazil was the last region in the Atlantic with legal slavery. Slavery was an important aspect of the economy, as it had been in Cuba, because Brazil was a major sugar producer, but by this time it was apparent that global trends were tilted in favor of emancipation. Brazilian abolitionists were able to point to the massive Brazilian slave revolts of the nineteenth century, while the British, one of the major purchasers of Brazilian sugar, continued to press for emancipation. Political leaders became particularly worried about slave revolts during Brazil's wars with neighboring regions in 1865–70. By 1871, the Brazilian government passed the first of several gradual emancipation laws; the 1871 law mandated free birth for all subsequently born children, and later laws progressively moved the legal boundaries of slavery further south. Northern slave owners often tried to subvert the intent of such laws by selling their slaves to southern plantations just ahead of legal emancipation. Finally, in 1888, 1.2 million slaves were freed by the Golden Law – thus ending slavery in the Atlantic.

Timeline: abolition

1661 Barbados slave code

1675 Slave rebellion in Barbados

1685 *Code Noir* decreed by French Crown

1692 Slave rebellion in Barbados

1712 New York Slave Revolt

1733 Slave rebellion in Saint John

1739 Stono Rebellion in South Carolina

1760 Tacky's Rebellion in Jamaica

1772 *Somersett's Case* makes slavery illegal in England

1777 Emancipations begin in the Northern U.S. states

1781 *Zong* incident

1789 Olaudah Equiano's autobiography published

1791–1804 Haitian Revolution

1794 France abolishes slavery

1800 Gabriel Prosser rebellion planned in Virginia

1802 France reestablishes slavery in its colonies

1807 British ban slave trade

1808 United States bans slave trade

1811 German Coast Uprising, Louisiana

1811 Abolition begins in Spanish territories in the New World and in European countries

1815 Simón Bolívar negotiates abolition with Alexandre Pétion

1816 Bussa Rebellion in Barbados

1822 Denmark Vesey rebellion planned in South Carolina

1823 Demerara slave revolt in Guyana

1831 Mary Prince's autobiography published

1831 Nat Turner's rebellion in Virginia

1831–2 Great Jamaican Slave Revolt

1833 British ban slavery in the British Empire in the Atlantic

1835 Malê Revolt in Bahia, Brazil

1841 *United States v. The Amistad*

1845 Frederick Douglass' autobiography published

1852 Harriet Beecher Stowe publishes *Uncle Tom's Cabin*

1857 *Dred Scott v. Sandford*

1859 John Brown raid on Harpers Ferry

1861 Harriet Jacobs' autobiography published

1861–5 American Civil War

1863 Emancipation Proclamation

1867 Slavery abolished in Spain

1868–78 Ten Years' War in Cuba initiates the ending of slavery in Cuba

1873 Slavery abolished in Puerto Rico (then a Spanish colony)

1888 Golden Law of Brazil ends slavery in the Atlantic

Notes

1 Adam Smith, *An Inquiry into the Nature and Causes of the Wealth of Nations*, 9th Ed. (London: W. Strahan and T. Cadell, 1799), 88. This was first published in 1776.

2 Olaudah Equiano, *The Interesting Narrative of the Life of Olaudah Equiano* (London: T. Wilkins, 1789).
3 Eric Williams, *Capitalism and Slavery* (Chapel Hill: University of North Carolina Press, 1944), 136.
4 Toussaint L'Ouverture, Letter to the Directory, 5 November, 1797, in *The Haitian Revolution*, Nick Nesbitt, ed. (New York: Verso, 2008), 35.
5 William Lloyd Garrison, *Liberator*, September 3, 1831, in *William Lloyd Garrison and the Fight Against Slavery: Selections from the Liberator*, William E. Cain, ed. (Boston: Bedford, 1994), 82.
6 Eric Williams, 208.

Part V
The paradox of modernity

17 Industrialization

In tandem with the intellectual and cultural changes of the Enlightenment, the late eighteenth century saw the beginning of the incredible transformation in technology that is commonly called the Industrial Revolution. Its roots lay in the new scientific discoveries and attitudes of the previous century. The first signs of change appeared in Britain, the center of wealth and power, from which it spread rapidly to Canada, the United States, and Western Europe and thence to the rest of the world. Although industrialization was – and is – a global transformation, its spread has also been uneven. Industrialization developed along routes accessible to transport or energy sources. England, the first country to industrialize, was an ideal zone not only because of its economic and political dominance, but also because it contains significant coal deposits which are also located near navigable waterways. In every region, industrial growth was regionally located; in the United States, for example, the Northern states industrialized, while the South remained largely rural and dependent on the export of raw agricultural products.

The most fundamental change of the Industrial Revolution was in the usage of energy; in previous centuries, the main source of productive energy had been animal and human, with increasing use of water and wind power. However, in the Industrial Revolution, first steam, then mineral sources such as coal, oil, gas and, finally, electricity were used as sources of power, setting off a continuous wave of development that continued into the twentieth century and beyond. The technological developments of the Industrial Revolution occurred gradually, but there were a few key developments, among them Lewis Paul and John Wyatt's patent for the first mechanized cotton-spinning apparatus in 1738 and James Watt's redesign of the steam engine in the 1770s so that it could run a machine effectively. In the eighteenth and nineteenth centuries, the new power sources were revolutionary because they were far more productive and efficient than previous sources, allowing mechanized production of goods, initially textiles. Along with factories, the Industrial Revolution brought rapid long-distance transportation, including rail lines and steamships, and the first form of instant communication, the telegraph (see Figure 17.1).

The Industrial Revolution occurred in part because it also overlapped with other major societal changes in demography and agriculture – it is sometimes termed the "Triple Revolution" for that reason. At first, England and then the rest of northern Europe saw a growth of population in the eighteenth century that was caused by environmental factors – an end to what has been termed the "mini Ice Age" of the previous century which allowed for more productive agriculture – and more clearly human-induced changes, such as an end to the major wars of the seventeenth century and a decline in death rates caused by better sanitation, more food, and the advent of smallpox inoculation. "Inoculation" was an earlier form of smallpox prevention using the introduction of weakened smallpox virus and adopted beginning in the early eighteenth century in England, as opposed to "vaccination" with the cowpox virus, which was also developed in England at the end of the eighteenth century. These changes also seem to have led to increases in the birth rate, which rose and then began to decrease again at the end of the eighteenth century with greater access to birth control and education for women. Demographic change was supported by concurrent agricultural changes that enormously increased agrarian productivity, allowing more food to be produced on the land and also bringing more land under production. These included improvements in crop rotation, fertilizer, the use of new crops such as potatoes and sugar beets, and the development of more productive crops and animal breeds. Fewer people were needed to work the land, while there was more food available to sustain the growth of large populations and enable them to cluster in expanding cities. This created two spurs for industrialization: the rising incomes of some portions

Figure 17.1 Telegraph chart commemorating the first telegraph cable laid across the Atlantic Ocean by H.H. Lloyd & Company, 1858. Map reproduction courtesy of the Norman B. Leventhal Map Center at the Boston Public Library.

of the population and the increasing population in general created new purchasers of cheap industrial products, while they also pushed people off the land and created a population of laborers needed to work in the new industrial factories.

These developments transformed economic relationships in modern society. Industrialization was closely tied to capitalism as an economic theory that emphasized efficiency, productivity, and the rationally managed flow of capital. On one hand, the tremendous productive capacity of industrialization lowered prices and enormously magnified the output of manufactured products, creating great fortunes for businessmen and entrepreneurs. It raised living conditions for many through expanded opportunities for profit and growth. Goods that had once been luxuries, such as ceramic or glass dishware, household adornments, extra clothing, and books, were now available to many. Industrialization thus supported the continued growth of the middle class, which became a substantial portion of the population of industrialized countries.

On the other hand, in line with capitalism's disregard for social relationships or communal values, industrialization created an impoverished working class that labored in exploitative workplaces and subsisted on inadequate wages while living under wretched conditions. This working class had been detached from the traditional economy of family- and village-based livelihoods of the past to become components in a vast industrial machine. Unrestrained capitalism dictated the extraction of the greatest amount of labor at the lowest cost, leading to extreme poverty and abusive relationships between workers and owners that included low wages, long hours, hazardous conditions, child labor, and lack of redress for mistreatment. Indeed, most urban workers were worse off than their ancestors had been. Children in particular were expected to work long hours under dangerous conditions and did not receive schooling. They were seen as desirable employees by industrialists because they could be paid a small percentage of an adult male's wage. Women, too, were paid much less than men.

The industrial work conditions of the nineteenth century were the preconditions for the radical movements of the nineteenth and early twentieth centuries, including both socialism and labor movements, which critiqued the uncontrolled capitalism of the nineteenth century and emphasized social equality as the precondition for modern society. Discontent from the increasing inequality of modern society led to new political tactics – workers' unions and strike actions – and growing efforts by middle-class reformers. Workers demanded better wages and working conditions, while reformers were galvanized by investigations of working conditions that exposed severe abuses, such as the 1832 Sadler Report on child labor in Britain or the 1842 Parliamentary Commission on child labor in the mines. Nonetheless, it took a long time before these demands were met, as social norms adjusted slowly. Among the earliest piece of legislation was the 1819 Cotton Mills and Factory Act in Britain, which was seen as a progressive piece of legislation at the time, although it only mandated that child workers had to be at least nine years old and could not work longer than twelve-hour days. However, these conditions were gradually alleviated in the industrial West during the nineteenth and early twentieth centuries.

The social changes incurred by industrialization continued to present unexpected challenges and consequences. As workers in the West increasingly began to question the inequality of their societies, their menial and unregulated work was increasingly transferred out of Western countries to regions with fewer protections for workers, a trend that continues today. Perhaps ironically, the new industrial capitalist system was also a factor in the disappearance of slavery, as the productivity of the wage relationship was manifestly greater than that of slave labor. It was likewise instrumental in the ending of serfdom in eastern Europe, which occurred during the nineteenth century.

Industrialization helped Western societies continue in the trajectory of global dominance begun by their assumption of power over the wealth of the Atlantic, which was then invested in the increasingly productive manufacturing industry and in other industrial processes during the nineteenth century. Industrial strength became a key component of the rise of American power after the American Civil War. In addition to the wealth deriving from Atlantic sources, the United States and Europe were fortunate to possess abundant supplies of coal, which was a critical source of power during the Industrial Revolution. Another unanticipated consequence of industrialization was the emergence of pollution and environmental damage particularly associated with the combustion of oil and coal, another legacy that contemporary societies still struggle with today.

The Industrial Revolution increased the speed of globalization, tying world societies and international markets together in unprecedented ways. For example, as whale oil came into demand for lamp lighting and as an industrial lubricant on both sides of the Atlantic, whaling off the East Coast of the United States became one of the most lucrative global industries. As Atlantic whale populations were depleted, whalers turned to the Pacific, taking part in voyages of several years' duration that brought Americans in contact with South Pacific societies until industrial chemists finally developed more efficient mineral sources for oil. Similarly, the effects of Eli Whitney's invention of the cotton gin in the 1790s exemplified the global effects of industrialization. His device, intended as a labor-saving modification to the cotton cloth manufacturing process, greatly increased the potential value of cotton production and thus escalated slavery in the American South, creating strong ties between the South and Britain, which consumed the cotton in its industrial factories. As famously pointed out by nineteenth-century socialist economist Karl Marx, this relationship put thousands of Africans to work in Southern cotton fields, put thousands of Britons to work in English factories, and impoverished millions of previously independent textile makers in India. Even after the U.S. Civil War, these economies remained tied together. In response to the North's blockades of Southern ports during the war, the British were readily able to turn to their new Asian colonies in Egypt and India to supply the demand – although by this time they were obtaining raw cotton produced by menial agricultural laborers instead of finished textiles from artisan families at a higher cost as they had in previous centuries. In the meantime, the industrialization of the North enabled its victory over the largely agricultural South. Thus, capitalist relationships triumphed, while African slaves, British factory workers, and Indian cotton harvesters were linked together in supporting the success of British and American industrialists with their labor. The natural affiliation of the two industrialized giants – the U.S. North and Great Britain – emerged as the most durable connection of this era despite their occasional enmity in the past.

Industrialization was also an important foundation for colonialism, the spread of which will be discussed in greater detail in the following chapters. Technologies of the industrial era were fundamental in making colonialism possible, including the enhanced transportation and communication made possible by steamships, railways, and telegraph lines. The "All Red Line" (or web of telegraph cables that connected disparate parts of the British Empire) was seen as a crucial support for British imperial governance. Another critical development enabling colonialism was the invention of automatic weapons, particularly the Gatling gun, first utilized effectively by the North in the U.S. Civil War, and the Maxim gun, used by British colonialists in Africa and Asia. In addition, the new markets created by industrialization furnished additional incentives for colonialism. Colonizing countries aimed to control access to raw materials required for industrial processes such as rubber and palm oil (used as a lubricant) while seeking markets in which to sell manufactured goods.

Industrialization had a complex legacy. It was, in many ways, the culmination of the process begun in 1492 when Europeans first established control over the Americas. It helped create the modern world that we live in today and contributed substantially to raising the standard of living in the West and for middle classes around the globe. Yet this occurred at the cost of exploitative relationships in which urban workers realized little, if any, gain. Thus, the Industrial Revolution also ushered in an era of radicalism in which workers, socialists, and reformers challenged many of the central assumptions of capitalist society. In addition, unequal labor relationships have been recapitulated in the developing world, and they continue to cause problems globally. Finally, human-induced environmental damage, first becoming significant during the Industrial Revolution, persists as a global concern.

Timeline: industrial inventions

1589 Stocking frame – first mechanical knitter

1709 Coke used to smelt iron ore

1712 First functioning steam engine

1733 Flying shuttle – first weaving machine

1738 Mechanized cotton-spinning machine

1765 Spinning jenny – a more efficient weaving machine

1769 Water frame

1775 Efficient steam engine

1779 Spinning mule – fully automated weaving machine

1792 Gas lamp

1793 Cotton gin

1801 Steam locomotive

1803 First working steamboat

1821 Electric motor

1823 Telegraph

1824 Portland cement

1828 Hot-blast process used in smelting iron

1839 Daguerreotype – first photograph

1858 Trans-Atlantic telegraph cable

1859 Gasoline engine

1861 Gatling gun

1876 Telephone

1878 Microphone

1879 Incandescent lamp

1884 Maxim gun

1885 Automobile

1888 Radio

1892 Cinematograph

1903 Powered flight

18 Migration

A significant percentage of the industrial workers on the western side of the Atlantic were immigrants. Immigration caused significant demographic change in both North and South America during the nineteenth century. It had obviously been a factor in peopling the Americas since 1492, but the numbers of European migrants greatly increased during the nineteenth century. Taken as a whole, the nineteenth-century Atlantic experienced the largest movement of people in history, comprising tens of millions of people leaving their homelands. Perhaps the most important factor was the advent of transoceanic steamship routes, which greatly shortened the duration of voyages across the Atlantic from two months to two weeks, thus significantly reducing the risks of crossing the ocean.

Immigrants came for a multitude of reasons, both to avail themselves of the opportunities available in the Americas and to escape adverse circumstances in the lands they departed from. They came in order to take advantage of plentiful and cheap farmlands and urban work opportunities, especially in factories and construction. Rumors of easy wealth provided an incentive for many. For most Europeans, the new countries in the West were more socially fluid and more tolerant of differences in religion and class than the countries they had left behind. In addition, many fled life-threatening circumstances such as persecution, poverty, or famine or escaped from societies that denied the right of free expression. Most immigrants crossed the ocean because of a combination of such reasons.

The majority of nineteenth-century immigrants were Europeans. Europe experienced rapid demographic growth in the nineteenth century, doubling its population, and the New World helped absorb some of these extra people. Immigrants came from Britain, Ireland, eastern Europe, German-speaking regions, Italy, Portugal, Scandinavia, and Spain; there were also smaller flows of people from other parts of Europe. In addition, Asians, including Chinese, Indians, and Japanese, as well as Arabs and Armenians from the Middle East, also crossed the ocean seeking new homes in the Americas.

Immigrants spread across the Americas, but the greatest numbers went to the four biggest areas geographically: the United States, Argentina, Canada, and Brazil. Countries in the Americas that still possessed relatively low populations and high amounts of available land, like Argentina and Canada, often attempted to lure immigrants by providing incentives, especially farmland. The largest receiver of immigrants was the United States, which gained over 25 million immigrants from the mid-nineteenth century through the early twentieth century. Next was Argentina, with about 12 million immigrants; Canada gained about 1.5 million immigrants, although it lost some who entered Canadian ports but continued their travels to the United States; and Brazil received slightly over 2 million European immigrants in addition to the 2.5 million slaves brought forcibly during the nineteenth century. Immigration to the United States and Canada continued at high rates through the beginning of the twentieth century, bringing more Europeans to the Americas.

Virtually all immigrants hoped to better their economic prospects, but many, perhaps most, were also escaping bad conditions at home. Frequently, they were fleeing for their lives. Irish immigration greatly increased during the years of the Potato Famine and afterward, with 1 million leaving Ireland during the famine and another 3 million leaving in the half century thereafter. Eastern European Jews fled deadly pogroms, which greatly intensified during the nineteenth century. German socialists came to escape imprisonment and experience greater freedom of expression.

The majority of immigrants were peasants, expelled from their traditional societies as landlords consolidated land and as agriculture became more efficient, requiring fewer people. Most migrants were young men, though people of every age migrated, and there was considerable variation among groups depending on their circumstances. People who fled persecution, such as Russian Jews, were more likely to arrive with their families. Close to half of Irish immigrants were women because of the high numbers of single women in the post-famine era when peasant marriage required a couple's inheritance of a land holding.

Movement occurred in many directions during this era. A significant percentage of nineteenth-century migrants did not emigrate far from their homes – many merely moved from the countryside to the nearest city, thus promoting European industrialization, or moved within Europe – for instance, many Irish migrants went to England. Some did cross the Atlantic, but not permanently, becoming migrant laborers, such as Italian and Spanish peasant laborers who harvested crops in Europe, then traveled to South America to work there during the later harvest season and returned home by the beginning of the planting season. In addition, there was also significant immigration to Australia during this century.

Immigrants typically found that life in the New World was harder than they had expected. It took them considerable time for them to adapt and learn a foreign language. Each successive wave of immigrants experienced prejudice until the next group arrived – then the previous group often joined in with rejection of the newcomers. Despite most immigrants' belief that they would find limitless opportunity in their new land, many experienced poverty and exploitation. They often had difficulty adjusting to the expectations of the new society; frequently, it was their children who were first able to find success.

For the receiving societies, the flood of immigrants created significant change, especially in the cities, where most immigrants clustered. They provided workers for the factories, thus reinforcing industrialization and bolstering the economy, especially in the United States. Immigrants also brought dynamic productive energy to their new societies, bringing new ideas, youthful vigor, and the willingness to work hard. They transformed the societies they entered, especially in the countries with the highest rate of immigration. This was particularly true in areas where initially small populations were combined with high rates of immigrants. Around half of Argentina's population was foreign-born by the end of the nineteenth century and was mainly composed of Italians and Spaniards plus some eastern European Jews. However, it was the United States that became famous as a melting pot of the world's cultures, even though they represented a much smaller proportion of the overall population. The United States experienced both high population growth and high rates of immigration, growing from a population of 6 million to 80 million during the nineteenth century. At the same time, net national wealth and the standard of living rose to become the highest in the world. By about 1900, the United States had taken over from Britain as the world's richest nation and greatest industrial power, an attainment that was possible in large part because of the immigrants who had entered during the previous century. While immigration boosted the populations of emerging regions in the Americas, it also helped absorb the excess population growth of nineteenth-century Europe.

Asian laborers

Although most immigrants of the nineteenth century were Europeans, a substantial subset were Asians, who often had very different experiences of immigration than their European counterparts. Indentured Asian laborers, often called by the derogatory term "coolies," were brought to the Americas to replace disappearing slave labor. Most came from China or India. While many of these laborers signed indenture contracts similar to those of indentured servants in previous centuries, they were typically deceived about their conditions of work and were often kept as laborers past the official termination of their contracts. Unlike European migrants, a significant number, perhaps the majority, had been kidnapped into forced labor. Although both the Chinese government and the British government of India made some efforts to protect the workers, often their lives were similar to those of the slaves they had replaced. Chinese workers ended up in Peru, Chile, Cuba, and other parts of the Spanish Caribbean; the British Caribbean colonies; and the United States and Canada, where they comprised a considerable percentage of the laborers on the United States' first Transcontinental

Railroad and the Canadian Pacific Railway. Indians were more likely to travel voluntarily, going all over the British Empire, including into the British Caribbean islands, Trinidad and Tobago, Guyana, and the Dutch colony of Suriname. In the last three areas, people of Indian descent today make up about a quarter of the population. Both the Chinese and Indians left a significant imprint on their destinations, adding their cultural practices, religions, and life experiences to the mixture of cultures that arose in the Americas. Although they arrived under exploitative circumstances, their presence in the receiving countries gradually moved these societies toward greater tolerance and social acceptance.

19 Atlantic societies in the nineteenth century

The nineteenth century was the period in which the new countries of the western Atlantic established themselves as nations. For the first time, they began to demonstrate a political hierarchy that would continue into the twentieth century, with the nations of the Northern Hemisphere, including the United States, Canada, and Western Europe, rapidly industrializing and prospering economically. The southern countries located in Latin America, Brazil, and Africa were entering the world economy from an unequal basis and were beginning to increasingly lag behind in technology and wealth.

Expansion of the United States

During the nineteenth century, the new United States was finding its feet amid other Atlantic nations. In its early days, a number of factors seemed ready to undermine the young government, including trenchant political argument about the reach of the federal government and attempts to continue antigovernment rebellion over economic and tax grievances, as in the Whiskey Rebellion (1791–4) and Shays' Rebellion (1786–7). There were also international pressures such as the Quasi War (1798–1800), an undeclared war fought on the side of Britain against France and Spain, and the Barbary Wars (1801–5 and 1815) in which the United States resisted the North African Barbary states' practice of exacting tribute from American ships in the Mediterranean. However, the United States' victory in North Africa signaled its increasing ability to hold its own in the international sphere.

U.S. territory grew significantly with the 1802 Louisiana Purchase, which added the former eastern half of Spain's Louisiana territory, by this time owned by the French, and with the acquisition of Florida as a result of Andrew Jackson's victory against the Spanish-allied Seminoles in the First Seminole War (1817–18). Warfare also erupted in the northern portion of the Americas as Britain and the United States jostled over control of North America. The War of 1812, initiated by the United States, was the new nation's first true declaration of war as a result of building grievances over trade, border disputes with Canada, the impressment or kidnapping of American sailors to serve in the British navy, and the thwarting of U.S.

expansionism westward by British alliances with Native American groups. Native Americans fought on both sides, with the Creeks' Red Sticks movement and Tecumseh's Shawnee allied with the British, while other factions of Creeks and Cherokees supported the Americans. As in the American Revolutionary War, the British offered sanctuary to thousands of fleeing American slaves who were manumitted and later resettled in Canada.

The Treaty of Ghent of 1814 ended the war at a high point for the Americans, in part because the British had been more invested in the concurrent Napoleonic Wars on the European Continent, which threatened the island of Britain more directly. There was little change in political relationships between the opponents, but the war solidified long-standing societal trends. Canada remained British, but nationalism grew on both sides of the border. For Native Americans, the outcome of the war was an enormous loss of Southern land previously controlled by the Creeks. The United States and Britain remained political allies and major trading partners, while Britain, after its victory in the Napoleonic Wars, was left on the path to becoming the biggest world power, consolidating its victories over colonial territories in Asia, Africa, the Mediterranean, and the Atlantic, ceded by Spain, the Netherlands, and France.

A further war which helped establish the young United States was the Mexican-American War (1846–8), which was fought over control of the territories southwest of the first twenty-eight U.S. states. American forces rapidly incorporated the remainder of what is now the American West, including Arizona, California, New Mexico, and Texas, as well as other states, enormously expanding the territory controlled by the United States. This was to intrude on some conflicts of the later nineteenth century, setting the stage for disputes about the extension of slavery into the newly acquired territories, enabling the philosophy of Manifest Destiny, and setting in motion the increasing encroachment of American settlers into lands that had been mainly occupied by Native Americans. In the Spanish-American War in 1898 between Spain and the United States, the United States took over control of Guam, the Philippines, Puerto Rico, and Cuba, though the latter remained nominally independent.

By the end of the nineteenth century, the United States was rapidly becoming a major world power. It had become a leader in industrialization, a crucial factor in its victory of the Northern United States over the South in the U.S. Civil War. After the war, there was a period of economic prosperity and growth, often called the Gilded Age, bolstered by economic benefits stemming from expansion into the western territories; the surge of immigrants from Europe; and, perhaps most importantly, the dynamic growth of technology, transportation, and communication. The increasing presence of the United States in world affairs paralleled its economic power. Nonetheless, significant inequality continued to exist between rich and poor, the middle class and workers, blacks and whites, and men and women. This period also saw an intensification of attempts by underprivileged groups to obtain political and social equality.

Canada

During the first half of the nineteenth century, Canada was a British colony, having been acquired from France during the Seven Years' War. Due to the immigration of almost a million people from Britain and Ireland during the Great Migration in the first half of the century, the majority of the settlers were English-speaking by mid-century. Canada's history was often tied to that of its more populous neighbor, United States. During the War of 1812, the British military barely managed to thwart a planned U.S. invasion of southern Canada, which was perceived to be sheltering Native American groups attacking American frontier settlements. In the meantime, Canadians, like Americans before them, increasingly began to develop a sense of settler identity that translated into a desire for political autonomy, culminating in the unsuccessful Rebellions of 1837.

Canada, like the other white settler colonies of the British Empire, began a path to political autonomy during the nineteenth century, with individual provinces first unified and given partial political autonomy beginning in the 1840s. By 1867, Canada was almost entirely self-governing, with Australia soon to follow. This sharply contrasts with the British government's determination to cling to control over colonies with populations composed mainly of indigenous peoples, like India or its African possessions. Ireland's independence, somewhere between these two poles, was repeatedly debated in the British Parliament during the late nineteenth century, with increasing support for Irish independence. However, a Home Rule bill was not passed in Parliament until the early twentieth century, and in the end, Ireland only achieved independence (and partition) as a result of the Irish War of Independence (1919–21).

The challenge of welding together a multicultural society that included French and English setters, Native Americans, Métis peoples, Afro-Canadians, and Asian and European immigrants was navigated somewhat better than in the United States, in part because Canadian slavery, never very extensive, was ended with the 1833 ending of slavery in the British Empire and also because peoples of Native American descent made up a significantly larger portion of the population. Nonetheless, Canada was faced with an early crisis in the rebellions of the Métis peoples in Saskatchewan and Manitoba (1869–70 and 1885). The country was also challenged by boundary disputes with the United States; conflicts over French, English, and First Nation identity; and an 1896 gold rush. The federation of Canadian provinces continued throughout the early twentieth century.

Latin America after independence

Latin America lagged behind Canada, Europe, and the United States but experienced many of the same trends that occurred in northern America and Europe. However, a significantly different aspect was continuing and severe social inequality that was not redressed by the revolutions of the early nineteenth century. Although elites continued to exercise significant amounts of power all over the world, this pattern was much more marked in Latin America than elsewhere in the Western world, in the United States, Canada, and Western Europe, leaving the majority of people in South America poor and uneducated. As elsewhere, elites were more likely to be white, while the poor and disenfranchised were often of African, Native American or, from the nineteenth century, Asian backgrounds.

In part, this pattern occurred because of the trajectory of independence movements. The Spanish monarchy had seen itself as the overlord of Native Americans as well as of transplanted Spaniards, and although it had allowed many depredations against Amerindians, it had also expressed tolerance toward them and had made some efforts to acknowledge their rights. Much as in the American Revolution, the newly formed governments composed of creole elites believed themselves to be fighting against overseas domination and establishing democracy, as well as wiping away the economic protectionism of Spain with modern capitalism and individualism. Yet they also continued to accept racist values that held contempt for blacks and natives but which were now unmitigated by the Spanish government's sense of benevolent patronage. Much as in the new United States, the new countries aimed to assert control over territories that were under native control, but Latin America as a whole also possessed a larger Amerindian population. One of the most vicious of these colonial wars was Argentina's conquest of the fertile Patagonian plains in the late 1870s, which entailed the annihilation of the Indian tribes living in the region. Although there remained some native groups like the Maya in the Yucatán who resisted colonialist policies or urban activists who promoted greater equality, their voices were mostly drowned out in their societies. By the beginning of the twentieth century, most of Latin America possessed societies in which mainly white elites controlled politics with little attention paid to the interests and needs of an impoverished non-white underclass. Democracy was often adhered to more in theory than in practice, and poverty, lack of education, discrimination, and lack of Spanish-language skills often kept indigenous groups from exercising their rights. However, at the same time in some areas such as Mexico, increasing pride in mestizo heritage began to develop in the early twentieth century.

Latin America's economy was also less well developed as it entered the industrial age. Unlike Canada, Europe, and the United States, which had developed powerful industrial and commercial sectors, the economies of Latin American states focused on exchanging raw materials for industrially manufactured products. In some cases, such exports were considerable, and trade did generate wealth, but primarily for economic elites. Nonetheless, urban growth and modern infrastructure did develop in Latin America, including steamships, railroads, telegraphs, factories, and electricity. However, the development of industrial infrastructure came at a price:

Latin American countries required cash investments, imported materials, and foreign experts, especially from Britain and the United States, resulting in significant debts and foreign control over considerable amounts of Latin American land, businesses, and capital.

Latin America was also subject to informal colonialism by the United States, justified by the Monroe Doctrine of 1823, named for President James Monroe, who was in office from 1817 to 1825. The initial guiding principle was that the United States would act to block political or economic interference in the Americas; the doctrine was intended to prevent European colonization efforts in the wake of Latin American independence movements. As the United States gained military strength, it began to increasingly enforce this policy, and it evolved into a rationalization for U.S. interventions in Latin America in the former's own interests. It also became a justification for the annexation of the western territories and for expansionist clashes such as the Mexican-American War (1846–8). It was also invoked in the Spanish-American War in 1898 between Spain and the United States, which developed out of American intervention in the Cuban War of Independence. The Monroe Doctrine was also used to justify neocolonialist protectionist policies that benefited American corporations in Latin America beginning from the early twentieth century. The United States continued to intervene in Latin American affairs during the twentieth century, although that is mainly beyond the scope of this book; one of the most widely cited examples is U.S. support for Panama's secession from Colombia in 1903, subsequently followed in 1904 with the commencement of U.S.-sponsored construction work on the Panama Canal.

Africa and the end of the slave trade

The slave trade continued in the Atlantic until the late 1860s, while internal slavery persisted longer in some areas. Even after the slave trade ended, its damaging effects still endured, with localities that had formerly participated in the trade left politically unstable, corrupt, and underdeveloped. While African institutions might have recovered on their own over time, they were not given the opportunity. Within a generation, African societies were confronted with colonialism, an onslaught that they were unable to stem. In addition to subjecting Africans to oppressive regimes designed to support the interests of European colonizers, colonization stifled African modernization and innovation.

Both before and after the last recorded slave ship voyages in 1866, European explorers, some of them missionaries, had been coming to Africa in small numbers. At first they did not dominate or subjugate Africans. Instead, they cooperated with African authorities as they mapped the African continent, noting geographical features, especially rivers, and trade opportunities, as well as weak states that could be manipulated. Initially, such trips were very risky because of the dangers of malaria, until the use of quinine, derived from Peruvian cinchona bark, enabled Europeans to penetrate the interior safely.

In 1884, very little of Africa was under European control, though there was considerable contact between coastal regions and Europeans and Americans. The Back-to-Africa Movement had resulted in settlements of repatriated slaves, like the British colony of Sierra Leone with its capital of Freetown, established in 1787. Freetown was founded by a population of African Americans who had fled to the British during the American Revolution and had then come to Africa via Canada. Colonies of former slaves also included the French colony of Libreville, which was founded in Gabon by slaves freed from a Brazilian ship in 1848, and Liberia, which was colonized by repatriated former U.S. slaves in 1820; the latter declared independence in 1847. In addition, Europeans had established footholds in a few areas along the western shores of Africa, such as the small long-standing Portuguese settlements along the Angolan and Congolese coasts. At the end of the eighteenth century, Egypt was occupied by France and then Britain but had become semi-autonomous again by mid-century. Around the same time, the British took control over most of the former Dutch possession of Cape Colony in South Africa. The French had gradually encroached on northern Africa through the nineteenth century, beginning with the conquest of Algiers in 1830. However, the majority of interactions between Europeans and Africans consisted of legitimate trade sanctioned by African states.

20 Continued colonialism

Nineteenth-century colonialism was essentially a continuation of the patterns of behavior that had been manifested in the Americas since 1492. By the nineteenth century, as northern European states took the place of Spain as colonizing empires, few territories remained available in the western Atlantic. Nineteenth-century colonialism in Latin America, mainly the purview of the United States under the terms of the Monroe Doctrine, primarily remained informal, operating through political and economic influence and occasional military intervention rather than direct control, but colonialism was more openly expressed in other parts of the world. Newly imperial states thus turned to Africa in the eastern Atlantic and Asia when they sought to consolidate empires. In Asia and Africa, imperial conquest was made possible by the new technologies of the industrial age – the telegraph, steamship, and Maxim gun, as well as by the new wealth produced by industrialization. With these means, the conquest of Africa was rapid, mainly completed in the fifteen years from 1885 to 1900, unlike imperialism in Asia, which occurred more gradually as the Portuguese, English, Dutch, Russians, and French slowly extended control over southeastern and northern regions. The United States also stepped in, taking over control of the Philippines from Spain. During the nineteenth century, Europeans apportioned and took possession of previously uncolonized regions of the world. By the turn of the century, European countries, especially Britain and France, dominated much of the rest of the world.

Although an industrial power as well, the United States did not engage extensively in Asian and African colonialism. In part, this was because, as a former colony, there was an element of anticolonial ethos, but more germanely because it was less desirable and more difficult for the United States than for European nations. The United States was still establishing itself as a world power and was concurrently expanding along its borders, a process which absorbed much of its potential colonial energy. The conquest of the West was a form of colonialism in itself, including extensive encroachment into territory held by Mexico and Native Americans, and remained the focus of American expansionism for most of the nineteenth century. The concept of "Manifest Destiny," while challenged by some, provided a sense of entitlement and an almost transcendent impetus to westward expansion. Indeed, the interests of the United States seemed to rest more clearly in the Western Hemisphere, which included imposing some control over the economies of Latin American states in accordance with the Monroe Doctrine but occasioned less interest in faraway Asia and Africa. Nonetheless, the United States did engage in some ventures of overt colonization away from its borders. After the purchase of Alaska from Russia in 1867, the United States annexed Hawaii in 1898, effectively endorsing the coup instigated by American fruit growers and businessmen four years previously. In the same year, as a consequence of the Spanish-American War, it acquired Cuba temporarily, as well as Guam, the Philippines, and Puerto Rico from Spain. During World War I, it purchased the U.S. Virgin Islands from Denmark.

European colonialism differed from American western expansion in that its aims were not necessarily to expand settled territories. Instead, much as in the United States' colonization of its island territories, Asian and African regions were conquered, and then European administrations were imposed on them. However, unlike the territories that the United States had obtained from Spain, European colonies consisted mainly of formerly independent regions. Colonialism occurred in the late nineteenth century because it became possible at that time, facilitated by emerging technologies in the industrialized world and also by a lull in European warfare, especially as the century of revolutions essentially drew to a close. In addition, it was enabled by a new era of citizen armies that willingly backed nationalist interests. However, it also required motivating causes.

Incitements for colonialism can be grouped into economic, political, and moral interests. Economically, colonies had the potential to give colonizing countries control over markets in indigenous raw materials, produce plantation crops, and obtain these resources by utilizing cheap labor. In addition, colonial markets provided an opportunity to profit from the sale of European manufactured goods. In the political realm, imperial advances provided glory and prestige, promoted nationalistic ideals, and blocked the ambitions of rival countries. Colonies also meant control over strategic zones and a source of additional troops for imperial armies. Wars of conquest served to divert the attention of the public at home from contentious domestic issues such as persistent economic inequality and the lack of political representation, and they provided an outlet for the energies of a growing population. Moral causes for colonialism were closely related to political inspirations; there was a deeply entrenched perception that non-Western societies were backward and would benefit from the guidance of Europeans. Indeed, in many cases, colonial administrations were preceded by Christian missionaries with whom they worked closely, although in some cases missionaries critiqued the process of conquest. Further, the late nineteenth century was the age of eugenics, a pseudo-science that purported to apply a Darwinist analysis to human societies. According to the many who ascribed to these views, various human societies differed both in cultural development and biologically. Europeans and whites were seen as exemplars of the highest stage of human development with a natural destiny to dominate and, in more extreme versions, to exterminate other human groups. This was a philosophy that was not widely discredited until after World War II. Even in their less virulent variations, eugenics and racist theories convinced many of the appropriateness and even obligation for Europeans to engage in colonialism. Together, opportunity, interest in economic gain, and political and moralistic ideologies united to unleash a wave of colonialism in the last fifteen years of the nineteenth century.

Colonialism in Africa

Asian and Pacific colonization mainly occurred gradually, with the British and Dutch growing their Asian empires from initial foundations in southeast Asia and the British and Russians competing for control of Central Asia in the "Great Game" during much of the nineteenth century, though there was a spate of rapid colonization in the late nineteenth century, especially by the French. In the Atlantic, the main target for colonization was Africa, where colonization occurred rapidly during the last fifteen years of the nineteenth century. During the nineteenth century, there had been some interest in European and American exploration of Africa, which purported to reveal the mysteries of "darkest" Africa to a Western reading public but which also mapped important geographical figures, such as the courses of important rivers, and detailed the availability of useful resources. It was not until the end of the century, though, that Europeans were ready to move into Africa in force. Interest in colonization of Africa caught fire in the 1880s. Conquest of African territories was suddenly made much more possible once the first prototype of the Maxim gun, the first machine gun, was made available to European military forces in 1884. That same year, representatives of the most important European powers met in Prussia at the Berlin Conference to apportion Africa among themselves. This meeting served not only to legitimize the conquest of Africa but also to prevent tensions that might arise from more than one European nation claiming the same territory. The participants partitioned the entire African continent, allocating territories to various European states, with the largest shares going to the most powerful, Britain and France. Regions of Africa were allocated based on initial footholds held by various European nations, a policy referred to as "effective occupation," and also based on the relative political influence of the participating nations. The new territories were demarcated on a map concentrating on European interests rather than aligning with existing borders. Little attention was paid to existing political, ethnic, cultural, or linguistic boundaries within Africa itself.

In a swift wave of conquest, Europeans occupied almost all of Africa during the next fifteen years, an event referred to as "The Scramble for Africa." The French took control over much of northern and western Africa, while the British acquired a large swath of land that included most of eastern and southern Africa, including the remaining Dutch territories in South Africa and Egypt. The Portuguese consolidated their control over inland portions of Angola and Mozambique; the Belgian King Leopold I attained the Congo, incongruously named the Congo Free State; Germany gained colonies in both the west and east in what would become Togo, Cameroon, Namibia, and Tanzania; Italy took Libya and Somalia in northern Africa; and Spain also took control over a small portion of the northwest. The German colonies, together with Ottoman territories in the Middle East, were lost in the aftermath of World War I, leaving Britain and France the two remaining large colonial powers. The naked avarice of this rapid flurry of occupation was clearly shown by King Leopold's famous injunction to his ambassador at the Berlin Conference to get him a share of the "magnificent African cake" and by British tycoon and colonial leader Cecil Rhodes' statement that as the earth had already been "nearly parceled out," he wished he could "annex the planets" in space.[1]

The colonization of Africa, like the colonization of the American continents in previous centuries, was accompanied by extreme violence. Among the worst depredations occurred in the Congo Free State, where laborers were forced to cultivate rubber under a slave-labor-like system. Rampant abuses, including murder, torture, rape, starvation, and mutilation, resulted in the extermination of more than 10 million people, a situation that was later mitigated somewhat by the eventual transfer of control over the colony from the Crown to the Belgian state in 1908. In Namibia, the Germans exterminated the majority of the Herero people after they rebelled in 1904. In the Second Boer War (1899–1902), fought between the British and Dutch over control over South Africa, more than 100,000 Dutch women and children and 100,000 Africans were interned in camps, of whom only about three quarters survived.

Many areas tried to resist colonialism, with some temporary successes, such as a short-lived Zulu victory against British forces in South Africa in 1878. Guinean leader Samori Ture was able to obtain repeating rifles through political networks and hold off French colonialism by guerrilla warfare until 1898. Ultimately, however, only Abyssinia (Ethiopia) and Liberia were able to maintain their independence. The latter was protected by its status as a client of the United States. The Ethiopians were successful in holding off the invasion of Italian troops in a series of military encounters, culminating in the 1896 Battle of Adwa. A slight lag in the onset of Italian colonialism had enabled the farsighted Emperor Menelik II to obtain and train troops in the latest weaponry, including machine guns.

Motivations

There were a number of distinct incentives for European powers to colonize African territories in particular. Imperial expansion in Africa involved obtaining or maintaining strategic footholds in areas like Egypt (especially after the completion of the Suez Canal in 1869), Gibraltar, or the Cape of Good Hope, all of which eventually became territories under British influence. As elsewhere, economic considerations were paramount. African colonial plantations were a source of cheap labor that produced large yields of agricultural products inexpensively, including cocoa, coffee, cotton, palm oil, rubber, sisal fiber, and tea. The African colonies also were a source of plentiful natural resources, including diamonds, copper, gold, iron, ivory, and tin. In addition, the colonies served as markets for European manufactured goods. African colonial administrations also provided significant employment for Europeans who came to the colonies as officials, businessmen, soldiers, managers, engineers, traders, clerks, police, and teachers.

As colonialism took shape, the profit motive continued to dominate imperial interests. While the abuses of the Congo Free State were extreme, it was not unusual for European corporations leasing vast swaths of land to use force to coerce agricultural laborers to work in the plantations. Many countries became dependent on the cultivation of one or two crops grown on huge plantations for the export market, replacing the self-sustaining small farms of indigenous farmers. In addition to suffering under coercive labor practices, Africans were forced to pay exorbitant taxes that returned little in the way of benefits. Europeans ran steamship, rail, and telegraph lines across the continent to support colonial infrastructure but created few institutions devoted to African interests.

In support of economic and political incentives, colonialism was also justified by racism. Many, perhaps most, Europeans believed that European culture was superior to African culture. Africans were seen as backward in morality and religion in addition to lagging behind Europeans technologically. This perspective validated the conquest of Africans who, it was believed, would be enriched and civilized by their contact with whites. Some claimed that it was the "white man's burden" to impose civilization on barbaric and childlike peoples. While there were missionaries who were sincere in their intention to proselytize or who sometimes engaged in humanitarian activities such as the establishment of medical clinics or schools, in many cases the missionizing ideal was based on an assumption of superiority and often tied into the colonial government establishment. Africans were encouraged or forced to give up African culture, although this was articulated differently by individual colonial administrations. For instance, the official rhetoric in French areas was that Africans who adopted French culture would eventually achieve French citizenship, with their nation incorporated into the French polity, while in British areas, African countries were to eventually develop into self-governing states under the tutelage of British administrators. Under neither regime were these goals expected to be realizable in the near future.

Consequences

The most significant result of colonialism was the appropriation of African sovereignty. Colonialism left Africans politically and economically dependent. Much like Native Americans on the western side of the Atlantic, Africans became an underclass in their own ancestral lands. Demographically, colonization and the wars of conquest that were necessitated by it led to loss of life, starvation, and disease. The result of these factors was cultural and social disorientation, with long-lasting consequences that still endure even in the aftermath of colonialism in the late twentieth and early twenty-first centuries. With the traditional channels of power disrupted, Africans were less able to set up stable political and social structures, a situation that was later exacerbated by Cold War interventions during the twentieth century. In the social sphere, African norms were also disrupted, and Africans were pushed to accommodate European models. The role of elders in guiding society and maintaining concord was diminished but not replaced by other cohesive institutions. The status of women shrank. In most traditional African societies, at least in non-Islamic areas, land ownership had been in the hands of lineages or family groups, and much of the administration of land and market production was in the hands of women, giving them significant social and economic power. When colonial governments imposed laws and taxes on Africans, they identified male heads of households as the official representatives for families, limiting the ability of women to hold authority in the community. Finally, the existence of inequality between Europeans and Africans furthered racism both within African countries and in Europe.

Economically, colonized African countries were disadvantaged in the world market. Their reliance on single crops meant that they had little ability to negotiate prices with the European country that was their main trading partner. Additionally, monocrop agriculture meant that African economies had little resilience if prices fell because of competition or crop failures. Most of the fertile land within Africa was owned or controlled by whites, while indigenous farmers were pushed into marginal lands or became landless laborers on farms, on railways, or in construction. Most people were impoverished yet expected to pay steep taxes. Infrastructure was mostly based on the needs of Europeans rather than Africans. In some areas, a service elite composed of local people was trained to serve as clerks and lower officials, but in others, immigrants, especially Indians, were brought in to take that role, creating social friction.

In the end, colonialism also caused problems for the colonizers themselves. Despite attempts to reduce antagonism through collaboration, as in the Berlin Conference, colonialism ultimately worsened competition between European powers. In the short term, this resulted in competitive colonial wars, as in South Africa. In the long term, colonial rivalry can be seen as a contributing factor in the outbreak of World War I. And during the later twentieth century, the conflicts that broke out as many former colonies attempted to achieve independence were destructive, costly, and demoralizing.

Controversially, some have claimed that colonialism provided benefits, though ironically the greatest benefits come from institutions that enabled Africans to resist colonialism. Europeans did establish systems of formal education in many of the African territories that they controlled. Though such institutions aimed at training lower-level government functionaries rather than political leaders, they did provide access to education and modern political theory to an elite cadre of Africans. It is notable that almost all leaders of African independence movements in the twentieth century were educated in colonial schools, in many cases run by missionaries. Another less ambiguous benefit was the introduction of Western medicine. In addition, European colonizers did develop some infrastructure in Africa in addition to schools, including hospitals, electrical power, rail lines, harbors, water and sewage lines, telegraph lines and, later, telephone lines. Primarily, these were meant to benefit white colonists and were constructed near areas where whites were settled, but they also provided the basis for modern development. Finally, the establishment of Christianity, while hostile to native African traditions, also became a vehicle for resistance against colonialism. The Christian tradition's support for equality and justice seemingly challenged the oppression and inequality of colonial societies while urging Africans to abandon ethnic and economic differences that prevented political cohesion. An example was the extension of the Jehovah's Witness–based Watch Tower sect in Malawi in the early twentieth century, which syncretically incorporated African values and supported African nationalism. Also, while missionaries generally supported colonial administrations, in some instances they promoted greater equality for Africans and even furthered nationalist aims. Yet it will always be impossible to ascertain the extent to which these "benefits" would have been adopted in African states on their own had they been able to remain independent. It seems probable that colonization stunted rather than promoted African acquisition of many of these institutions.

Note

1 Leopold is quoted in Adam Hochschild, *King Leopold's Ghost* (Boston: Houghton Mifflin, 1999), 58; and Cecil Rhodes and W. T. Stead, *The Last Will and Testament of Cecil John Rhodes* (London: "Review of Reviews" Office, 1902), 190.

21 Conclusions

The nineteenth century was a time in which the concept of the Atlantic as a coherent global zone was breaking down. The new industrial technologies, especially steamships and the telegraph, rapidly increased globalization, connecting all parts of the world through rapid transportation and communication. By the end of the century, new technologies made international commerce, intellectual connections, and warfare possible on a scale never before imagined. Indeed, Atlantic society changed very considerably during the nineteenth century. This period saw an increase in the standard of living for Western Europeans and Americans in particular as newly developed industrial and productive capacities raised overall wealth, while rising workers' movements and middle-class reformers had fought to improve working-class conditions. Growing nationalism also possessed a democratizing aspect, as it claimed cohesion among all the citizens of a nation. European nations increasingly began to look outward, competing to colonize Asia and Africa, a development which was made possible by industrialization and which depended on but also reinforced nationalistic ideals.

The paradox of modernity

Columbus' voyage had inaugurated a period of European dominance. By the twentieth century, the leading role was taken by the United States, a society founded in the course of the Atlantic connection. The world of the nineteenth century was divided by nationalism but was also increasingly integrated; disenfranchised people remained oppressed but were becoming increasingly vocal in defense of their rights. The new societies that had grown up in the Atlantic did not replicate earlier European, African, or Native American societies. Although set up in the mold of dominant Europeans, they demonstrated new syncretic societies that would continue to grapple with contested visions of opportunity, equality, and freedom.

By the end of the nineteenth century, the emerging geopolitical pattern was one of national differences. Modern industrialized nations possessed a large middle class and advanced infrastructures that included railways, sewer systems, and postal and educational systems. They were often democratic and generally were characterized by the continuing emergence of greater equality, though demographic factors such as gender, race, poverty, religion, and immigrant status still presented social barriers. This included the United States, Canada, and Western Europe. Transitional nations, such as those in Latin America, were independent, but significant segments of their populations remained poverty stricken. These countries were typically not fully democratic, and although they possessed some modern infrastructure, they also had economies that were at least partially agricultural, with large peasant populations. Finally, underdeveloped nations, usually colonized in the late nineteenth century, occupied a dependent position, though sometimes their populations included small groups of elites or educated clerical classes. They had little infrastructure, uneducated populations, and agriculture-based economies. This included African as well as some Asian regions.

The Atlantic world in the nineteenth century was characterized by these kinds of inequalities and inconsistencies. In particular, there was a sharp contrast between the fortunes of those who were elites – usually, but not always, white middle- and upper-class males – and those who were disenfranchised – the poor, women, and people of color. The Enlightenment, the era of revolutions, and especially the Industrial Revolution had ushered in immense new wealth and opportunity that were gradually becoming available to increasing numbers of people. The century also saw the development of new acknowledgment of human rights and human equality that was manifested through revolutions; the appearance of egalitarian political philosophies; abolitionism; increases in state-sponsored services such as public education; and suffrage, labor, and women's rights movements.

All of these political and intellectual trends originated in the Atlantic world, especially in its central contradictory reality: slavery. Paradoxically, both Western slavery and abolitionism were born in the Atlantic. Yet Atlantic society was full of such contradictions. Despite the growth of humanitarian sentiment and the growing consensus against slavery, the nineteenth century continued to be an era of extreme discrimination and inequality. Industrialization was built on the backs of urban and, to some degree, rural workers. Poor workers everywhere failed to see the promise of rising expectations and incomes. At the same time, around the globe, Europeans competed to colonize new territories in Asia and Africa, a development which was made possible by industrialization and the new democratic nationalism. The philosophy of human rights and equality was contradicted by eugenics, which was frequently used to justify colonialism and disenfranchise colonial peoples. Globalization meant that nations themselves replicated unequal labor relationships, with colonized countries transformed into vast plantations with gulag-like conditions. Likewise, as the United States expanded its global political presence, it colonized increasing amounts of Native American land while imposing restrictions on the autonomy of Latin American states through the Monroe Doctrine. In the Southern United States, the end of Reconstruction meant a loss of rights that African Americans had achieved in the wake of the Civil War and inaugurated an epidemic of lynching inflicted upon African American men. In fact, blacks, though freed from the threat of slavery by the end of the century, faced high levels of discrimination, racism, and disenfranchisement throughout the Atlantic world.

Yet despite the pervasive inequality of the nineteenth century, the era also saw the promise of further equality. Many of the issues that would be fought out in the twentieth century were first articulated in the nineteenth century as greater forms of oppression, such as slavery, were successfully dismantled. Rather than accepting their fate as in centuries past, poor and disenfranchised peoples everywhere continued to resist and engage in sustained movements for their rights. This was an era of tremendous inequality but also tremendous promise. These contradictions were borne out in the twentieth century, which did see a greater expansion of rights, although this was achieved with much struggle and bloodshed, and two world wars that exceeded all previous conflicts in their death tolls and barbarity. The promise of equality, born in the Enlightenment and in the Atlantic world, continued to inspire people around the world to fight for human and civil rights, a critical cornerstone of human values in the modern world.

Sources for further reading

Many who read this book will want to study some of the topics addressed in greater depth. Much of the published material on Atlantic history focuses on investigations of particular problems or issues that are explored in great complexity. What follows are some suggestions on selected readings that will give a more detailed perspective on many of the issues discussed in this book, with a few topics listed in greater detail. I have focused particularly on works which are either recent or particularly important. It should be apparent that many of the individual books and articles could be listed under a number of categories, though they only appear in one place in this bibliography. With the exception of the first three sections, the topics are arranged in alphabetical order.

The dominance of the West

Abu-Lughod, Janet Lippman. *Before European Hegemony: The World System A.D. 1250–1350* (New York: Oxford University Press, 1989).

Crosby, Alfred W. *The Columbian Exchange: Biological and Cultural Consequences of 1492* (Westport, CT: Greenwood Press, 1972).

Curtin, Philip. *The World and the West: The European Challenge and the Overseas Response in the Age of Empire* (Cambridge, UK: Cambridge University Press, 2000).

Diamond, Jared. *Guns, Germs, and Steel: The Fates of Human Societies* (New York: W.W. Norton & Co., 1997).

Frank, Andre Gunder. *ReOrient: Global Economy in the Asian Age* (Berkeley: University of California Press, 1998).

Parthasarathi, Prasannan. *Why Europe Grew Rich and Asia Did Not: Global Economic Divergence, 1600–1850* (New York: Cambridge University Press, 2011).

Pomeranz, Kenneth. *The Great Divergence* (Princeton, NJ: Princeton University Press, 2000).

Wallerstein, Immanuel. *The Modern World System: Capitalist Agriculture and the Origins of the European World Economy in the Sixteenth Century* (New York: Academic Press, 1974).

Generalist works on Atlantic history

Bailyn, Bernard. *Atlantic History: Concept and Contours* (Cambridge, MA: Harvard University Press, 2005).

Bailyn, Bernard, and Patricia Denault, eds. *Soundings in Atlantic History: Latent Structures and Intellectual Currents, 1500–1830* (Cambridge, MA: Harvard University Press, 2009).

Benjamin, Thomas. *The Atlantic World: Europeans, Africans, Indians and Their Shared History, 1400–1900* (Cambridge, UK: Cambridge University Press, 2009).

Benjamin, Thomas, Timothy Hall, and David Rutherford, eds. *The Atlantic World in the Age of Empire* (Boston: Houghton Mifflin, 2001).

Cañizares-Esguerra, Jorge. *The Atlantic in Global History: 1500–2000* (Upper Saddle River, NJ: Prentice Hall, 2006).

Canny, Nicholas. "Atlantic History: What and Why." *European Review*, Vol. 9, No. 4 (2001), pp. 399–411.

Canny, Nicholas, and Philip Morgan, eds. *The Oxford Handbook of the Atlantic World: 1450–1850* (Oxford: Oxford University Press, 2011).

Coclanis, Peter. "Atlantic World or Atlantic/World?" *William and Mary Quarterly*, Third Series, Vol. 63, No. 4 (Oct. 2006), pp. 725–742.

Egerton, Douglas R., Alison Games, Jane G. Landers, and Kris Lane. *The Atlantic World: A History, 1400–1888* (Wheeling, IL: Harlan Davison, 2007).

Falola, Toyin, and Kevin Roberts, eds. *The Atlantic World: 1450–2000* (Bloomington: Indiana University Press, 2008).

Games, Alison, and Adam Rothman, eds. *Major Problems in Atlantic History: Documents and Essays* (Boston: Houghton Mifflin, 2008).

Greene, Jack P., and Philip D. Morgan, eds. *Atlantic History: A Critical Appraisal* (Oxford: Oxford University Press, 2009).

Klooster, Wim, and Alfred Padula, eds. *The Atlantic World: Essays on Slavery, Migration, and Imagination* (Upper Saddle River, NJ: Pearson, 2005).

Kupperman, Karen Ordahl. *The Atlantic in World History* (New York: Oxford University Press, 2012).

Primary sources cited in the narrative
(non-English works listed in translated editions)

Clarkson, Thomas. *An Essay on the Slavery and Commerce of the Human Species* (London: J. Phillips, 1788).

Columbus, Christopher. *The Four Voyages of Christopher Columbus*, J.M. Cohen, trans. (Harmondsworth, UK: Penguin, 1969).

Douglass, Frederick. *Narrative of the Life of Frederick Douglass, An American Slave* (Boston: Anti-Slavery Office, 1845).

Equiano, Olaudah. *The Interesting Narrative of the Life of Olaudah Equiano* (London: T. Wilkins, 1789).

Garrison, William Lloyd. *William Lloyd Garrison and the Fight Against Slavery: Selections from the Liberator* (Boston: Bedford, 1994 [mid-nineteenth century]).

Guaman Poma de Ayala, Felipe. *The First New Chronicle and Good Government: On the History of the World and Incas up to 1615*, Roland Hamilton, trans. (Austin: University of Texas Press, 2009 [1615]).

Hakluyt, Richard. *The Principal Navigations, Voyages, Traffiques and Discoveries of the English Nation*, 12 Vols. (Glasgow: J. MacLehose and Sons, 1903–1905 [1598–1600]).

Jacobs, Harriet. *Incidents in the Life of a Slave Girl* (Boston: Author, 1861).

La Cruz, Juana Inés de. *Poems, Protest, and a Dream: Selected Writings*, Margaret Sayers Peden, trans. (New York: Penguin, 1997 [late seventeenth century]).

La Vega, Garcilaso de. *The Royal Commentaries of the Incas*, Alian Gheerbrant, trans. (New York: Orion Press, 1961 [1609, 1617]).

Las Casas, Bartolomé de. *A Short Account of the Destruction of the Indies*, Nigel Griffin, trans. (London: Penguin, 1992 [1555]).

Léry, Jean de. *History of a Voyage to the Land of Brazil*, Janet Whatley, trans. (Berkeley: University of California Press, 1990).

Locke, John. *Two Treatises of Government*, Peter Laslett, ed. (New York: Cambridge University Press, 1988 [1689]).

L'Ouverture, Toussaint. *The Haitian Revolution*, Nick Nesbitt, ed. (New York: Verso, 2008).

Marx, Karl, and Friedrich Engels. *Manifesto of the Communist Party* (New York: International Publishers, 1948 [1848]).

Mill, John Stuart. *On Liberty and the Subjection of Women* (London: Penguin, 2006 [1859, 1869]).

Montaigne, Michel de. *The Complete Essays* (Stanford, CA: Stanford University Press, 1976 [1580]).

Prince, Mary. *The History of Mary Prince, a West Indian Slave* (London: F. Westley and A.H. Davis, 1831).

Rhodes, Cecil, and W.T. Stead. *The Last Will and Testament of Cecil John Rhodes* (London: "Review of Reviews" Office, 1902).

Sahagún, Bernardino de. *We People Here: Nahuatl Accounts of the Conquest of Mexico*, James Lockhart, ed. (Eugene, OR: Wipf and Stock Publishers, 2004).

Smith, Adam. *An Inquiry into the Nature and Causes of the Wealth of Nations*, 9th Ed. (London: W. Strahan and T. Cadell, 1799 [1776]).

Stowe, Harriet Beecher. *Uncle Tom's Cabin* (Oxford: Oxford University Press, 1998 [1852]).

Vespucci, Amerigo. *The Letters of Amerigo Vespucci*, Clements R. Markham, trans. (London: Hakluyt Society, 1894 [1504]).

Abolition and emancipation

Afigbo, A. E. *The Abolition of the Slave Trade in Southeastern Nigeria, 1885–1950* (Rochester, NY: University of Rochester Press, 2006).

Blackburn, Robin. *The Overthrow of Colonial Slavery* (New York: Verso, 1988).

Blanchard, Peter. "The Language of Liberation: Slave Voices in the Wars of Independence." *Hispanic American Historical Review*, Vol. 82 (2002), pp. 499–523.

Brown, Christopher Leslie. *Moral Capital: Foundations of British Abolitionism* (Chapel Hill: University of North Carolina Press, 2006).

Carey, Brycchan, and Geoffrey Plank. *Quakers and Abolition* (Urbana, IL: University of Illinois Press, 2014).

Conrad, Robert Edgar. *The Destruction of Brazilian Slavery, 1850–1888* (Berkeley: University of California Press, 1972).

Craton, Michael. *Testing the Chains: Resistance to Slavery in the British West Indies* (Ithaca, NY: Cornell University Press, 2009).

Davis, David Brion. *The Problem of Slavery in the Age of Emancipation* (New York: Random House, 2014).

Drescher, Seymour. *From Slavery to Freedom: Comparative Studies in the Rise and Fall of Atlantic Slavery* (New York: New York University Press, 1999).

Drescher, Seymour, and Christine Bolt. *Capitalism and Anti-Slavery: British Mobilization in Comparative Perspective* (Oxford: Oxford University Press, 1987).

Drescher, Seymour, Pieter C. Emmer, and João Pedro. *Who Abolished Slavery? Slave Revolts and Abolitionism* (New York: Berghahn, 2010).

Holt, Thomas C. *The Problem of Freedom: Race, Labor, and Politics in Jamaica and Britain, 1832–1938* (Baltimore, MD: Johns Hopkins University Press, 1992).

Matthews, Gelien. *Caribbean Slave Revolts and the British Abolitionist Movement* (Baton Rouge: Louisiana State University Press, 2006).

Midgley, Clare. *Women Against Slavery: The British Campaigns, 1780–1870* (New York: Routledge, 1995).

Rugemer, Edward Bartlett. *The Problem of Emancipation: The Caribbean Roots of the American Civil War* (Baton Rouge: Louisiana State University Press, 2008).

Schmidt-Nowara, Christopher. *Empire and Antislavery: Spain, Cuba, and Puerto Rico, 1833–1874* (Pittsburgh: University of Pittsburgh Press, 1999).

Schmidt-Nowara, Christopher. *Slavery, Freedom, and Abolition in Latin America and the Atlantic World* (Albuquerque: University of New Mexico Press, 2011).

Scott, Rebecca. "Defining the Boundaries of Freedom in the World of Cane: Cuba, Brazil and Louisiana after Emancipation." *American Historical Review*, Vol. 99, No. 1 (1994), pp. 70–102.

Scott, Rebecca J. *Slave Emancipation in Cuba: The Transition to Free Labor, 1865–1899*, 2nd Ed. (Pittsburgh: University of Pittsburgh Press, 2000).

Temperley, Howard, ed. *After Slavery: Emancipation and Its Discontents* (London: Frank Cass, 2000).

Africa in the Atlantic world

Curtin, Philip. *African History: From Earliest Times to Independence* (London: Longman, 1995).

Heywood, Linda. *Contested Power in Angola, 1840s to the Present* (Rochester, NY: University of Rochester Press, 2000).

Hochschild, Adam. *King Leopold's Ghost* (Boston: Houghton Mifflin, 1999).

Law, Robin. *Ouidah: The Social History of a West African Slaving Port, 1727–1892* (Athens: Ohio University Press, 2005).

Lovejoy, Paul. *Transformations in Slavery: A History of Slavery in Africa*, 2nd Ed. (New York: Cambridge University Press, 2000 [1983]).

Northrup, David. *Africa's Discovery of Europe, 1450–1850*, 2nd Ed. (Oxford: Oxford University Press, 2008).

Rodney, Walter. *How Europe Underdeveloped Africa* (Washington, DC: Howard University Press, 1981).

Thornton, John. *Africa and Africans in the Making of the Atlantic World, 1400–1800*, 2nd Ed. (Cambridge, UK: Cambridge University Press, 1998).

Thornton, John. "Legitimacy and Political Power: Queen Njinga, 1624–1631." *The Journal of African History*, Vol. 32, No. 1 (March 1991), pp. 25–40.

Afro-Atlantic culture

Beckles, Hilary, and Verene Shepherd. *Caribbean Freedom: Society and Economy from Emancipation to Present* (Kingston, Jamaica: Randle, 1993).

Beckles, Hilary, and Brian Stoddart. *Liberation Cricket: West Indies Cricket Culture* (Manchester, UK: Manchester University Press, 1995).

Bilby, Kenneth. "Swearing by the Past, Swearing to the Future: Sacred Oaths, Alliances, and Treaties Among the Guianese and Jamaican Maroons." *Ethnohistory*, Vol. 44, No. 4 (Autumn 1997), pp. 655–689.

Carney, Judith A. *Black Rice: The African Origins of Rice Cultivation in the Americas* (Cambridge, MA: Harvard University Press, 2001).

Falola, Toyin, and Matt D. Childs. *The Yoruba Diaspora in the Atlantic World* (Bloomington: Indiana University Press, 2004).

Gilroy, Paul. *Black Atlantic: Modernity and Double Consciousness* (Cambridge, MA: Harvard University Press, 1993).

Gomez, Michael Angelo. *Exchanging Our Country Marks: The Transformation of African Identities in the Colonial and Antebellum South* (Chapel Hill: University of North Carolina Press, 1998).

Hall, Gwendolyn Midlo. *Africans in Colonial Louisiana: The Development of Afro-Creole Culture in the Eighteenth Century* (Baton Rouge: Louisiana University Press, 1992).

Heuman, Gad. *Between Black and White: Race, Politics, and the Free Coloreds in Jamaica, 1792–1865* (Westport, CT: Greenwood Press, 1981).

Heywood, Linda. *Central Africans and Cultural Transformations in the American Diaspora* (Cambridge, UK: Cambridge University Press, 2002).

Heywood, Linda, and John Thornton. *Central Africans, Atlantic Creoles, and the Foundation of the Americas, 1585–1660* (New York: Cambridge University Press, 2007).

Inikori, Joseph. *Africans and the Industrial Revolution in England: A Study in International Trade and Economic Development* (New York: Cambridge University Press, 2002).

Landers, Jane G. *Atlantic Creoles in the Age of Revolutions* (Cambridge, MA: Harvard University Press, 2011).

Morgan, Philip D. *A Slave Counterpoint: Black Culture in Eighteenth-Century Chesapeake and Low Country* (Chapel Hill: University of North Carolina Press, 1998).

Spear, Jennifer M. *Race, Sex, and Social Order in Early New Orleans* (Baltimore, MD: Johns Hopkins University Press, 2009).

British and colonial America

Anderson, Fred. *Crucible of War: The Seven Years' War and the Fate of Empire in British North America, 1754–1766* (New York: Knopf, 2000).

Anderson, Fred. *A People's Army: Massachusetts Soldiers and Society in the Seven Years' War* (Chapel Hill: University of North Carolina Press, 1984).

Armitage, David, and Michael J. Braddick, eds. *The British Atlantic World, 1500–1800* (New York: Palgrave Macmillan, 2002).

Beckles, Hilary. *A History of Barbados: From Amerindian Settlement to Nation-State* (Cambridge, UK: Cambridge University Press, 1990).

Breen, T. H., and Timothy Hall. *Colonial America in an Atlantic World* (New York: Pearson, 2004).

Buckner, Phillip. *Canada and the British Empire* (Oxford: Oxford University Press, 2010).

Canny, Nicholas. "The Ideology of English Colonization: From Ireland to America." *William and Mary Quarterly*, Third Series, Vol. 30, No. 4 (Oct. 1973), pp. 575–598.

Canny, Nicholas. *Making Ireland British, 1580–1650* (Oxford: Oxford University Press, 2001).

Canny, Nicholas, and Anthony Pagden, eds. *Colonial Identity in the Atlantic World* (Princeton, NJ: Princeton University Press, 1987).

Fischer, David Hackett. *Albion's Seed: Four British Folkways in America* (Oxford: Oxford University Press, 1989).

Games, Alison. *The Web of Empire: English Cosmopolitanisms in an Age of Expansion* (Oxford: Oxford University Press, 2008).

Gould, Eliga. *The Persistence of Empire: British Political Culture in the Age of the American Revolution* (Chapel Hill: University of North Carolina Press, 2000).

Greene, Jack P. *Pursuits of Happiness: The Social Development of Early Modern British Colonies and the Formation of American Culture* (Chapel Hill: University of North Carolina Press, 1988).

Greene, Jack P., and J. R. Pole, eds. *Colonial British America* (Baltimore, MD: Johns Hopkins University Press, 1984).

Jacobs, Jaap. *New Netherland: A Dutch Colony in Seventeenth-Century America* (Leiden, Netherlands: Brill, 2005).

Jarvis, Michael. *In the Eye of All Trade: Bermuda, Bermudans, and the Maritime Atlantic World, 1680–1783* (Chapel Hill: University of North Carolina Press, 2010).

Katz, Stanley N., John Murrin, and Douglas Greenberg, eds. *Colonial America: Essays in Politics and Social Development*, 3rd Ed. (New York: Knopf, 1993).

Landsman, Ned. *From Colonials to Provincials: American Thought and Culture, 1680–1760* (Ithaca, NY: Cornell University Press, 2000).

Lepore, Jill. *The Name of War: King Philip's War and the Origins of American Identity* (New York: Vintage, 1999).

Louis, William Roger, Nicholas P. Canny, Alaine M. Low, P. J. Marshall, and A. N. Porter. *The Oxford History of the British Empire* (Oxford: Oxford University Press, 1998–1999).

Mancall, Peter C. *The Atlantic World and Virginia, 1550–1624* (Chapel Hill: University of North Carolina Press, 2007).

Mancall, Peter C. *Envisioning America: English Plans for the Colonization of North America, 1580–1640* (Boston: Bedford St. Martin's, 1996).

Mancall, Peter C. *Hakluyt's Promise: An Elizabethan's Obsession for an English America* (New Haven, CT: Yale University Press, 2007).

Mancke, Elizabeth, and Carole Shammas, eds. *The Creation of the British Atlantic World* (Baltimore, MD: Johns Hopkins University Press, 2005).

Menard, Russell. *Economy and Society in Colonial Maryland* (New York: Garland, 1985).

Morgan, Philip, ed. *Diversity and Unity in Early America* (New York: Routledge, 1993).

Olwell, Robert, and Alan Tully, eds. *Cultures and Identities in Colonial British America* (Baltimore, MD: Johns Hopkins University Press, 2006).

Pestana, Carla, and Sharon Salinger, eds. *Inequality in Early America* (Hanover, NH: University Press of New England, 1999).

Rhoden, Nancy, ed. *English Atlantics Revisited: Essays Honouring Professor Ian K. Steele* (Montreal, Canada: McGill-Queen's University Press, 2007).

Stern, Philip. "British Asia and British Atlantic: Comparisons and Connections." *William and Mary Quarterly*, Vol. 63, No. 4 (2006), pp. 693–712.

Vickers, Daniel, ed. *A Companion to Colonial America* (Oxford: Blackwell, 2003).

Empires in the Atlantic

Banks, Kenneth J. *Chasing Empire Across the Sea: Communications and the State in the French Atlantic, 1713–1763* (Montreal, Canada: McGill-Queen's University Press, 2006).

Benton, Lauren. *A Search for Sovereignty: Law and Geography in European Empires, 1400–1900* (Cambridge, UK: Cambridge University Press, 2010).

Bowen, H. V., Elizabeth Mancke, and John G. Reid. *Britain's Oceanic Empire: Atlantic and Indian Ocean Worlds, c.1550–1850* (Cambridge, UK: Cambridge University Press, 2012).

Daniels, Christina, and Michael V. Kennedy. *Negotiated Empires: Centers and Peripheries in the Americas, 1500–1820* (New York: Routledge, 2002).

Diffie, Bailey W., and George D. Winius. *Foundations of the Portuguese Empire, 1415–1580* (Minneapolis: University of Minnesota Press, 1977).

Elliot, John. *Empires of the Atlantic World: Britain and Spain in America 1492–1830* (New Haven, CT: Yale University Press, 2007).

Gómez, Nicolás Wey. *The Tropics of Empire: Why Columbus Sailed South to the Indies* (Cambridge, MA: MIT Press, 2008).

Goodfriend, Joyce D., Benjamin Schmidt, and Annette Stott, eds. *Going Dutch: The Dutch Presence in America 1609–2009* (Leiden, Netherlands: Brill, 2008).

Gould, Eliga. "Entangled Histories, Entangled Worlds: The English Speaking Atlantic as a Spanish Periphery." *American Historical Review*, Vol. 112 (June 2007), pp. 764–786.

Greer, Allan. *The People of New France* (Toronto: University of Toronto Press, 1997).

Kagan, Richard L., and Geoffrey Parker, eds. *Spain, Europe and the Atlantic World* (Cambridge, UK: Cambridge University Press, 1995).

Mancke, Elizabeth. *The Fault Lines of Empire* (New York: Routledge, 2004).

Pagden, Anthony. *Lords of All the World: Ideologies of Empire in Spain, Britain and France c.1500–c.1800* (New Haven, CT: Yale University Press, 1995).

Seed, Patricia. *Ceremonies of Possession in Europe's Conquest of the New World, 1492–1640* (New York: Cambridge University Press, 1995).

Immigration

Bailyn, Bernard. *The Peopling of British North America* (New York: Knopf, 1986).

Bailyn, Bernard. *Voyagers to the West: A Passage in the Peopling of America on the Eve of the Revolution* (New York: Knopf, 1986).

Bailyn, Bernard, and Philip Morgan, eds. *Strangers Within the Realm* (Chapel Hill: University of North Carolina Press, 1991).

Burnard, Trevor. "European Migration to Jamaica, 1655–1780." *William and Mary Quarterly*, Third Series, Vol. 53 (1996), pp. 769–796.

Canny, Nicholas, ed. *Europeans on the Move: Studies on European Migration, 1500–1800* (Oxford: Oxford University Press, 1994).

Cressy, David. *Coming Over: Migration and Communication Between England and New England in the Seventeenth Century* (Cambridge, UK: Cambridge University Press, 1987).

Daniels, Roger. *Coming to America* (New York: HarperCollins, 1990).

Fogleman, Aaron. *Hopeful Journeys: German Immigration, Settlement, and Political Culture in Colonial America, 1717–1775* (Philadelphia: University of Pennsylvania Press, 1996).

Games, Alison. *Migration and the Origins of the English Atlantic World* (Cambridge, MA: Harvard University Press, 1999).

Miller, Kirby. *Emigrants and Exiles: Ireland and the Irish Exodus to North America* (Oxford: Oxford University Press, 1985).

Racine, Karen, and Beatriz G. Mamigonian, eds. *The Human Tradition in the Atlantic World, 1500–1850* (Lanham, MD: Rowman and Littlefield, 2010).

Schrier, Arnold. *Ireland and the American Emigration, 1850–1900* (Minneapolis: University of Minnesota Press, 1958).

Indentured servants

Galenson, David. *White Servitude in Colonial America* (Cambridge, UK: Cambridge University Press, 1981).

Grubb, Farley. "The Transatlantic Market for British Convict Labor." *The Journal of Economic History*, Vol. 60, No. 1 (March 2000), pp. 94–122.

Menard, Russell. *Migrants, Servants, and Slaves: Unfree Labor in Colonial British America* (Aldershot, UK: Ashgate, 2001).

Palmer, Colin. *The World of Unfree Labour: From Indentured Servitude to Slavery* (Aldershot, UK: Ashgate, 1998).

Salinger, Sharon. *"To Serve Well and Faithfully": Labor and Indentured Servants in Pennsylvania, 1682–1800* (Cambridge, UK: Cambridge University Press, 1987).

Wareing, John. "Preventive and Punitive Regulation in Seventeenth-Century Social Policy: Conflicts of Interest and the Failure to Make 'Stealing and Transporting Children and Other Persons' a Felony, 1645–73." *Social History*, Vol. 27, No. 3 (2002), pp. 288–308.

Latin American society and culture

Adelman, Jeremy, ed. *Colonial Legacies: The Problem of Persistence in Latin American History* (New York: Routledge, 1999).

Andrews, George Reid. *Afro-Latin America, 1800–2000* (New York: Oxford University Press, 2004).

Anna, Timothy E. *The Mexican Empire of Iturbide* (Lincoln: University of Nebraska Press, 1990).

Anna, Timothy E. *Spain and the Loss of America* (Lincoln: University of Nebraska Press, 1983).

Carrera, Magali. *Imagining Identity in New Spain: Race, Lineage, and the Colonial Body in Portraiture and Casta Paintings* (Austin: University of Texas Press, 2012).

Fontaine, Pierre-Michel, ed. *Race, Class, and Power in Brazil* (Los Angeles: Center for Afro-American Studies, 1985).

Hanke, Lewis. *The Spanish Struggle for Justice in the Conquest of America* (Philadelphia: University of Pennsylvania Press, 1949).

MacLachlan, Colin M. *Spain's Empire in the New World: The Role of Ideas in Institutional and Social Change* (Berkeley: University of California Press, 1988).

O'Flanagan, Patrick. *Port Cities of Atlantic Iberia, c. 1500–1900* (Aldershot, UK: Ashgate, 2008).

Safier, Neil. *Measuring the New World: Enlightenment Science and South America* (Chicago: University of Chicago Press, 2008).

Schwartz, Stuart B. *Sovereignty and Society in Colonial Brazil* (Berkeley: University of California Press, 1981).

Studnicki-Gizbert, Daviken. *A Nation upon the Ocean Sea: Portugal's Atlantic Diaspora and the Crisis of the Spanish Empire, 1492–1640* (Oxford: Oxford University Press, 2007).

Szuchman, Mark D., and Jonathan C. Brown, eds. *Revolution and Restoration: The Rearrangement of Power in Argentina, 1776–1860* (Lincoln: University of Nebraska Press, 1994).

Weber, David J. *Bárbaros: Spaniards and Their Savages in the Age of Enlightenment* (New Haven, CT: Yale University Press, 2005).

Weber, David J. *The Spanish Frontier in North America* (New Haven, CT: Yale University Press, 1992).

Native American lifeways and encounters with colonists

Axtell, James. *Beyond 1492: Encounters in Colonial North America* (Oxford: Oxford University Press, 1992).

Banner, Stuart. *How the Indians Lost Their Land: Law and Power on the Frontier* (Cambridge, MA: Harvard University Press, 2005).

Bourne, Russell. *The Red King's Rebellion: Racial Politics in New England, 1675–1678* (Oxford: Oxford University Press, 1991).

Bragdon, Kathleen. *Native Peoples of Southern New England, 1500–1650* (Norman: University of Oklahoma Press, 1999).

Bragdon, Kathleen. *Native Peoples of Southern New England, 1650–1775* (Norman: University of Oklahoma Press, 2009).

Clendinnen, Inga. *Ambivalent Conquests: Maya and Spaniard in Yucatán, 1517–1570* (Cambridge, UK: Cambridge University Press, 1987).

Clendinnen, Inga. *Aztecs: An Interpretation* (Cambridge, UK: Cambridge University Press, 1991).

Clendinnen, Inga. *The Cost of Courage in Aztec Society: Essays on Mesoamerican Society and Culture* (New York: Cambridge University Press, 2010).

Cook, Noble David. *Born to Die: Disease and New World Conquest, 1492–1650* (Cambridge, UK: Cambridge University Press, 1998).

Cook, Noble David. *People of the Volcano: Andean Counterpoint in the Colca Valley of Peru* (Durham, NC: Duke University Press, 2007).

Demos, John. *The Unredeemed Captive: A Family Story from Early America* (New York: Knopf, 1994).

Gallay, Alan. *Indian Slavery in Colonial America* (Omaha: University of Nebraska Press, 2010).

Gump, James O. "A Spirit of Resistance: Sioux, Xhosa, and Maori Responses to Western Dominance, 1840–1920." *Pacific Historical Review*, Vol. 66, No. 1 (Feb. 1997), pp. 21–52.

Horn, Rebecca. *Postconquest Coyoacan: Nahua-Spanish Relations in Central Mexico, 1519–1650* (Palo Alto, CA: Stanford University Press, 1997).

Kupperman, Karen. *Indians and English: Facing Off in Early America* (Ithaca, NY: Cornell University Press, 2000).

Kupperman, Karen. *Settling with the Indians: The Meeting of English and Indian Cultures in America, 1580–1640* (Totowa, NY: Rowman and Littlefield, 1980).

Lee, Wayne, ed. *Empires and Indigenes: Intercultural Alliance, Imperial Expansion, and Warfare in the Early Modern World* (New York: New York University Press, 2011).

León-Portilla, Miguel, and Lysander Kemp. *The Broken Spears: The Aztec Account of the Conquest of Mexico* (Boston: Beacon Press, 1962).

MacCormack, Sabine. *Religion in the Andes* (Princeton, NJ: Princeton University Press, 1991).

Mancall, Peter C., and James H. Merrell. *American Encounters: Natives and Newcomers from European Contact to Indian Removal, 1500–1850* (New York: Routledge, 2000).

Merrell, James H. "I Desire All That I Have Said . . . May Be Taken Down Aright": Revisiting Teedyuscung's 1756 Treaty Council Speeches." *William and Mary Quarterly*, Vol. 63, No. 4 (Oct. 2006), pp. 777–826.

Merrell, James H. *The Indians' New World: Catawbas and Their Neighbors from European Contact Through the Era of Removal* (Chapel Hill: University of North Carolina Press, 1989).

Merrell, James H. *Into the American Woods: Negotiators on the Pennsylvania Frontier* (New York: Norton, 1999).

Nash, Gary. *Red, White, and Black: The Peoples of Early America* (Englewood Cliffs, NJ: Prentice Hall, 1974).

Plane, Ann Marie. *Colonial Intimacies: Indian Marriage in Early New England* (Ithaca, NY: Cornell University Press, 2000).

Plank, Geoffrey. *An Unsettled Conquest: The British Campaign Against the Peoples of Acadia* (Philadelphia: University of Pennsylvania Press, 2003).

Restall, Matthew, ed. *Beyond Black and Red: African-Native Relations in Colonial Latin America* (Albuquerque: University of New Mexico Press, 2005).

Richter, Daniel J. "War and Culture: The Iroquois Experience." *William and Mary Quarterly*, Third Series, Vol. 40 (1983), pp. 528–559.

Salisbury, Neal. *Manitou and Providence: Indians, Europeans, and the Making of New England, 1500–1643* (Oxford: Oxford University Press, 1982).

Schwartz, Stuart. *Victors and Vanquished: Spanish and Nahua Views of the Conquest of Mexico* (Boston: Bedford, 2000).

Sheehan, Bernard. *Savagism and Civility: Indians and Englishmen in Colonial Virginia* (Cambridge, UK: Cambridge University Press, 1980).

Silver, Timothy. *A New Face on the Countryside: Indians, Colonists, and Slaves in South Atlantic Forests, 1500–1800* (Cambridge, UK: Cambridge University Press, 1990).

Usner, Jr., Daniel J. *Indians, Settlers, and Slaves in a Frontier Exchange Economy: The Lower Mississippi Valley Before 1783* (Chapel Hill: University of North Carolina Press, 1992).

White, Richard. *The Middle Ground: Indians, Empires, and Republics in the Great Lakes Region, 1650–1815* (Cambridge, UK: Cambridge University Press, 1991).

Wright, Jr., J. Leitch. *Creeks and Seminoles: The Destruction and Regeneration of the Muscogulge People* (Omaha: University of Nebraska Press, 1990).

Pirates and sailors

Cordingly, David. *Under the Black Flag: The Romance and Reality of Life Among the Pirates* (New York: Random House, 1996).

Creighton, Margaret S., and Lisa Norling. *Iron Men, Wooden Women: Gender and Seafaring in the Atlantic World, 1700–1920* (Baltimore, MD: Johns Hopkins University Press, 1996).

Lane, Kris. *Pillaging the Empire: Piracy in the Americas, 1500–1750* (Armonk, NY: M.E. Sharpe, 1998).

Linebaugh, Peter, and Marcus Rediker. *The Many-Headed Hydra: Sailors, Slaves, Commoners, and the Hidden History of the Revolutionary Atlantic* (Boston: Beacon Press, 2000).

Newman, Simon P. "Reading the Bodies of Early American Seafarers." *William and Mary Quarterly*, Third Series, Vol. 55, No. 1 (Jan. 1998), pp. 59–82.

Rediker, Marcus. *Between the Devil and the Deep Blue Sea: Merchant Seamen, Pirates, and the Anglo-American Maritime World, 1700–1750* (Cambridge, UK: Cambridge University Press, 1987).

Rediker, Marcus. "'Under the Banner of King Death': The Social World of Anglo-American Pirates, 1716 to 1726." *William and Mary Quarterly*, Third Series, Vol. 38, No. 2 (Apr. 1981), pp. 203–227.

Rediker, Marcus. *Villains of All Nations: Atlantic Pirates in the Golden Age* (Boston: Beacon Press, 2004).

Religion

Barnes, Sandra T. *Africa's Ogun: Old World and New* (Bloomington: Indiana University Press, 1997).

Bremer, Francis J. *First Founders: American Puritans and Puritanism in an Atlantic World* (Durham: University of New Hampshire Press, 2012).

Cañizares-Esguerra, Jorge. *Puritan Conquistadors: Iberianizing the Atlantic, 1550–1700* (Stanford, CA: Stanford University Press, 2006).

Davis, David Brion. *In the Image of God: Religion, Moral Values, and Our Heritage of Slavery* (New Haven, CT: Yale University Press, 2001).

Gossai, Hemchand, and Nathaniel Samuel Murrell, eds. *Religion, Culture and Tradition in the Caribbean* (New York: St. Martin's Press, 2000).

Greer, Allan. *The Jesuit Relations: Natives and Missionaries in Seventeenth-Century America* (Boston: Bedford, 2000).

Haefeli, Evan. *New Netherland and the Dutch Origins of American Religious Liberty* (Philadelphia: University of Pennsylvania Press, 2012).

Hall, David D. *World of Wonder, Days of Judgment: Popular Religious Belief in Early New England* (New York: Knopf, 1989).

Schwartz, Stuart. *All Can Be Saved: Religious Tolerance and Salvation in the Iberian Atlantic World* (New Haven, CT: Yale University Press, 2008).

Souza, Laura de Mello e. *The Devil and the Land of the Holy Cross: Witchcraft, Slavery, and Popular Religion in Colonial Brazil*, Diana Whitty, trans. (Austin: University of Texas Press, 2004).

Stannard, David E. *The Puritan Way of Death: A Study of Religion, Culture, and Social Change* (Oxford: Oxford University Press, 1977).

Sweet, James H. *Domingos Álvares, African Healing, and the Intellectual History of the Atlantic World* (Chapel Hill: University of North Carolina Press, 2011).

Revolutions in the Atlantic

Armitage, David. *The Declaration of Independence: A Global History* (Cambridge, MA: Harvard University Press, 2007).

Bailyn, Bernard. *The Ideological Origins of the American Revolution* (Boston: Harvard University Press, 1967).

Bender, Thomas, Laurent Dubois, and Richard Rabinowitz, eds. *Revolution!: The Atlantic World Reborn* (New York: New York Historical Society, 2011).

Dubois, Laurent. *Avengers of the New World: The Story of the Haitian Revolution* (Cambridge, MA: Belknap Press, 2004).

Geggus, David. *The Impact of the Haitian Revolution in the Atlantic World* (Columbia: University of South Carolina Press, 2001).

Gould, Eliga H., and Peter S. Onuf, eds. *Empire and Nation: The American Revolution in the Atlantic World* (Baltimore, MD: Johns Hopkins University Press, 2005).

Greene, Jack P., and J.R. Pole, eds. *A Companion to the American Revolution* (Malden, MA: Blackwell, 2003).

James, C.L.R. *The Black Jacobins: Toussaint L'Ouverture and the San Domingo Revolution* (New York: Vintage Books, 1963).

Klooster, Wim. *Revolutions in the Atlantic World: A Comparative History* (New York: New York University Press, 2009).

Langley, Lester D. *The Americas in the Age of Revolution, 1750–1850* (New Haven, CT: Yale University Press, 1996).

Nash, Gary. *Race and Revolution* (Lanham, MD: Rowman & Littlefield, 2001).

Nash, Gary. *The Unknown American Revolution: The Unruly Birth of Democracy and the Struggle to Create America* (New York: Viking, 2005).

Nash, Gary. *The Urban Crucible: The Northern Seaports and the Origins of the American Revolution* (Cambridge, MA: Harvard University Press, 1986).

Offutt, William M. *Patriots, Loyalists, and Revolution in New York City, 1775–1776* (Boston: Longman, 2011).

O'Shaughnessy, Andrew Jackson. *An Empire Divided: The American Revolution and the British Caribbean* (Philadelphia: University of Pennsylvania Press, 2000).

Palmer, Robert R. *The Age of the Democratic Revolution: A Political History of Europe and America, 1760–1800* (Princeton, NJ: Princeton University Press, 1959).

Thornton, John. "'I Am the Subject of the King of Congo': African Political Ideology and the Haitian Revolution." *Journal of World History*, Vol. 4, No. 2 (Fall 1993), pp. 181–214.

Wood, Gordon. *The Radicalism of the American Revolution* (New York: Vintage, 1993).

Slavery and the slave trade

Altink, Henrice. "Slavery by Another Name: Apprenticed Women in Jamaican Workhouses in the Period 1834–8." *Social History*, Vol. 26, No. 1 (2001), pp. 40–59.

Anderson, Robert Nelson. "The *Quilombo* of Palmares: A New Overview of a Maroon State in Seventeenth-Century Brazil." *Journal of Latin American Studies*, Vol. 28, No. 3 (1996), pp. 546–566.

Beckles, Hilary. *Black Rebellion in Barbados: The Struggle Against Slavery, 1627–1838* (Bridgetown, Barbados: Antilles Publications, 1984).

Beckles, Hilary. *Natural Rebels: A Social History of Enslaved Black Women in Barbados* (New Brunswick, NJ: Rutgers University Press, 1989).

Beckles, Hilary. *White Servitude and Black Slavery in Barbados, 1627–1715* (Knoxville: University of Tennessee Press, 1989).

Berlin, Ira. *Many Thousands Gone: The First Two Centuries of Slavery in North America* (Cambridge, MA: Harvard University Press, 1998).

Blackburn, Robin. *The Making of New World Slavery* (New York: Verso, 1992).

Bush, Barbara. *Slave Women in Caribbean Society, 1650–1838* (Bloomington: Indiana University Press, 1990).

Costa, Emília Viotti da. *Crowns of Glory, Tears of Blood: The Demerara Slave Rebellion of 1823* (Oxford: Oxford University Press, 1994).

Curtin, Philip. *The Atlantic Slave Trade: A Census* (Madison: University of Wisconsin Press, 1969).

Curtin, Philip. *The Rise and Fall of the Plantation Complex* (Cambridge, UK: Cambridge University Press, 1990).

Curtin, Philip, and Paul Lovejoy. *Africans in Bondage: Studies in Slavery and the Slave Trade* (Madison: University of Wisconsin Press, 1986).

Davis, David Brion. *Inhuman Bondage: The Rise and Fall of Slavery in the New World* (Oxford: Oxford University Press, 2006).

Davis, David Brion. *The Problem of Slavery in the Age of Revolution, 1770–1823* (Ithaca, NY: Cornell University Press, 1975).

Dunn, Richard S. *Sugar and Slaves: The Rise of the Planter Class in the English West Indies, 1624–1713* (Chapel Hill: University of North Carolina Press, 1972).

Eltis, David. *The Rise of African Slavery in the Americas* (Cambridge, UK: Cambridge University Press, 2000).

Eltis, David, and David Richardson. *Atlas of the Transatlantic Slave Trade* (New Haven, CT: Yale University Press, 2010).

Fogel, Robert William. *Time on the Cross: The Economics of American Negro Slavery* (New York: Norton, 1989).

Gaspar, David Barry, and Darlene Clark Hine. *More Than Chattel: Black Women and Slavery in the Americas* (Bloomington: Indiana University Press, 1996).

Genovese, Eugene D. *From Rebellion to Revolution: Afro-American Slave Revolts in the Making of the Modern World* (Baton Rouge: Louisiana State University Press, 1979).

Hall, Gwendolyn Midlo. *Slavery and African Ethnicities in the Americas* (Chapel Hill: University of North Carolina Press, 2005).

Heuman, Gad. *Out of the House of Bondage: Runaways, Resistance, and Marronage in Africa and the New World* (London: Frank Cass, 1986).

Heuman, Gad, and James Walvin, eds. *The Slavery Reader* (London: Routledge, 2003).

Hoffer, Peter Charles. *Cry Liberty: The Great Stono River Slave Rebellion of 1739* (Oxford: Oxford University Press, 2010).

Huggins, Nathan Irvin. *Black Odyssey: The Afro-American Ordeal in Slavery* (New York: Vintage, 1979).

Inikori, J. E., and S. L. Engerman, eds. *The Atlantic Slave Trade: Effects on Economies, Societies, and Peoples in Africa, the Americas, and Europe* (Durham, NC: Duke University Press, 1992).

Jarvis, Michael J. "Maritime Masters and Seafaring Slaves in Bermuda, 1680–1783." *William and Mary Quarterly*, Third Series, Vol. 59, No. 3 (July 2002), pp. 585–622.

Jordan, Winthrop. *White Over Black: American Attitudes Toward the Negro, 1550–1812* (Chapel Hill: University of North Carolina Press, 1968).

Klein, Herbert S. *African Slavery in Latin America and the Caribbean* (Oxford: Oxford University Press, 2007).

Lepore, Jill. *New York Burning: Liberty, Slavery, and Conspiracy in Eighteenth-Century Manhattan* (New York: Vintage, 2006).

Lovejoy, Paul, and Nicholas Rogers, eds. *Unfree Labour in the Development of the Atlantic World* (New York: Routledge, 1994).

Menard, Russell. *Sweet Negotiations: Sugar, Slavery, and Plantation Agriculture in Early Barbados* (Charlottesville: University of Virginia Press, 2006).

Miller, Joseph C. *Way of Death: Merchant Capitalism and the Angolan Slave Trade, 1730–1830* (Madison: University of Wisconsin Press, 1988).

Morgan, Edmund S. *American Slavery, American Freedom: The Ordeal of Colonial Virginia* (New York: Norton, 1975).

Morgan, Kenneth. *Slavery and the British Empire: From Africa to America* (Oxford: Oxford University Press, 2007).

Northrup, David. *The Atlantic Slave Trade* (Boston: Houghton Mifflin, 2002).

Rawley, James, and Stephen D. Behrendt. *The Transatlantic Slave Trade: A History* (Omaha: University of Nebraska Press, 2009).

Rediker, Marcus. *The Amistad Rebellion: An Atlantic Odyssey of Slavery and Freedom* (New York: Viking, 2012).

Rediker, Marcus. *The Slave Ship: A Human History* (New York: Viking, 2007).

Schwartz, Stuart. *Slaves, Peasants, and Rebels: Reconsidering Brazilian Slavery* (Urbana: University of Illinois Press, 1996).

Schwartz, Stuart. *Sugar Plantations in the Formation of Brazilian Society: Bahia 1550–1835* (Cambridge, UK: Cambridge University Press, 1986).

Sheridan, Richard. *Sugar and Slavery: An Economic History of the British West Indies, 1623–1775* (Kingston, Jamaica: Canoe Press, 1994).

Smallwood, Stephanie. *Saltwater Slavery: A Middle Passage from Africa to American Diaspora* (Cambridge, MA: Harvard University Press, 2008).

Williams, Eric. *Capitalism and Slavery* (Chapel Hill: University of North Carolina Press, 1944).

Trade, markets, and economies

Braund, Katherine. *Deerskins and Duffels: The Creek Indian Trade with Anglo-America, 1685–1815* (Lincoln: University of Nebraska Press, 1993).

Davis, Ralph. *The Rise of the Atlantic Economies* (Ithaca, NY: Cornell University Press, 1973).

Emmer, Pieter. *The Dutch in the Atlantic Economy, 1580–1880: Trade, Slavery and Emancipation* (Aldershot, UK: Ashgate, 1998).

Glaisyer, Natasha. "Networking: Trade and Exchange in the Eighteenth-Century British Empire." *The Historical Journal*, Vol. 47, No. 2 (June 2004), pp. 451–476.

Hancock, David. *Citizens of the World: London Merchants and the Integration of the British Atlantic Community, 1735–1785* (Cambridge, UK: Cambridge University Press, 1995).

Hunter, Phyllis Whitman. *Purchasing Identity in the Atlantic World: Massachusetts Merchants, 1670–1780* (Ithaca, NY: Cornell University Press, 2001).

Knight, Franklin W., and Peggy K. Liss, eds. *Atlantic Port Cities: Economy, Culture, and Society in the Atlantic World, 1650–1850* (Knoxville: University of Tennessee Press, 1991).

Liss, Peggy K. *Atlantic Empires: The Network of Trade and Revolution, 1713–1826* (Baltimore, MD: Johns Hopkins University Press, 1983).

Mintz, Sidney. "The Caribbean as a Socio-Cultural Area." *Cahiers d'Histoire Mondiale [Journal of World History]*, Vol. 9, No. 4 (1966), pp. 916–941.

Mintz, Sidney. *Sweetness and Power: The Place of Sugar in Modern History* (New York: Penguin, 1985).

Schwartz, Stuart. *Tropical Babylons: Sugar and the Making of the Atlantic World, 1450–1680* (Chapel Hill: University of North Carolina Press, 2004).

Smith, S. D. "Gedney Clarke of Salem and Barbados: Transatlantic Super-Merchant." *The New England Quarterly*, Vol. 76, No. 4 (Dec. 2003), pp. 499–549.

United States

Fischer, David Hackett, and James C. Kelly. *Bound Away: Virginia and the Westward Movement* (Charlottesville: University of Virginia Press, 2000).

Owsley, Jr., Frank. *Struggle for the Gulf Borderlands: The Creek War and the Battle of New Orleans, 1812–1815* (Gainesville: University Press of Florida, 1981).

Taylor, Alan. *The Civil War of 1812: American Citizens, British Subjects, Irish Rebels, & Indian Allies* (New York: Vintage, 2011).

Wood, Gordon. *Empire of Liberty: A History of the Early Republic, 1789–1815* (Oxford: Oxford University Press, 2011).

Yokota, Kariann. *Unbecoming British: How Revolutionary America Became a Postcolonial Nation* (Oxford: Oxford University Press, 2011).

Witchcraft

Boyer, Paul, and Stanley Nissenbaum. *Salem Possessed: The Social Origins of Witchcraft* (Cambridge, MA: Harvard University Press, 1974).

Breslaw, Elaine. *Tituba, Reluctant Witch of Salem: Devilish Indians and Puritan Fantasies* (New York: New York University Press, 1996).

Demos, John. *Entertaining Satan: Witchcraft and the Culture of Early New England* (Oxford: Oxford University Press, 1992).

Macfarlane, Alan. *Witchcraft in Tudor and Stuart England*, 2nd Ed. (London: Routledge, 1991).

Norton, Mary Beth. *In the Devil's Snare: The Salem Witchcraft Crisis of 1692* (New York: Alfred A. Knopf, 2002).

Thomas, Keith. *Religion and the Decline of Magic* (London: Penguin, 2012 [1971]).

Women in the Atlantic world

Applewhite, Harriet, and Darlene G. Levy, eds. *Women and Politics in the Age of Democratic Revolution* (Baltimore, MD: Johns Hopkins University Press, 1983).

Brown, Kathleen. *Good Wives, Nasty Wenches, and Anxious Patriarchs: Gender, Race, and Power in Colonial Virginia* (Chapel Hill: University of North Carolina Press, 1996).

Carr, Lois, and Lorena Walsh. "The Planter's Wife: The Experience of White Women in Seventeenth-Century Maryland." *William and Mary Quarterly*, Third Series, Vol. 34, No. 4 (1977), pp. 542–571.

Catterall, Douglas, and Jodi Campbell. *Women in Port: Gendering Communities and Social Networks in Atlantic Port Cities, 1500–1800* (Leiden, Netherlands: Brill, 2012).

Gaspar, David, and Darlene Hines. *More Than Chattel: Black Women and Slavery in the Americas* (Bloomington: University of Indiana Press, 1996).

Norton, Mary Beth. "'The Ablest Midwife That Wee Knowe in the Land': Mistress Alice Tilly and the Women of Boston and Dorchester, 1649–1650." *William and Mary Quarterly*, Third Series, Vol. 55, No. 1 (Jan. 1998), pp. 105–134.

Pagan, John Ruston. *Anne Orthwood's Bastard: Sex and Law in Early Virginia* (Oxford: Oxford University Press, 2002).

Ransome, David. "Wives for Virginia." *William and Mary Quarterly*, Third Series, Vol. 48, No. 1 (1991), pp. 3–18.

Salinger, Sharon. "'Send No More Women': Female Servants in Eighteenth-Century Philadelphia." *The Pennsylvania Magazine of History and Biography*, Vol. 107, No. 1 (1983), pp. 29–48.

Shepherd, Verene, Bridget Brereton, and Barbara Bailey. *Engendering History: Caribbean Women in Historical Perspective* (New York: St. Martin's Press, 1995).

Suranyi, Anna. "'Willing to Go if They Had Their Clothes': Early Modern Women and Indentured Servitude." In *Challenging Orthodoxies: The Social and Cultural Worlds of Early Modern Women*, Melinda Zook and Sigrun Haude, eds. (Farnham, Surrey, UK: Ashgate, 2014).

Ulrich, Laurel Thatcher. *A Midwife's Tale: The Life of Martha Ballard, Based on Her Diary, 1785–1812* (New York: Knopf, 1990).

Van Kirk, Sylvia. *Many Tender Ties: Women in Fur-Trade Society, 1670–1870* (Norman: University of Oklahoma Press, 1993).

Index